Remo F. R[...]

Return
of the
World Soul

Wolfgang Pauli, C.G. Jung
and the Challenge
of Psychophysical Reality

Part II: A Psychophysical Theory

Pari Publishing

"What is still older is always the newer"

Wolfgang Pauli

Copyright © Remo F. Roth 2012

First published in Italy in 2012 by Pari Publishing Sas.
All rights reserved. No part of this publication may be reproduced, transmitted or stored in a retrieval system, in any form or by any means, without permission in writing from Pari Publishing Sas, application for which must be made to the publisher.

A catalogue record for this book is available from the British Library

ISBN 978-88-95604-16-9

Book and cover design: Andrea Barbieri
Cover image: Avalon, A., *Die Schlangenkraft, Die Entfaltung schöpferischer Kräfte im Menschen*, Bern, 1975

Quotations from the letters of Wolfgang Pauli reproduced with permission from the Pauli Committee, CERN, CH-1211 Geneva 23, Switzerland

Quotations from the letters of C.G. Jung reproduced with permission from Princeton University Press, © the C.G. Jung Estate

Quotations from C.G. Jung, Collected Works reproduced with permission from Princeton University Press

dr.remo.roth@psychovision.ch
www.paulijungunusmundus.eu

Pari Publishing

Via Tozzi 7, 58045 Pari (GR), Italy
www.paripublishing.com

Dedicated to my Hermetic partner Eva

Table of Contents

Preface 1

6 The Essence—
A psychophysical theory and its application for the understanding of paranormal phenomena 5

6.1   The hypotheses 6
6.1.1   A new interpretation of the Hermetic alchemical Axiom of Maria Prophetissa 6
6.1.2   The bipolarity of the energy term: spirit-psyche and matter-psyche 16
6.1.3   C.G. Jung's typology, the Logos ego and the Eros ego 18
6.1.4   Observational methods of Logos and Eros, and the synchronicity quest 22
6.1.5   The spaceless and timeless psychophysical reality or *unus mundus*, and psychophysical nonlocality 25
6.2   The six demands of Pauli's Fludd/flood synchronicity 30
6.3   'Disinfected' Matter in the Heavens, C.G. Jung's archetypes and physical matter as *being* 31
6.4   Matter and archetypes as *potential being* and their actualization in the quantum leap 33
6.5   The blue color in the World-clock vision as the causal *Logos philosophicus* versus the acausal *Logos Spermatikos* 35
6.6   Synchronicity as an incarnation in the mental/spiritual world versus magical Hermetic incarnation in the material world 38
6.7   The saviour of the universe as the son of the apocalyptic sun woman, the world soul and the vegetative body 39
6.8   The elements and processes of the Hermetic alchemical *coniunctio* as the basis of a psychophysical theory 45
6.9   C.G. Jung's depth psychology and the Hermetic alchemical myth 48

6.10	Quantum physics and Wolfgang Pauli's epistemological insights compared to the Hermetic alchemical myth	49
6.11	An overview on the necessary elements and processes of a new psychophysical theory	52
6.12	Solving the psychophysical problem: the psychophysical theory and its application for the understanding of paranormal phenomena	56
6.12.1	The task: explaining the Hermetic alchemical twin process with the help of a neutral language	56
6.12.2	The translation into a modern language of the Hermetic alchemical exchange of attributes happening during *coniunctio*	59
6.12.2.1	The collapse of the wave function or (acausal) quantum leap in the act of measurement and in the radioactive beta decay	59
6.12.2.2	The psychophysical radioactive beta decay, the acausal production of the matter-psyche, and the twin process	61
6.12.2.3	The observation of dreams and visions out of the unconscious	68
6.12.2.4	Synchronicity described in the neutral language	71
6.12.2.5	The Kappa synchronicity—an example of a spontaneously realized meaning of a synchronicity	76
6.12.3	Description of the paranormal magic processes in the neutral language	81
6.12.3.1	The twin process of Hermetic magic and the crucial role of the individual	81
6.12.3.2	The Pauli effect as a psychokinetic phenomenon and the 'synchronous synchronicity'	88
6.12.3.3	Marie-Louise von Franz' anticipation of the *fenestra aeternitatis* and the solution of the problem of physical incarnation out of the *unus mundus*	105
6.12.3.4	UFO encounter, the artificial fission of the atom and the observation of incarnation into our world by the extraverted Eros ego	111
6.12.3.5	UFO abduction and the observation of incarnation in the *unus mundus* by the introverted Eros ego	124
6.13	Symptom-Symbol Transformation—conscious 'UFO abduction' for the cure of disease	135
6.14	Body-Centered Imagination—conscious 'UFO abduction' for the healing of the world's disease	142
6.14.1	The theory of Body-Centered Imagination	142
6.14.2	Body-Centered Imagination with the turtle and the UFO, who lead me to Anubis in the beyond resulting in a rotation as a dance with the UFO:	147

6.15 A case example of Symptom-Symbol Transformation: The Cure of Multiple Sclerosis 160
6.16 Interpretation of some of Pauli's most decisive dreams, visions and auditions as an empirical confirmation of the psychophysical theory 170
6.16.1 'People who know what rotation is' 170
6.16.2 The radioactive experiment of the revenant and the death of the neutrino 181
6.16.3 The secret laboratory, the radioactive isotope unknown to Pauli, and the sun eclipse 190
6.16.4 The new house dreams: the vegetative body, the Seal of Solomon and the singular quantum leap 199
6.16.5 Brass tones engraved in a metal plate and eggs as a confirmation of the psychophysical theory 217
6.16.6 The 'Chinese revolution,' the *Spiegler* (the maker of reflections) and the twin process 223
6.16.7 Wolfgang Pauli's fine structure constant/death room synchronicity.. 230
6.16.8 The Nobel laureate's visual-auditive experience of the dancing Chinese woman, the Seal of Solomon, the quintessence and the square, and the World-clock vision..................................... 234

CONCLUSIONS AND OUTLOOK 243

BIBLIOGRAPHY 251

Preface

C.G. Jung was conscious of the fact that his depth psychological theory cannot be the definite answer. Already in 1948, in the Foreword to Esther Harding's book *Psychic Energy, Its Source and Its Transformation*[1] he writes:

> The pioneer in a new field rarely has the good fortune to be able to draw valid conclusions from his total experience. The efforts and exertions, the doubts and uncertainties of his voyage of discovery have penetrated his marrow too deeply to allow him the perspective and clarity which are necessary for a comprehensive presentation. Those of the second generation, who base their work on the groping attempts, the chance hits, the circuitous approaches, the half truths and mistakes of the pioneer, are less burdened and can take more direct roads, envisage farther goals. They are able to cast off many doubts and hesitations, concentrate on essentials, and, in this way, map out a simpler and clearer picture of the newly discovered territory. This simplification and clarification redound to the benefit of those of the third generation, who are thus equipped from the outset with an over-all chart. With this chart they are enabled to formulate new problems and mark out the boundary lines more sharply than ever before.

In relation to the psychophysical problem in particular, Jung realized the incompleteness of his theory. As he writes in a letter dated March 7, 1953 to Wolfgang Pauli, he was especially convinced that he had not solved the problem of the so-called *coniunctio*[2]:

> The problem of the coniunctio must be kept for the future; it is more than I can cope with, and my heart reacts if I exert myself too much along these lines. My essay on the 'Der Geist der Psychologie' ['On the Nature of the Psyche'[3]] of 1946 resulted in a serious attack of tachycardia, and synchronicity brought on the rest.

---

[1] *Pantheon Books, Random House, Inc., N.Y., Bollingen Series X, 1948; today also in* CW 18, § 1126.
[2] AaA, p. 101; PJB, p 103; WB 4/II, p. 67; *definition of the* coniunctio *see in* Return of the World Soul, Part I (2011)
[3] *In* CW 8, §§ 343-442

As we have seen in Part I of *Return of the World Soul*[4], Wolfgang Pauli, the quantum physicist and Nobel laureate who had an intense oral and written dispute with the depth psychologist, was also convinced that Jung's quaternity, postulated as the structure of the (Logos) Self and center of the collective unconscious, did not solve the problem of the *coniunctio*. He summarizes his criticism in the following statement that had occupied us very intensely in Part I[5]:

> *As long as quaternities are kept 'up in the heaven'* at a great distance from people...no fish will be caught, *the hierosgamos* [equivalent to coniunctio; RFR] *is absent, and the psychophysical problem remains unsolved.* [Emphasis mine]

The reader may remember that the background of this statement was Pauli's insight that alchemy was split into two: on the one hand Neoplatonic alchemy with its tendency to spiritualize matter and let it ascend into Heaven; shared with Jung's quaternity. On the other hand Hermetic alchemy, with its representants Paracelsus, Michael Meier, Gerhard Dorn (Dorneus) and Robert Fludd, the physicians, who defined an intermediate world to which the spirit had to descend and thus matter was able to ascend to it. This intermediate world, represented by the Seal of Solomon or Star of David, they called the *lapis*, the stone, the alchemic gold. Out of it, in the process that Gerhard Dorn called the *unio corporalis* and other alchemists the *coniunctio*, the final result was distilled, the red tincture or quintessence. Thus, only Hermetic alchemy was, at least in symbolical terms, able to find a unification of matter and spirit.

In his last collaboration with his friend Werner Heisenberg in the years 1957 and 1958 Pauli also tried to find a unification; a unification on the physical level, of Einstein's General Relativity Theory and quantum mechanics[6], the so-called world formula. Then, however, he realized that this was not possible, and he distanced himself from their joint theory[7]. With the help of his apt wit he formulated the problem in a letter to his colleague George Gamow as follows[8]:

---

[4] Remo F. Roth, Return of the World Soul, Wolfgang Pauli, C.G. Jung and the Challenge of Psychophysical Reality, Part I: The Battle of the Giants, Pari Publishing, Pari, Italy, 2011
[5] AaA, p. 95; originally in PJB, p. 96; also in WB 4/II, p. 55
[6] See letter [2912] of Weisskopf to Pauli from March 7, 1958; WB 4/IVB, p. 1015
[7] See Pauli's letter [2959] from April 7, 1958 to Heisenberg; WB 4/IVB, p. 1124
[8] Attachment to letter [2897] to Gamow from March 1st, 1958; WB 4/IVB, p. 998

This is to show the world, that I can paint like Tizian:

Only technical details are missing.   W. Pauli

Since the unsuccessful attempt of Heisenberg and Pauli several other efforts had been made to formulate such TOEs, Theories of Everything, for example the string and the superstring theory. In my opinion, they will fail since they do not integrate the psychophysical level of reality, and thus neither paraphysics, as Pauli demanded[9]. As we will see in section 6.1.1 my hypothesis consists in the inclusion of a new interpretation of the alchemical Axiom of Maria Prophetissa, a feminine alchemist of the 2nd or 3rd century. It shows that we have to look for another, hitherto unknown form of energy—in Pauli's 'neutral language' I call it matter-psyche; in contrast to outer spirit-psyche (physical energy) and inner spirit-psyche (Jung's objective psychic energy). Further, we have to include Pauli's demand of 'a third type of law of nature'[10] besides the causal laws of Newton and Einstein on the one hand, and the quantum physical laws on the other. My book tries to formulate such a psychophysical theory and its energetic processes. In this way I think that I have fulfilled Pauli's demand of finding 'something entirely new, in other words something very "crazy"'[11].

/ / /

---

[9] WB 4/II, p. 327; letter [1667] to Marie-Louise von Franz
[10] WB 4/II, p. 310-311 (letter to Kröner), p.335-336 [in Die Klavierstunde (The Piano Lesson) in letter to M.-L. von Franz] and p. 387-389 (letter to Heisenberg)
[11] See motto of Chapter 6

I would like to thank my proofreader Lyle Fuller, in Canada, for his careful review of the manuscript. I thank Veronica Goodchild Ph.D., Clinical Psychology, Pacifica Graduate Institute, Carpinteria, California for the interesting discussions on the subject of the book. Further, I thank Pari Publishing and in particular Maureen Doolan and Andrea Barbieri for a pleasant collaboration.

6 The Essence— A psycho-physical theory and its application for the understanding of paranormal phenomena

> *I now completely agree with Bohr [that our theory] is not crazy enough. Something entirely new, in other words something very 'crazy' is needed.*
>
> Wolfgang Pauli to C.S. Wu[12]

---

[12] Pauli (one month before his early death) in a letter from Nov 17, 1958 [WB 4/IV, p. 1331] concerning Heisenberg's and his unified field theory he presented in New York on Feb 1st, 1958 to Niels Bohr, C.S. Wu, Oppenheimer, Pais, etc. [WB 4/IV, p. 871]. Abraham Pais writes: '[Pauli] had requested to be allowed to give a "secret" seminar on his recent work with Heisenberg at Columbia University, by invitation only. Actually he spoke in the overfilled large lecture hall in Pupin Laboratory. I was present and vividly recall my reaction: this was not Pauli I had known for so many years. He spoke hesitantly. Afterward, a few people, including Niels Bohr and myself, gathered around him. Pauli said to Bohr: "You may well think that all this is crazy." To which Bohr replied: "Yes, but unfortunately it is not crazy enough".' [WB 4/IV, p. 898]

6.1 The hypotheses

6.1.1 A new interpretation of the Hermetic alchemical Axiom of Maria Prophetissa

Maria Prophetissa, also called the Jewess[13], was a female alchemist. The axiom was named after her. We do not know exactly when she lived. One source talks of the second, the other of the third century A.D.[14] Thus, she lived at the very beginning of the aeon of Pisces, and her Axiom belongs to the ancient alchemy.

Figure 6.1:
Maria Prophetissa[15]

---

[13] CW 12, § 209
[14] *Jung dates it to the 2nd—3rd century;* CW 10, § 738
[15] *From Maierus, Michael,* Symbola aureae mensa, *Frankfurt 1617; also in CW 12, p. 191*

The Axiom of Maria, which, as I mentioned previously in Part I, is not complete in the published English translation of C.G. Jung's *Collected Works*, goes as follows:

> One becomes two, two becomes three, and out of the third comes the One as the fourth[16]. Like this the two become one[17].

At the end of Chapter 3 of Part I, I have shown that C.G. Jung tried to find the psychophysical archetype at the background of whole numbers. There, he hypothesized, lies the key to a union of the quantitative and the qualitative, of physics and depth psychology, since numbers are both. This idea was further developed by Marie-Louise von Franz in her book *Number and Time (Zahl und Zeit)*[18]. In order to unite the quantitative with the qualitative aspect of numbers she postulates the existence of the so-called one-continuum[19]. This corresponds to the idea

> To consider [the monas] running right through the whole number series. One can compare it to a 'field' in which the individual numbers represent activated points.

She then exemplifies this idea with the first five whole numbers. Number two symbolizes the symmetry quality of the one-continuum, and consequently the bipolarity principle. Number three would be the symmetry axis in the bipolarity of the One. This would correspond to a 'retrograde process, which means 'a reflection leading from two back to the primal one.' In the case of number four this idea leads to the Axiom of Maria Prophetissa, which Marie-Louise von Franz interprets therefore as 'the number three, taken as a [qualitative] unity related back to the primal one, becomes the fourth.'

We will see that my interpretation of the development of the first into the fourth is different. Though I integrate Marie-Louise von Franz' hypothesis of the qualitative one-continuum, I will extend it and show that the Axiom tells us on

---

[16] ČW 12, § 209

[17] GW 13, § 187, *footnote 160: 'So wird aus zweien ein einziges'. For unknown reasons, the last sentence is missing in the English edition of C.G. Jung's* Collected Works, *i.e., in CW, Volume 13, § 187, footnote 81. Also, though the depth psychologist cites the Axiom several times, this is the only quote (in the original German edition) in which the last sentence is included.*

[18] Marie-Louise von Franz, Zahl und Zeit, Psychologische Überlegungen zur einer Annäherung von Tiefenpsychologie und Physik, *Stuttgart, 1970; English translation:* Number and Time, Reflections Leading toward A Unification of Depth Psychology and Physics, *Northwestern University Press, Evanston, 1974*

[19] *For the following see* Number and Time, *p. 63-64.*

the one hand that the second must contain the qualitative aspect of the first, further, the third the qualitative aspects of the second and of the first, and the fourth even the qualitative aspects of all the three. On the other hand I will also show that the statement of the Axiom that the third must become one in the fourth implicitly means that the third is split, and that this split must be overcome by a unification process in the fourth, as in the above 'the two become one.' Further, I will also include the energy term. Thus, these differences lead also to a completely different interpretation of the whole Axiom.

As we realized from C.G. Jung's hypothesis, our task consists in the unification of the quantitative with the qualitative aspect of whole numbers. Since symbolically seen the term 'quantitative' corresponds to the masculine principle and 'qualitative' to the feminine, it becomes obvious that the background of such a task is the archetype of the *coniunctio*, the Holy Wedding of Hermetic alchemy.

/ / /

As C.G. Jung writes in his article *A Psychological Approach to the Dogma of the Trinity*[20], nonascertainability[21] is the qualitative aspect of number one:

> Unity, the absolute One, cannot be numbered, it is indefinable and unknowable.

From the qualitative point of view, the most common unity symbol is the point and also the circle. This is why the empty circle is the oldest known God-image. We find it engraved in stones already in prehistoric times. However, we have to accept that this god-image is nonascertainable wholeness, i.e. a metaphysical statement. And from a quantitative point of view the One is of course number one.

Mathematical number theory takes number one as decisive to explain the series of whole numbers. It tells us that the series develops as follows: Number one comes first. Then we add another unity and get number two. The result of this addition is called the successor; in this case number two is the successor of number one. Then we add again a unity and get number three, the successor of number two. We continue and receive number four as the successor of number three, etc. This is what mankind regards as the series of natural numbers. It is however only the quantitative series.

After the creation of the first two integers, of number one and number two, one can add them and receives like this the quantitative number three. The

---

[20] CW 11, §§ 169
[21] CW 11, § 180

most remarkable attribute of the addition of 1 and 2 (where the latter is the successor of the former), is that this mathematical operation creates the successor of number two, number three: the addition 1+2=3 possesses thus the attribute that number one and its successor, number two, added together create the successor of the higher number, the successor of the successor. This is an absolutely unique attribute—a unique quality—of the first three whole numbers. We can also express this characteristic in a negative way: the addition of number two and number three does not result in number four, the successor of number three, but is number five; 3+4 is not equal to 5, the successor of 4 (it is 7), and so on. Since number three as the third is followed by something completely different, the progress from the third to the fourth, as we realized before, is symbolically described as the '2000-year-old problem' (C.G. Jung) of the Axiom.

Mathematical number theory however, does not take into consideration this unique qualitative relationship between the first three numbers. Therefore, as shown above, it goes on in the quantitative way and adds 1 to 3; 3 plus the original one gives 4, etc.

From a qualitative point of view this way of creating the series of whole numbers is only correct until number three. The first corresponds to number one, the second corresponds to number two, and the third corresponds to number three. The operation 1+2=3 corresponds therefore to the addition of the ordinal numbers. Thus, the operation 'The first plus the second equals the third' is equivalent to the quantitative addition. The ordinal aspect is a qualitative attribute. Thus, for the first three numbers the addition of the quantities corresponds to the addition of the qualities.

Further, we can interpret the term 'the addition of the qualities' as the inclusion of the quality of the first, oneness, into the second, and of the second, bipolarity (see below), and oneness, the quality of the first, into the third. This way we return to the above mentioned aspect of the so-called one-continuum of whole numbers, introduced by Marie-Louise von Franz in her book *Number and Time*. As we remember, the quality of the one-continuum in my interpretation means, however, that every successor should contain qualitative aspects of *all* the predecessors.

/ / /

Let us now concentrate on the qualitative aspect of the second number. Bipolarity is a necessary qualitative aspect of number two. Number two must however also contain the qualitative aspect of unity, oneness. Thus, the two are secretly one. Here we meet again the *coniunctio* archetype, which I am dealing with in this book. The masculine and the feminine godhead of Hermetic alchemy have sexual intercourse, i.e., become one, and like this create the third, the child.

The same process is realized in Taoism. There, in a simultaneous process yin and yang, the bipolar principle of the Tao, create the oneness of the Tai Gi tu. Further we have seen that a necessary attribute of the *coniunctio* is the exchange of attributes: yin becomes yang, and yang becomes yin. With such a process the Tai Gi tu implicitly contains also an energetic aspect (see figure 5.1 in Part I).

/ / /

Let us now consider the qualitative definition of the third. It should include the quality of the first, unity, as well as the second, bipolarity. Further, there must also exist a qualitative aspect of the third itself.

The quality of unity is expressed in the symbol of the Holy Spirit (or the Trinity): the equilateral triangle pointed upwards.

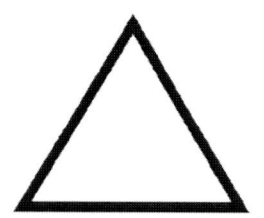

Figure 6.2a:
The triangle pointed upwards as symbol of
the Holy Spirit and the Trinity

In a modern neutral language we can define the symbol of the Holy Spirit as the energetic aspect of the Christian God. We can thus conclude that *the third is an expression of the energy term*. Since the third is equivalent to number three, the latter must also be a symbol of the energy term. This is in fact the case: to define the energy term, we always need three elements: the above and the below, and the third as the flow in-between. Or in electricity: the positive and the negative pole, and the electrical current that flows from one to the other. With the energy term, besides the qualitative aspect of number one, the qualitative three-aspect is also included in the third.

When we talk about energy, a qualitative term, we implicitly always include thus the quantitative aspect of the third, number three. Energy is number three, so to speak. Since number three cannot be represented as the sum of two identical numbers, the qualitative aspect of the third, the energy term, can only be unipolar. However, according to the hypothesis of the one-continuum, the third should also contain the qualitative aspect of the second, bipolarity. Since the inclusion of bipolarity corresponds to an archetypal necessity, in accordance with the above conclusion, however, it cannot be realized in the third. It nevertheless prevails in a different way, namely in a chronological process C.G. Jung called enantiodromy[22]: the energetic principle develops into its contrary, into its qualitative opposite. In a religious-psychological terminology this means that Christ, the son aspect of the Trinity (of the Three-Oneness), of the one solar energy, creates out of Himself the anti-Christ, the devil, darkness. In science, the one continuous energy of classical physics gives rise to the discontinuous energy term of quantum physics. Further, the principle of causality is necessarily infiltrated by the principle of acausality—which is also true in Jung's depth psychology. In ethics the necessary inclusion of the opposition always leads to the fact that good implies evil.

It is thus an inherent quality of the third and thus of the energy term, to be *split*. Since it is marked by this split, the third cannot be a union, the qualitative One, either, though the energy term can be presented as the equilateral triangle. As we will soon see, this is one of the most important characteristics implicitly contained in the Axiom.

Since we are used to arguing completely quantitatively and neglect and repress the qualitative aspect of numbers, the qualitative aspect of the third and of the energy term, its inherent opposition, is not at all obvious to us. This is *precisely the great problem we unconsciously suffer from. One of the most important qualitative aspects of the third (and thus of the energy term), its being an opposition in itself, is repressed. This way the third is split into a conscious and accepted part, the quantitative number three and the 'masculine' energy term on the one hand, and a repressed qualitative part, 'feminine energy,' on the other. The general unconsciousness of this split is the deepest reason why the energy term is everywhere defined as unipolar until today.*

The qualitative amplification of the third and of number three leads us back to early quantum physics. It was a great shock for the community of physicists when Max Planck discovered that in specific cases the energy term is not continuous, as assumed in Newton's differential equations, but it is quantized. Energy is emitted in quanta, i.e., in some sort of *whole numbers*, and not continuously. The necessary conclusion of this revolutionary discovery is that energy can 'jump' over the zero point, and thus physical energy, always defined as positive, can become negative. Early quantum physics thus stumbled upon the bipolarity of energy. At this time physics had the possibility to define the bipolar energy term. However, such an extension was not possible because the mathematical expression of the energy term is completely quantitative, and therefore does not contain a qualitative element. As I will comment later[23], Paul A.M. Dirac redefined negative

---

[22] CW 6, §§ 716-718
[23] See section 6.12.2.5, *where I present my Kappa synchronicity*

energy as antimatter in a completely metaphysical way in 1928. The bipolarity of energy was excluded from physics and science in general, and the process of the quantitative-qualitative development from the third to the fourth was eliminated.

Since mathematics started to dominate the philosophy of nature in the 17th century (Galilei, Kepler, Newton) and created modern science, classical physics and science in general consider only the quantitative aspect of the third, i.e., measurable physical energy. As the above demonstrates, though in 1928 quantum physics was confronted by the bipolarity of energy, it went on applying the unipolar energy term. We can consider it a historical synchronicity that C.G. Jung, in 1912, sixteen years before this crucial development, defined the objective psychic energy term also in a unipolar way[24]. Consequently, later Pauli found the complementary relationship of physics and depth psychology. In the following I will call the energetic aspect of this fact the complementarity between outer spirit-psyche and inner spirit-psyche, between physical energy and psychical energy.

Further, since the two-ness of the energy term always breaks through—if not consciously accepted, then in an unconscious way—it is a logically consistent development that with the definition of synchronicity C.G. Jung created a contradiction. On the one hand objective psychic energy is quantitative-causal, for example in his complex theory, on the other it is qualitative-acausal[25], as in his synchronicity theory. We will see that this discrepancy comes from the fact that with synchronicity the qualitative aspect of the energy term—I will call it the matter-psyche aspect—is at work, as opposed to the quantitative/causal psychology of the complexes.

/ / /

Let us now return to the Axiom. The inclusion of the quality of the first, the unity, into the second, and of the second, bipolarity, and the unity into the third is the content of the first part of the Axiom:

One becomes two, two becomes three

---

[24] In his book Wandlungen und Symbole der Libido, 1911/12, *published in English as* The Psychology of the Unconscious. A Study of the Transformations and Symbolisms of the Libido. A Contribution to the History of the Evolution of Thought, *New York, 1916. The corrected version (without Freudian terms) is published today as CW 5; more in my digital publication* Holy Wedding, *http://paulijungunusmundus.eu/hknw/holy_wedding_alchemy_modern_man_contents.htm*

[25] *In synchronicity the energy term is qualitative since in the two events a potentially increased meaning is shown.*

As we realized, since number one is equivalent to the first, number two equivalent to the second and number three to the third, we can also write: 'the first becomes the second, the second becomes the third,' which means that the second also contains unity, the third also unity and bipolarity.

If we look at it this way, the first part of the Axiom as I interpret it encompasses the qualitative aspect of the one-continuum as well as the (quantitative) successor idea of number theory. It describes the union of the opposites, and becomes a *coniunctio* of the quantitative and the qualitative aspects of the first three numbers.

However, as we have seen, the *simultaneous* coexistence of the two aspects of bipolarity is not possible in the third. Thus, as an inevitable consequence an alternating time process starts: out of one aspect the other is created and vice versa. A mostly unconscious enantiodromia takes place, which leads to the opposite principle: the 'masculine' energetic unity, (the triangle pointing upwards, the Holy Ghost), transforms into the 'feminine' energetic unity, (the triangle pointing downwards). This way the split in the third, the opposition of two hostile principles becomes visible. Only one of these principles can be true at a given moment. Thus, the third cannot be a real union of the opposites either, a union the *coniunctio* is aiming at. Already here we can thus anticipate that such a unity and unification can only be reached in the fourth.

It is exactly this split of the third principle *as well as its solution* that is described in the second part of the Axiom:

And out of the third comes the One as the fourth

First we realize that obviously also Maria supposes in her Axiom that the third and number three are equivalent. This is why three is replaced by the third in the second part. Then, however, she does not conclude, as one would assume, that the third and number three transform into number four as the fourth. She informs us that the essential characteristic of the fourth is its unity. Obviously such a statement implies that unification can only take place in the fourth, and thus the third principle is not yet a unity, as derived from the split into the opposites, where one part is always repressed and/or demonized.

Secondly, in contrast to mathematical number theory, the axiom does not continue in a quantitative but in a qualitative way. Thus, it does not talk of the development of number three into number four, but of the transformation of the third into the fourth as unity. Though number four as 2/2 would contain the quality of bipolarity, such bipolarity could not be expressed energetically, because number four only includes number one besides number three. As we remember, number one is the nonascertainable and non-energetic principle. This leads to the conclusion that in contrast to the first three numbers the fourth and number four cannot be regarded as equivalent. The fourth seems to be something completely different—but what could it be?

According to the above hypothesis of the one-continuum the fourth, besides the quantitative characteristics of its predecessors, i.e., 1, 2 and 3 must also possess the qualitative characteristics of unity, bipolarity and 'Trinity,' or 'triad', (i.e., the equilateral triangle). Since the third is also equivalent to the energy principle, the fourth must also contain it. This way we receive an enlarged addition, which contains the quantitative as well as the qualitative aspects of the first *three* principles:

$$1 + 2 + 3 = 6$$

And

The first + the second + the third = the fourth

Thus we can conclude:

The fourth corresponds to number 6.

Further, the combination of the terms 'bipolarity' and 'triad' leads to the term 'double triad.' As number three corresponds to the energetic principle, this one is now also included, though as bipolarity.

The only symbol that unifies the above quantitative, qualitative and energetic characteristics is the Seal of Solomon, or the Star of David (see figure 4.4 in Part I). Thus we obtain the result:

The fourth corresponds to the Seal of Solomon.

As we have seen, the Seal of Solomon is a main symbol of Hermetic alchemy. It can be constructed from the hexagon, which can itself be easily constructed from the circle using the radius. Since the circle is the symbol of unity and the Seal is so intimately connected to it, it also becomes a symbol of unity. Thus, the circle as well as the hexagon and the Seal describe the unity aspect of the fourth.

As is evident from the figure, the Seal also contains the qualitative aspect of bipolarity, which is represented by the two interlocked equilateral triangles, where the triangle pointed upwards symbolizes the 'masculine' energy, its contrary the 'feminine' energy. This is emphasized by the fact that this representation of the triangle has always been a symbol of the female pelvis[26].

---

[26] *Every woman who has given birth knows that the doctors measure this triangle to verify if the pelvis is big enough to give birth to the child without a Cesarean section.*

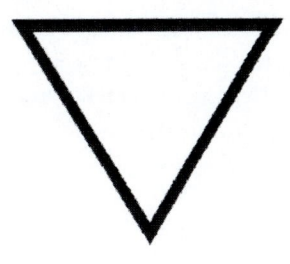

Figure 6.2b:
The triangle pointed downwards as symbol of the female pelvis

We realize further that with the inclusion of the two equilateral triangles (the qualitative aspect of the third), the energetic principle is present. It can be embedded as the preconscious wholeness, namely as the male-female bipolarity. This latter characteristic leads us back to the last sentence of the Axiom, which is in fact also realized:

Like this the two become one

This statement means that the deeply unconscious split of the third and of the energy term is extinguished in the fourth of the Seal of Solomon. In the Seal the simultaneous coexistence of 'masculine' and 'feminine' energy, of quantitative and qualitative, of causal and acausal energy is obtained and maintained in its dynamism. We will see later that this characteristic is the necessary precondition for what I call the twin process, in which a singular quantum leap happens.

/ / /

As we remember, C.G. Jung stated that unity is nonascertainable. He further showed[27] that everything must be developed up to number three to become recognizable. Thus, it is true that the second (i.e., number two) is already a bipolarity, however, such a bipolarity is not yet recognizable. We first must include the third, which means advancing to an energetic view. Only then does the God-image become recognizable. Further, we have to consider that the energy term must be bipolar, which leads immediately to the double triad and to the Seal. It is therefore the Seal of Solomon, and not C.G. Jung's quaternity that corresponds to the *observable* God-image. Only this double-triadic background of the archetypal

---

[27] *CW 11, § 180*

or even psychophysical processes allows human observation, which, as we know, leads to the incarnation into the space-time restricted world of the here and now.

Every physicist knows that only energetic processes are observable. As we realized in Chapter 5, such energetic processes become observable in the collapse of the wave function or quantum leap, in which *potential being* transforms into *actual being*. In Hermetic alchemy Gerardus Dorneus called this process *unio corporalis*, other Hermetic alchemists used the term *coniunctio*. In a neutral language I define this process as the singular acausal quantum leap. As we will see in the course of this chapter such spontaneous acausal events are observable in one's own body when one practices Body-Centered Imagination on the one hand, and on the other in the outside world as UFOs/'ETs' encounter and abduction phenomena.

6.1.2 The bipolarity of the energy term: spirit-psyche and matter-psyche

My interpretation of the Axiom gives us the means to define a bipolar energy term. As we remember, one of the most important results of Jung's and Pauli's epistemological discussion was the idea that what we call matter, psyche (Psyche in my definition) or spirit is just a nonascertainable X we can only metaphysically talk about. As Pauli then unsuccessfully tried to show the depth psychologist, this X, especially its collective psyche aspect, is however neither *nonbeing*—the scientific metaphysical belief—nor *being*, as Jung proposes, but *potential being*. We have further seen that Pauli defines the transformation of the wave function into the real object in the moment of the act of measurement precisely in this way:

{(Nonobservable X = *potential being*) → *actual being*}

The same process happens in the moment of the spontaneous decay of a radioactive atom, independently of man's conscious will. We can therefore take this model of quantum physics and define a psychophysical process. Then the process looks like this:

{(Nonobservable X = *potential being* = psychophysical reality = *unus mundus*) → observed spirit-psyche}

CHAPTER 6   17

Since we have seen that depth psychology and physics are complementary, we can further define an outer and an inner process:

A: {(Nonobservable X = *potential being*
= psychophysical reality
= *unus mundus* = **matter**)

→

(observed *outer* spirit-psyche
= observed physical energy)}

And

B: {(Nonobservable X = *potential being*
= psychophysical reality
= *unus mundus* = **spirit**)

→

(observed *inner* spirit-psyche
= observed objective psychic energy[28])}

With these definitions I underline the fact that the quantum leap leads to an observable result, to *actual being* in the here and now. Further I emphasize the idea that the inner process, the creation of a dream or a vision, is as observable as the physical quantum leap. The difference is that in the case of physical observation, in the act of measurement, the event is triggered by the conscious will, while in the case of the observation of dreams it is spontaneous: we cannot 'make' dreams, they happen spontaneously. This is why in a symbolic language I call these inner processes also 'the spontaneous observation of the inner quantum leap.'

Since the energy term is defined as bipolar—in fact with the above differentiation is even tripolar—hypothetically, there is another possible process:

---

[28] In the meaning of C.G. Jung

C: {(Nonobservable X = *potential being*
= *psychophysical reality*
= *unus mundus* = **Psyche**)

→

(matter-psyche
= observed paranormal energy)}

The first process (*A*) is a description of the quantum physical act of measurement or act of observation in a neutral language (W. Pauli); further, it describes the (acausal) radioactive decay in a neutral language. The second (*B*) means the description of the realization of a dream and the third (*C*) the observation of paranormal phenomena in a neutral language.

With the definition of matter-psyche two problems arise. First we have to ask ourselves if matter-psyche is also split into an inner and an outer part. We will soon see that this is not the case. Second, the question arises whether matter-psyche is really observable. We will realize at the end of my remarks about the possible processes and their manifestation in nature that there are situations, in which matter-psyche is also observable. However, it can already be noted that such observability is always connected to an altered state of consciousness I call the Eros ego.

6.1.3 C.G. Jung's typology, the Logos ego and the Eros ego

Before defining the bipolarity of the consciousness, we will have to go back to Jung's typology and consider two very important statements he made about the subject. As a result of his breakdown in 1913 Jung developed a typology of consciousness, which he published in 1921 as *Psychologische Typen*[29] (*Psychological Types*[30]). He distinguishes four different functions: thinking, feeling, sensation and intuition. Since all of these functions can be extraverted or introverted, there

---

[29] Rascher Verlag, Zürich, 1921; Today in GW 6.
[30] Today in CW 6

are eight possible types. The depth psychologist calls 'main function' the most important function on which the ego is based. Further there are two auxiliary functions and an inferior function. C.G. Jung's own typology consists in thinking as the main function, intuition as the first, sensation as the second auxiliary function, and feeling as the inferior function.

Thinking and feeling are psychological opposites as are sensation and intuition. Thus, the typology can be demonstrated as a cross which we can turn around to have the main function at the top:

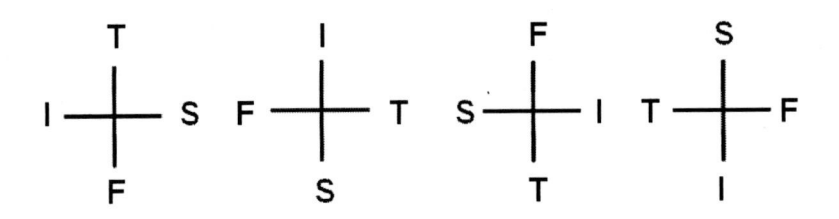

Figure 6.3:
The four possibilities of the main function
(T = thinking, S = sensation, F = feeling and I = intuition)

In science as well as in psychology the most common type is the extraverted thinking type[31]. By definition this type's inferior function is feeling. According to Jung the inferior function is very dangerous, as long as it is unconscious [32]. One of the main tasks in life would be to cope with this. If one does not try to integrate the inferior feeling, it begins to poison the thinking function and the person concerned becomes completely power- and will-possessed. Further, the negative feeling and the emotions attached to it begin to heavily disturb thinking. According to my experience this results in the typical sarcasm or even cynicism so widespread among scientists.

Based on these observations I define the Logos ego or Logos consciousness as the following typology: extraverted thinking as the main function, extraverted sensation as the first, intuition as the second auxiliary function, and repressed feeling as the fourth[33]. Thus, it corresponds to the first of the above images.

---

[31] *In physics and other sciences there are also many sensation types, for example the experimental physicist.*
[32] *As I show in my digital publication* Holy Wedding, *http://paulijungunusmundus.eu/hknw/holy_wedding_alchemy_modern_man_contents.htm, the repression of the inferior feeling function is the deepest background of his life crisis and breakdown of 1913 to 1918.*
[33] *If sensation is the first function it seems that in the scientific community not only feeling is repressed, but also intuition.*

All mainstream scientific research is based on Logos; one cannot do science with the help of the feeling function. Further, intuition is mostly like a mistress: one needs her, but does not show her in public. On the basis of C.G. Jung's typology this means that scientific research is by definition one-sided. It does not include the feeling function, and intuition is devaluated.

During my work of more than 30 years as a psychotherapist and healer I realized that there are many people who are marked by exactly the opposite typology. I call this consciousness the Eros ego and for a long time defined it as follows: introverted feeling as the main function, introverted sensation as the first, intuition as the second auxiliary function and thinking as the inferior function[34].

Some years ago I realized however that C.G. Jung's sensation function, the extraverted as well as the introverted, is based on the central nervous system (CNS), since sensation always deals with the five senses. The difference between extraverted and introverted sensation consists in the fact that in the case of introversion perception is accumulated with the contents of the unconscious. The introverted sensation type has therefore to be careful about how many perceptions they can stand.

It seems that in his seventies and eighties the great depth psychologist began to doubt the absolute truth of his typology. We know of two very interesting remarks which show this. One of them is from his 1952 synchronicity article[35]. C.G. Jung assumes that perhaps the cerebral cortex is not the only location of consciousness. He concludes this because in swoon states there exist observable phenomena of consciousness. This would mean that in such states the ego is not extinct but moved to another place.

To answer the question where such a complementary consciousness could be located, the depth psychologist first gives the example of the dance of bees described by the Nobel laureate Karl von Frisch. With their dance, the bees exchange information about the exact position of food, i.e., about its direction and distance. Jung then concludes[36]:

> This kind of message is no different in principle from information conveyed by a human being. In the latter case we would certainly regard such behaviour as a conscious and intentional act.

---

[34] *This does not mean, however, that feeling types cannot think, as already Marie-Louise von Franz realized. They can however only think about facts that are accompanied by a positive feeling. Further, there exists a type with introverted, vegetative sensation as the main function and feeling as the first auxiliary function (see text).*
[35] For the following see CW 8, §§ 954
[36] CW 8, § 956

Jung further remarks that bees 'have no cerebrospinal nervous system at all, but only a double-chain of ganglia[37].' The latter he compares with the human vegetative nervous system (VNS)[38], which could be the seat of this altered consciousness[39]. Thus he concludes that *'Von Frisch's observations prove the existence of transcerebral thought and perception,'* which is located in the VNS.

Already six years earlier, in 1946, Jung expressed a hypothesis, which surely let mainstream scientists and psychoanalysts doubt his mental health. He wrote[40]:

> If the unconscious can contain everything that is known to be a function of consciousness, then we are faced with the possibility that it too, like consciousness, possesses a subject, a sort of ego...*a second psychic system* coexisting with consciousness...[This would be] of absolutely revolutionary significance in that *it could radically alter our view of the world*. Even if not more than the perceptions taking place in such a second psychic system were carried over into ego-consciousness, we should have the possibility of enormously extending the bounds of our mental horizon. [Emphasis mine]

My observations as a psychotherapist and healer confirm Jung's hypotheses. They show further that this complementary ego, the Eros consciousness has its seat in the belly. Its physiological aspect, i.e., the independency of the brain and its ability to take decisions and influence the inner organs, was first described 25 years ago by Michael D. Gershon[41]. My observations eventually forced me to change the above definition of Eros consciousness or Eros ego complementary to the Logos ego: its sensation function is not related to the CNS, but to the VNS. This means that such an ego bound to live in the vegetative sensation has to be very introverted. In addition to the results of Gershon's research, my experience showed me that the belly brain, the seat of the Eros ego, is not only the ruler of the inner physiological processes as Gershon thinks, but is also able to produce inner images and specific inner perceptions[42]. The perception of such images and vegetative sensations is possible in the state of the Eros ego because it is deeply related to the VNS, to the gut brain or belly brain.

---

[37] CW 8, § 955

[38] In German, the sympathetic nervous system (which includes also the parasympathetic nervous system) is more accurately called the 'vegetative Nervensystem,' the vegetative nervous system. Thus I will use this term and its abbreviation VNS.

[39] CW 8, § 955

[40] CW 8, § 369

[41] See Gershon, M.D., The Second Brain, New York, 1998

[42] The exception is UFO encounter, in which the extraverted Eros ego is compelled to observe in the outside.

We will see that the definition of Eros consciousness is also decisive for the understanding of paranormal events. It helps us understand the Pauli effect, psychokinesis in general, UFO encounter and abduction, and also the method I developed to cure somatic, psychosomatic and specific psychological diseases: Body-Centered Imagination.

6.1.4 Observational methods of Logos and Eros, and the synchronicity quest

After the definition of the Logos ego and the Eros ego we can now have a look at the observational methods of the two complementary egos. It is obvious that the observational method of the Logos ego is the one used in the scientific experiment. Thinking and sensation, sometimes with the help of intuition create an experimental situation, in which the energetic changes in matter can be measured. An essential aspect of the experiment is that the conscious will decides the time and place of the experiment. Further, the experiment requires a completely extraverted focus of consciousness.

As I mentioned above, in quantum physics in the act of measuring, *an act of will*, the so-called quantum leap takes place. The mathematical formula that describes the different potential results of the act of measurement, the wave function, collapses. One and only one of the different possibilities becomes reality. Since no one knows which of them becomes reality the act of measurement is acausal, which means that there is no cause for the 'effect.' Since out of nothing something new is created, such an act actually is also a creation act. Out of the psychophysical reality, the *unus mundus*, something has been incarnated into our world of material reality.

The observational method of the Eros ego is different. First, it is completely introverted. It concentrates further on the 'gut brain' in the belly, the second brain independent from the head. This means that first, with the help of preparatory exercises the ego has to abandon the Logos. Only then it is able to concentrate on the vegetative aspects of the body.

A further difference between the Logos and the Eros ego is that the latter is completely without will. It just looks inside—and waits. During the time of concentration something might be observed, or not. In contrast to the observational method of the Logos ego, the scientific experiment, the time and place of this observation are completely accidental. Thus, if something is observed, a singular inner (acausal) quantum leap takes place. This is the main reason why, in a physical-symbolic language (W. Pauli) I also call the observational mode of the Eros ego *the observation of the singular inner quantum leap*. Such a method of observation corresponds to the above defined creation by observation in quantum physics. However, there are two decisive differences. First the observational act is completely introverted, and second, the ego has to be completely without will. This way the observational act leads to an accidental, acausal observation. This is the basis of Body-Centered Imagination.

A third difference between the observational act of quantum physics and BCI is that in physics the quantum leap happens in matter, whereas in the introverted observational method it also happens in the ego, more exactly in the Eros ego. This means that by replacing the quantum physical act by the psychophysical one we accept that the ego can also function acausally. This way the Eros ego becomes able to observe acausal creation acts out of or even in the *unus mundus*, the incarnation acts of the world soul.

/ / /

With the help of the above clarifications and extensions of some depth psychological and psychophysical terms, we can also define C.G. Jung's synchronicity principle in a more precise way. To do this, we have to look at the only synchronicity the depth psychologist ever published, the famous Scarab coincidence. He writes[43]:

> A young woman I was treating had, at a critical moment, a dream in which she was given a golden scarab. While she was telling me this dream I sat with my back to the closed window. Suddenly I heard a noise behind me, like a gentle tapping. I turned round and saw a flying insect knocking against the window-pane from outside. I opened the window and caught the creature in the air as it flew in. It was the nearest analogy to a golden scarab that one finds in our latitudes, a scarabaeid beetle, the common rose-chafer (Cetonia aurata), which contrary to its usual habits had evidently felt an urge to get into a dark room at this particular moment.

Jung continues[44]:

> The meaningful connection is obvious enough…in view of the approximate identity of the chief objects (the scarab and the beetle).

---

[43] *CW 8, § 843*
[44] *CW 8, § 845*

He then notes that the treatment of this patient was very difficult at first because she was caught in a strong rationalism and the possibility of the irrational phenomena was completely refused. She, therefore, needed a change of perspective whereby her consciousness could open to the irrational. Such a transformation of consciousness is almost exclusively represented by symbols of rebirth[45]:

> The scarab is a classic example of a rebirth symbol. The ancient Egyptian Book of What Is in the Netherworld describes how the dead sun-god changes himself at the tenth station into Khepri, the scarab, and then, at the twelfth station, mounts the barge which carries the rejuvenated sun-god into the morning sky.

The meaning of this synchronicity lies in the fact that Jung's patient was strongly shown that in her, symbolically speaking, a rebirth myth was constellated that had to be interpreted psychologically as a transformation of consciousness. This experience caused a deep affect which resulted in her opening up to the irrational and her recognition of the reality of the world of the unconscious.

Another very important aspect has to be considered. Jung was not at all concentrating on his client, as usual practice demands, but somehow 'dissolved' into space. Only this way was he able to listen to the noise at the window, and to open it in a *spontaneous act*. In slightly different words: he *unconsciously* was in the Eros state of the ego.

We know of a second synchronicity, in which we notice the same behaviour of C.G. Jung, the fox synchronicity I mentioned in Chapter 1[46]:

> For instance, I walk with a woman patient in a wood. She tells me about the first dream in her life that had made an everlasting impression upon her. She had seen a spectral fox coming down the stairs in her parental home. At this moment a real fox comes out of the trees not 40 yards away and walks quietly on the path ahead of us for several minutes. The animal behaves as if it were a partner in the human situation.

It is very unusual that a psychoanalyst goes for a walk with his patient. Thus, we can assume that Jung took another *spontaneous* decision. Only this way the coincidence of the dream fox and the real fox could happen. Since spontaneity belongs to Eros, we can conclude that in this second example the depth psychologist was unconsciously in the Eros state again.

I will come back to the specific behaviour—I call this the synchronicity quest—in the state of the Eros ego later[47]. Here I would only like to mention that

---

[45] CW 8, § 845
[46] Letters, Vol. 1, 1973, p. 395
[47] See section 6.12.2.4

with the discovery of the synchronicity quest in the early 1980s I became able to observe many more synchronicities. Since they are the real roots of creative thinking[48], my creativity was tremendously increased. Since then, whenever I write, I always feel that something is 'writing out of me,' and my task is that of the scribe.

6.1.5 The spaceless and timeless psychophysical reality or *unus mundus*, and psychophysical nonlocality

To define a further hypothesis we have to return to the correspondence between Pauli and Jung. Already in the first letters [29], [30] and [7][49] written between April and October 1934, the physicist and the depth psychologist began a discussion of parapsychological topics. Pauli refers to Jung's article *Seele und Tod*[50] (*The Soul and Death*) published that year. The depth psychologist doubts that psyche exclusively depends on the brain, since parapsychological facts, especially the 'spacial and temporal telepathic phenomena'[51], telepathy and precognition, show the contrary. Then he continues:

> The limitation of consciousness in space and time is such an overwhelming reality that every occasion when this fundamental truth is broken through must rank as an event of the highest theoretical significance, for it would prove that the space-time barrier can be annulled. The annulling factor would then be the psyche, since space-time would attach to it at most as a relative and conditioned quality. Under certain conditions it could even break through the barriers of space and time precisely

---

[48] *In a letter from Jan. 25, 1954 C.G. Jung calls this 'peculiar state of mind' 'an unconscious thinking that enables [one] to realize the natural progress of the mind in its own sphere,' and 'a natural thought-process in the unconscious.' (Letters, Volume 2, p. 146). He believes that these peculiar states of mind 'occur at the gateway of death.' I would say, also in the moment of the 'death' of the Logos ego when it consciously enters the Eros ego.*

[49] *Meier dates the letters [29] and [30] wrongly. The former is from April 28, 1934, the latter from May 24, 1934. Thus they have to be arranged before letter [7] from October 26, 1934.*

[50] *Today in GW 8, §§ 796; English translation in CW 8, §§ 796.*

[51] *For the following see CW 8, § 813*

because of a quality essential to it, that is, its relatively trans-spatial and trans-temporal nature.

Thus, Jung is convinced that[52]

> The psyche's attachment to the brain, i.e., its space-time limitation, is no longer as self-evident and incontrovertible as we have hitherto been led to believe.

The quotations show us that already in 1934 we find an argument similar to those from 1946 and 1952 I have discussed above. By 'psyche' Jung means 'objective psyche' and thus the objective psychic energy level, i.e., what I called inner spirit-psyche[53], with its center, the Logos Self. He is convinced that this deeper, collective layer of psyche reaches into a sphere, in which the usual meaning of space and time are relativized or even abolished. He even thinks that it is psyche itself that corresponds to the annulling factor, since it possesses a trans-spatial and trans-temporal quality.

As we have seen, during the following 18 years C.G. Jung refined this hypothesis and assumed that the trans-spatial and trans-temporal aspect of psyche corresponded to the vegetative nervous system. In 1952, concerning synchronicity he eventually writes[54]:

> [In the case of synchronicity] we must completely give up the idea of the psyche's being somehow connected with the brain, and remember instead the 'meaningful' or 'intelligent' behaviour of the lower organisms, which are without a brain [especially the bees with their dance, with which they exchange information; RFR].

In 1955, in his late work *Mysterium Coniunctionis*, at the age of 80, Jung concludes[55]:

> For just as a man has a body which is no different in principle from that of an animal, so *also his psychology has whole series of lower storeys* in which the spectres from humanity's past epochs still dwell, then the animal souls from the age of Pithecanthropus and the hominids, then the 'psyche' of the cold-blooded saurian, and, *deepest down of all, the*

---

[52] CW 8, § 813
[53] *In fact, Jung talks here of what I call the Psyche (with capital P), i.e., of matter-psyche. He cannot however distinguish it from inner spirit-psyche.*
[54] CW 8, § 947
[55] CW 14, § 279

transcendental mystery and paradox of the sympathetic and parasympathetic psychoid processes. [Emphasis mine]

Here again C.G. Jung assumes that the VNS, the sympathetic and parasympathetic nervous system, is the seat of specific psychical processes. Later, he anticipates that this trans-spatial and trans-temporal aspect of psyche must belong to a deeper level than the collective unconscious, the *unus mundus* or psychophysical reality, 'an invisible, potential form of reality that is only indirectly inferable through its effects' (W. Pauli)[56]. As already in 1911 the depth psychologist defined the energy term as unipolar[57], *he is however not in a position to distinguish the collective unconscious, the inner spirit-psyche principle, from the psychophysical reality with its energetic principle of matter-psyche, out of which real material incarnation is possible.* Thus he is not really able to explain paranormal phenomena. Further, as we have realized in section 5.2.1.6, this non-distinction leads to mixing the Anima with the *anima mundi*, feminine spirit-psyche with matter-psyche.

Wolfgang Pauli, however, comes closer to the solution of the problem. In letter [29P] he resumes Jung's idea of a possible trans-spatial and trans-temporal quality of the psyche, especially in connection with telepathy and precognition, which J.B. Rhine proved exactly the same year, in 1934. Pauli however objects that Jung's hypothesis is only meaningful if we can find observable events that prove it[58].

By 'observability' the physicist means of course the possibility of proving a hypothesis with empirical experiments. Further, he hints that in the observation of life phenomena (to which psyche belongs), the problem arises that as people have to stay alive, their examination is impossible in a physical experiment. He concludes that the examination of these phenomena is possible neither with causal-physical nor with quantum mechanical experiments. Then he asks the decisive question whether there is a possibility 'that there is *room left* for a new type of law of nature with life phenomena[59].'

As we see, as early as 1934 Pauli expressed a revolutionary idea that is still rejected today by mainstream scientists: physics is not sufficient to explain all the phenomena in the universe. Later this idea would cause a big conflict with

---

[56] AaA, p. 82
[57] In Wandlungen und Symbole der Libido, Beiträge zur Entwicklungsgeschichte des Denkens, *1911/12. English translation:* Psychology of the Unconscious. A Study of the Transformations and Symbolisms of the Libido. A Contribution of the History of the Evolution of Thought, *New York, 1916 (revised version in CW 5)*
[58] AaA, p. 25: '*Of course, it all depends on what position one adopts in the relationships of the hypothetical nonspation [and] nontemporal forms of being of the psyche to* observable *occurrences.*' [Emphasis mine]
[59] AaA, p. 26

Einstein, and Pauli would reproach him that he regarded 'as an imperfection of wave mechanics [quantum physics, RFR] within physics what in fact [is] an imperfection of physics within life[60].'

It was his insight that physics was too limited to understand life phenomena that lead Pauli in 1953 to the above mentioned formulation of the 'dritte Typus von Naturgesetzen'[61] (the third type of law of nature). With this formula he refers to a law to be found in the future, which besides the causality of classical physics and statistical causality of quantum physics obeys a third type of law of nature, and includes a world which possesses trans-spatial and trans-temporal quality[62]. I propose in this book such a third law: a singular inner quantum leap observable by the Eros ego, an acausal process which leads to new creation in the mind and even to incarnation phenomena in matter[63].

C.G. Jung remained all his life with his hypothesis of the VNS as the seat of a second consciousness, as we can see from a late letter[64]:

> We conclude therefore that we have to expect a factor in the psyche that is not subject to the laws of time and space, as it is on the contrary capable of suppressing them to a certain extent. In other words: this factor is expected to manifest the qualities of time- and spacelessness, i.e., 'eternity' and 'ubiquity.' Psychological experience knows of such a factor; it is what I call the archetype, which is ubiquitous in space and time, of course relatively speaking. It is a structural element of the psyche we find everywhere and at all times; and it is that in which all individual psyches are identical with each other, and where they function as if they were the one undivided Psyche the ancients called *anima mundi*.

Here, however, the decisive one-sidedness of C.G. Jung's depth psychological concept comes back. His inability to realize that the energy term must be defined as bipolar, and not unipolar, makes it impossible for him to distinguish spirit-psyche from matter-psyche. This way, he once again equalizes the collective unconscious ('psyche') and the *anima mundi*. Because of this inability he cannot realize the twin process, either.

It was especially the synchronicity phenomenon—the incarnation of preconscious knowledge of the *unus mundus* into the human mind that we will discuss below with the help of the terms of the neutral language—that lead Jung and

---

[60] AaA, p. 121

[61] WB 4/II, p. 310-311, 335-336 (in *Vorlesung an die fremden Leute / Klavierstunde*) and 387-389

[62] *Later Pauli's assumption will culminate in his dealing with the reincarnation hypothesis.*

[63] *Later I will show that synchronicity leads to spontaneous creation in the mind, whereas deeper processes lead to incarnation phenomena in matter and in the human body.*

[64] Letters, Volume 2, p. 398-399; Letter of Oct 21, 1957

Pauli to the above conclusions about the psychophysical reality without space and time in the physical meaning. Neither Jung nor Pauli did however find a solution to the problem of the third law of nature, though *they acknowledged that the unus mundus is spaceless and timeless. The reason is once again that they were not yet able to recognize its energetic principle, matter-psyche.*

In the course of my further remarks below we will come across even deeper phenomena, in which singular incarnation acts happen out of the spaceless and timeless *unus mundus* into the *material* world. In these spontaneous moments, in which spacelessness and new space created in our world touch each other, so to speak, inner and outer reality become alike, the 'point-space' and the 'all-space' unify. This is of course a modern formulation of the identity of microcosm and macrocosm as in Hermetic alchemy and Isaak Luria's *tikkun*. This way the subject-object boundary of the ego is also abolished. On the other hand the timelessness of the *unus mundus* touches the *kairos*, the qualitative and spontaneous time of incarnation. Eternity and the moment merge[65].

As synchronicity and these deeper events I call Hermetic magical phenomena[66] touch the psychophysical reality, the subject-object boundary is also abolished in these two paranormal phenomena. Thus, we can conclude that matter-psyche is, in contrast to spirit-psyche, not split into two, into an outer and inner energy aspect, as physical and objective psychic energy. This is why I also call the quality of the matter-psyche principle 'inner-outer.' What is happening in point A is happening everywhere simultaneously. In physics a similar behaviour is called nonlocality. Therefore, using the physical-symbolic language I call such behaviour in the psychophysical reality or *unus mundus* the psychophysical nonlocality.

---

[65] *Already in my early dreams this situation was symbolically expressed in the demand that I have to find the two holes of physics; the hole in physical space as well as the hole in physical time.*

[66] See section 6.12.3.1

6.2 The six demands of Pauli's Fludd/flood synchronicity

I would like to repeat here the interpretation of Pauli's Fludd/flood synchronicity, which, as we will see, can now be completed with a further, very important insight.

The Fludd/flood synchronicity at the foundation ceremony of the C.G. Jung Institute shows that this institution was challenged to solve the psychophysical problem (the second meaning of this synchronicity) on the basis of the unified psychophysical reality (W. Pauli) or of the *unus mundus* (Dorneus and Jung). The content of such a research should be an extended view of synchronicity and a theoretical description of the Pauli effect (the fourth meaning), which extends the parapsychological aspects of synchronicity, i.e., telepathy and precognition, with the principle of psychokinesis (the latter not explainable with the help of the synchronicity hypothesis). A further basis should be the bipolar Taoist energy concept of yin/yang (the fifth meaning), equivalent to the bipolar concept of Hermetic alchemy (the third meaning). Returning to the Hermetic worldview means thus also the inclusion of Taoism, since in both of them one form of energy can transform into the other and vice versa. This attribute corresponds to the 'fluidity,' the first meaning of Pauli's synchronicity. Because of the possibility of such a transformation or even transmutation in the Hermetic and Taoist worldview the complementarity between physics and Jung's depth psychology is overcome (the sixth and new meaning).

Such a process that overcomes complementarity happens in the *unus mundus* beyond the collective unconscious, physical matter and spacetime. Thus, neither physics nor depth psychology can explain it anymore. To describe it, the excluded third of Western philosophy, the *tertium non datur* is required. It is exactly the hypothesis of the psychophysical reality and of the singular (acausal) quantum leaps based on the twin process[67] that happen in and out of the psychophysical reality. These paranormal phenomena are complementary, as they are incarnation events on the level of objective psyche (synchronicity) *as well as* on the level of matter (Pauli effect, UFO encounter and abduction, BCI/SST). I will further show that both cases are observable.

---

[67] *Definition see below*

6.3 'Disinfected' Matter in the Heavens, C.G. Jung's archetypes and physical matter as *being*

As we have seen, it is impossible to solve the psychophysical problem with C.G. Jung's quaternity hypothesis based on *Answer to Job*: his addition of the Holy Mary to the Trinity in the Christian Heaven reduces her to 'disinfected' matter (W. Pauli). Disinfected matter is also infertile: acausality is not included. As we have further seen, Pauli's statement means that Jung's quaternity does not include the instinctive feminine aspect—as the Holy Mary does not possess an abdomen. Jung feels that something is missing, thus, in his other definitions of the quaternity he replaces the Holy Virgin by the devil[68]. Jung gets entangled in this contradiction because he cannot distinguish causal from acausal processes—the causality of the Christian God from the acausality of the devil, so to speak. Together with the Trinity, the Holy Mary is raised into Heaven, 'at a great distance from people.' (W. Pauli). This way the real feminine principle is not described at all, as the dark aspect of matter and of the instincts[69]—acausality—is left out. This aspect we find in Robert Fludd's 'intermediary realm,' as Wolfgang Pauli realized. In my interpretation it is the 'realm' of matter-psyche, the *unus mundus*, we should search in our own belly, and not in the 'heaven' of the head brain. Since this layer is situated between spirit and matter, it possesses a subtle consistency—the vegetative aspect of matter and of the body.

In a religious-psychological language we can express C.G. Jung's prejudice as the acceptance of only the virginal aspect of the Holy Mary, who was (by a nonrecurring miracle) fertilized by the Holy Ghost. Physically speaking this symbolic term can be translated into the (metaphysical) assumption of the *unique* big bang and the conservation of physical energy in its aftermath. In the language of medieval Hermetics it would mean that only *creatio ex nihilo* is possible, not *creatio continua*. In a neutral language we can call this aspect the conservation of the spirit-psyche of the universe. This conservation can be observed on the one hand as outer spirit-psyche (i.e., physical energy), and on the other as inner

---

[68] See for example CW 11, § 258
[69] As I show in my digital publication Holy Wedding, http://paulijungunusmundus.eu/hknw/holy_wedding_alchemy_modern_man_contents.htm the one-sided definition of the feminine principle leads Jung also to the definition of the Anima as feminine spirit-psyche (in my terminology), i.e., symbolic thinking. What I call matter-psyche, the paranormal aspect of outer as well as inner nature, the macrocosm as well as the microcosm, is absent from C.G. Jung's depth psychology and especially from his quaternity.

spirit-psyche (C.G. Jung's objective psychic energy). In fact, the depth psychologist considers inner energy as being conserved when he writes[70]:

> [Psychic] energy underlies the changes in phenomena, that *it maintains itself as a constant* throughout these changes. [Emphasis mine]

The dogma of the Assumption, Jung was so fascinated with, leads thus to a contradiction: on the one hand it is the theological way to express the liberation of energy out of 'disinfected' (and thus good) matter and its integration into the world of the spirit-mind-Logos. On the other hand, it is obvious that in psychoanalysis it is evil matter or the instincts that need to be 'cleaned' and raised into the 'Heaven' of the mind (the Neoplatonic prejudice). This contradiction is also at the background of C.G. Jung's inconsistent definition of the quaternity in the Heavens: sometimes the Trinity plus the Holy Mary, other times the devil replacing the mother of Christ.

Further, according to the Neoplatonic and Christian worldview such a quaternity is *being* in the Aristotelian sense. Speaking of *being* in a metaphysical realm is however itself metaphysics. For a natural scientist Jung's quaternity and the collective unconscious is thus *nonbeing*. However, the postulation of Jung's collective unconscious as *nonbeing* is also metaphysical. Further, as we have realized above, the scientific postulate of matter as *being* is metaphysics, as is Einstein's idea that 'I like to believe that the moon is still there even if we don't look at it[71].' Thus we are given the task to find a way out of the metaphysical assumptions of Jung's depth psychology as well as of physics and science in general. This I will do in the presentation of the psychophysical theory below.

---

[70] CW 8, § 3
[71] See for example http://www.thebigview.com/spacetime/uncertainty.html

6.4 Matter and archetypes as *potential being* and their actualization in the quantum leap

Let us briefly summarize: to avoid the metaphysical argument, which is not at all a scientific consideration, and in order to reach a true scientific empiricism, Pauli proposes that the terms matter, psyche and spirit are mere metaphysical (or transcendent) expressions. Thus, we cannot say anything about them: they can be *being* or *nonbeing*. This is why we can equate them and Jung calls the three of them the transcendent X. Instead of arguing for *being* or *nonbeing*, (as natural science and depth psychology do), one can replace the X by the hypothetical term of the unified psychophysical reality or *unus mundus*. Here Pauli uses an idea of Aristotle and postulates that there exists a third principle besides *being* and *nonbeing: potential being*. We can postulate that the 'contents' of the quantum physical wave function and the *unus mundus* consist of exactly this *potential being*. For a quantum physicist such a formulation is obvious, since the wave function describes in fact a mere potentiality.

With the help of *potential being* Pauli can explain on an epistemological level the collapse of the wave function or the quantum leap as the transformation of nonascertainable *potential being* into observable, i.e. ascertainable *actual being*. During the measurement an empirically observable reality in our world is created. This means that because of this event, in which something new is incarnated in our world, quantum physics does not remain in the metaphysical state of hypotheses about the *being* or *nonbeing* of X. In contrast to 'infertile' classical physics (Newton and Einstein), which uses metaphysical arguments regarding *being* and *nonbeing* (matter is *being* for them), quantum physics becomes 'fertile.' The process {*potential being* → *actual being*} happens during the act of measurement. It transforms something that only potentially existed into a new creation in our world. Quantum physics abandons this way the Neoplatonic worldview in favour of the Hermetic one. Thus Pauli can postulate that the act of observation is 'an act of creation[72].'

Apart from the collapse of the wave function in the act of observation well-known to physicists there is another kind of quantum leap. It is the natural, spontaneous quantum leap happening during the (acausal) decay of a radioactive atom. The difference between the two events is that the former happens as the consequence of an act of will—the physicist decides when and where he takes measurements—the latter is however completely independent of the will of the

---

[72] In letter [45P]; AaA, p. 55; PJB, p. 58, WB 4/I, p. 192

physicist. This means that this acausal decay is a natural phenomenon, which we cannot influence. *The radioactive decay, in the light of Pauli's epistemological prerequisite, becomes a creation and incarnation act.*

Since the singular radioactive decay of one specific atom is acausal, it can happen anytime, be it the next second or the next century. Thus, the singular decay is in principle not observable in a physical experiment fixed in space and time by will. Therefore, physics observes the mass of radioactive atoms and can derive statistically causal laws of their decay.

Since in the natural radioactive decay *potential being* spontaneously transforms into *actual being*, in a symbolic language I call it an incarnation act of the world soul. Thus, what quantum physics does not realize is that the decay of a single radioactive atom—created naturally or artificially—is such a unique incarnation act. Since the invention of the nuclear bomb and the nuclear power plants, where the decay is forced by human will, humankind identifies with the incarnation capacity of the world soul, which is nothing else but a self-deification. Since 1945, mankind plays the sorcerer's apprentice who, as I mentioned above[73], lost all control over the processes he launched. As I will show below, on a psychophysical level we can thus expect a physically non-observable but necessary 'side-effect' of artificial fission—as manifested in UFO encounter and abduction.

Pauli assumes that the quantum physical observational process and its effect, the transformation of *potential being* into *actual being* is also applicable to the depth psychological process. In other words, he applies the same epistemological background to Jung's depth psychology. He argues that archetypes are also *potential being* in the collective unconscious, the latter belonging to the nonascertainable X. Thus, archetypes are also a mere metaphysical (or transcendent) hypothesis, as the god of the theologians and the wave function of quantum physics. However, when we observe an incarnation out of this metaphysical world, out of the collective unconscious or out of the *unus mundus*, be it a dream, a vision or an audition, a synchronicity or a psychokinetic event, a content of this potential world becomes real. In both physical and depth psychological cases, in the moment of observation an incarnation takes place. We realize that with this brilliant idea of Pauli's, depth psychology ceases to be a metaphysical philosophy and becomes empirical and as such science.

The difference between the two modes of observation in physics and in depth psychology is that in the former we determine the time of the observation by will. In depth psychology this is impossible, since we cannot plan the 'experiment' by will; the contents of the unconscious appear spontaneously, i.e., acausally. Therefore, a depth psychological observation resembles much more the observation of a singular decay of a radioactive atom than the collapse of the wave function in the moment of the will-based act of observation.

---

[73] *See section 5.4.6 in Part 1*

6.5 The blue color in the World-clock vision as the causal *Logos philosophicus* versus the acausal *Logos Spermatikos*

Until the end of his life, C.G. Jung was unable to realize the difference between *being* and *potential being*. Thus, he was neither able to realize the difference of the definition of the archetypes as *being* or as *potential being*. This means that he did not understand the difference between the philosophical, theological and classical physical worldview on the one hand, and the view of quantum physics on the other; that is to say he could not make the difference between Neoplatonism and Hermeticism.

Wolfgang Pauli anticipated that these acausal events are represented in his World-clock vision, published by Jung for example in CW 12, § 307:

WOLFGANG PAULI'S VISION OF THE WORLD CLOCK:

There is a vertical and a horizontal circle, with a common centre. This is the world clock. It is supported by a black bird.

The vertical circle is a blue disc with a white border divided into 4 x 8 = 32 partitions. A pointer rotates on it.

The horizontal circle consists of four colors. Four little men with pendulums are standing on it, and around it there is a ring that was once dark and is now golden (formerly carried by children).

The 'clock' has three rhythms or pulses:

1. The small pulse: The pointer on the blue vertical disc advances by 1/32.
2. The middle pulse: One complete revolution of the pointer. At the same time the horizontal circle advances by 1/32.
3. The great pulse: 32 middle pulses are equal to one revolution of the golden ring.

Figure 6.4:
Pauli's vision of the World-clock[74]

In his attempt to interpret the vision C.G. Jung amplifies the blue color of the vertical disc with the coat of the Heavenly Queen[75], of the Virgin Mary. As we have seen, in a letter from October 8, 1953 to Fierz[76] Pauli, however, unmistakably rejects Jung's amplification. Though he realizes that the 'disinfected' matter of the Virgin Mary symbolizes infertility and the impossibility of the creation of something qualitatively new, he is however not yet able to see that in physical terminology the infertility, which he also recognizes as the main deficiency of Neoplatonic alchemy, means the principle of causality and especially of the energy conservation law, which, as we have seen, Jung also assumed as the basis of the energetic processes in the unconscious (with the exception of synchronicity).

Anticipating that his World-clock vision symbolizes an acausal process, Pauli amplifies with the blue color of Demeter's corn flower and the blue flower of German Romanticism. In contrast to the virginal infertility, the blue flower symbolizes fertility on the one hand, and magic on the other, the principle on which the singular acausal quantum leap[77] is based in my interpretation (see be-

---

[74] *Courtesy of W. Byers-Brown*
[75] *CW 12, § 320*
[76] *See section 3.3.9 in Part 1*
[77] *It is exactly this conclusion Pauli could not draw, since he was convinced of the energy conservation law and the complementarity between physics and depth psychology.*

low). The conflicting amplifications of the depth psychologist and of the quantum physicist thus root exactly in the difference between a causal and an acausal worldview. In ancient Greek philosophy it is the discrepancy between the (causal) Platonic *Logos philosophicus* and the acausal *Logos Spermatikos,* the Pneuma of the Stoa[78]. It is further the decisive difference between Neoplatonic and Hermetic alchemy. This is the deeper reason why Pauli states that while Neoplatonism (and science) is infertile, Hermetics however is fertile.

In a symbolic language I call the singular acausal process the self-fertilization of the world soul, which in a neutral language becomes the (magical) creation possibility out of matter-psyche of the *unus mundus* happening in the so-called *coniunctio,* the core process of Hermetic alchemy. Put in a neutral language, the Hermetic alchemical *coniunctio* becomes the singular acausal quantum leap, which happens in the intermediary realm of the psychophysical reality (Pauli) or *unus mundus* (Dorneus and Jung). To theoretically describe and empirically observe these self-fertilizations, we have thus to return to Hermetic alchemy on a higher level, while including the above epistemological results of Pauli and quantum physics in general as well as Jung's discovery of the collective unconscious (and the deeper reality of the *unus mundus,* the realm of the world soul).

/ / /

As we realized, during the 17th century Hermetics and with it acausality and magic was repressed, because mathematics entered the philosophy of nature. As a result of the birth of modern science, everything became explainable in a causal way (since mathematics is completely causal). Thus, the magical aspect of the material universe (in my neutral language its matter-psyche aspect) disappeared into the unconscious. Pauli, however, was convinced that this magical principle, he thought to be related to the Beyond, comes now back, for example in the Pauli effect that haunted him his entire life. Thus, the Nobel laureate demanded that physics was expanded with the inclusion of exactly this acausal principle (which according to my hypothesis expresses itself during the observable singular acausal quantum leap). Such expanded physics can only consist in the inclusion of some sort of paraphysics or parapsychology since this other principle is paranormal, especially psychokinetic (see the Pauli effect).

---

[78] *This other aspect of the bipolar energy term Hermetic alchemy of the Renaissance called the Pneuma or the* Logos spermatikos. *It is a form of energy that is not lead by the first cause, by God, but is the autochthonous energy form of the feminine principle. See Stadler, M.,* Renaissance: Weltseele und Kosmos, Seele und Körper, *in: Jüttemann, G., Sonntag, M., Wulf, Ch.,* Die Seele, Ihre Geschichte im Abendland, *Weinheim 1991, pp. 180-197.*

6.6 Synchronicity as an incarnation in the mental/spiritual world versus magical Hermetic incarnation in the material world

It was C.G. Jung who first discovered the mental/spiritual aspect of this new future science. What he called synchronicity was the empirically observable events of this world, the incarnations out of the collective unconscious or out of the *unus mundus*. Since in a synchronicity the outer world behaves symbolically in a way similar to the inner world, the archetype must somehow be 'transgressive' (C.G. Jung)[79], i.e. it must encompass both psyche and matter. However, the incarnation process of a synchronicity, the realization of the new insight, happens not in outer matter but 'only' in the mental/spiritual part of the universe.

We can therefore hypothetically assume that such an incarnation (i.e., the transformation of *potential being* in the *unus mundus* into *actual being*) is possible not only in the mental/spiritual, but also in the material world. This would mean that in the material/corporeal world totally new phenomena can be observed, and with the help of the observation they incarnate. According to my hypothesis UFO encounter and abduction are instances for these incarnations.

Hermetic alchemy described this type of incarnation. In a symbolic-mythological language it was called *coniunctio*. It is the sexual intercourse of a god and a goddess, of the king and the queen[80] with its fruit, the *infans solaris*, the red tincture or the quintessence, symbolizing the product of the acausal incarnation act in matter.

---

[79] *AaA, letter [46J], p. 62 (PJB, p. 64; WB 4/I, p. 204) of Jung: 'contingence of the archetype,' [Roscoe's translation is not correct], and 'transgressivity,' p. 63; see also Pauli's letter [47P], p. 67 (PJB, p. 69; WB 4/I, p. 215) : '"breaking of barriers through contingency" or "transgressivity" of the archetype.' Here it becomes clear that what is meant is 'of the archetype' and not 'with the archetype,' as Roscoe translates.*

[80] *See CW 14, Chapter IV*

6.7 The saviour of the universe as the son of the apocalyptic sun woman, the world soul and the vegetative body

As Pauli states, there exists a parallel myth to the *coniunctio*. It is the birth of the sun child from the apocalyptic sun woman. The sun child and the sun woman do not belong to the Christian Heaven, but to an intermediary world between Heaven and Earth, spirit and matter (see below). According to this myth the newborn sun child is nothing less than the *salvator macrocosmi*, the saviour of the universe compensatory to Jesus Christ, the *salvator microcosmi*, the saviour of the individual. It is the *salvator macrocosmi* that will come at the end of time, in contrast to the *salvator microcosmi*, Jesus Christ, who was at the origin of the Christian eon.

Since the myth of the saviour of the universe is so decisive, it will be one of the most important contents of this chapter. This is why we have to deal with this figure in more detail here. It is 'opposed to the "son of man,[81]"' to Jesus Christ. This opposition starts with the origins of the *filius macrocosmi*:

> In the sixteenth century Khunrath formulated for the first time the 'theological' position of the lapis [synonymous to the savior of the universe; RFR]…The 'Son of the Great World'…came…from those border regions of the psyche that open out into the mystery of cosmic matter. Correctly recognizing the spiritual one-sidedness of the Christ image, theological speculation had begun very early to concern itself with Christ's body, that is, with his materiality, and had temporarily solved the problem with the hypothesis of the resurrected body.

This idea is of course heretic, as we realize from another statement of Jung's[82].

> The alchemists…logically opposed to the son of the spirit a son of the earth and of the stars (or metals), and to the Son of Man or *filius microcosmi* [Jesus Christ; RFR] a *filius macrocosmi* [the *lapis*, the philosophical gold and the Seal of Solomon; RFR], thus unwittingly revealing that in alchemy there was an autonomous principle, which, while it did not replace the spirit, nevertheless existed in its own rights.

---

[81] *For the following see CW 13, § 127*
[82] *CW 14, § 150*

Here we see that C.G. Jung is close to the idea that besides the Heavenly mind/spirit principle there exist a material one, 'the *filius macrocosmi*, who... symbolize[s] the world-soul slumbering in matter[83].' The *filius* is identical with the *savior macrocosmi*; thus, the *savior macrocosmi* becomes equivalent to the world soul.

Since the depth psychologist was not able to realize that the energy term is bipolar, he always mixed up this complementary energetic principle with the one of the mind/spirit. Thus, he was neither able to define the bipolarity of the energy term as spirit-psyche (physical energy respectively objective psychic energy) versus matter-psyche, the feminine energetic principle (a magical-paranormal energy aspect), 'autonomous' and of 'its own rights,' the Pneuma of the Stoa independent from the 'first cause,' the Christian God.

The saviour of the material world is the child of 'fertile matter,' of the *prima materia*[84], and thus a principle which is of virginal origin[85]. However, in contrast to the Virgin Mary, this principle (the *anima mundi* or world soul), is able to acausally *create many times* out of the psychophysical reality. This principle corresponds to the medieval *creatio continua*, compensating the *creatio ex nihilo*, the Jewish-Christian singular 'big bang' of the Genesis. Since in the virginal conception (the principle of the feminine self-fertilization), the masculine part of mankind is absent, we can translate this virginity as (singular) acausality. If we remember Pauli's *bon mot* that acausality and the devil could have something in common[86], we realize that the *salvator macrocosmi* has to do with the evil principle. This common ground of the virginal conception (acausality) is also the reason why C.G. Jung, as we have seen, equates the Holy Virgin with the devil— residing however in the Heavens and not in the intermediary layer of Hermetic alchemy. As the devil, the fourth principle of the quaternity corresponds to acausality and thus to the self-fertilization of the world soul, but as the Virgin Mary it corresponds to 'disinfected' matter and thus to the Neoplatonic infertility of the causal-deterministic principle. This way the quaternity becomes a causal principle on the one hand, and on the other it is also acausal; this is how the discrepancy of Jung's two contradicting theories (W. Pauli) is created.

A further non-Christian precondition of the Hermetic alchemical *opus* is that the *lapis* or the alchemical gold can become the saviour of the material world and of the universe, only after being liberated by the alchemist's work. Thus[87],

> For the alchemist, the one primarily in need of redemption is not man, but the deity who is lost and sleeping in matter.

---

[83] *CW* 9/II, § 120
[84] *CW* 12, § 26; *CW* 14, § 15
[85] *CW* 14, § 355
[86] See section 3.3.9 in Part 1
[87] *CW* 12, § 420

And[88]

> The saviour and Preserver of the world...was extracted from matter by human art and, by means of the opus, made into a new light-bringer... The salvation or transfiguration of the universe is brought about by the mind of man.

When the alchemist thought that his work has redeemed the saviour, he could release 'his blood [which is] the quintessence, the red tincture[89].' The latter is synonymous to the 'rose-colored blood[90]' and is of 'vegetabile naturae.' Thus, the redeemed saviour must have something to do with vegetation, with the life of plants. Its energy seems not to move bodies, but to be related to the principle of the motionlessness of the body and matter. It is not physical energy, but an energy that out of motionlessness is able to change and even save the universe.

As we have realized, the *salvator macrocosmi* has first to be redeemed of matter. We have therefore to ask ourselves what such a procedure could look like, and what its goal could be. We find a very detailed description of this in Paracelsus' work *De vita longa*, about which C.G. Jung wrote a longer essay[91]. There we find three crucial paragraphs. The first reads as follows[92]:

> [The *salvator macrocosmi*] is the astral man, the manifestation of the macrocosm in the microcosm...who 'tasted not death'...the deathless Original Man, to whom the mortal man can be approximated by means of the alchemical opus. As a result of this approximation the powers and attributes of the *homo maximus* flow like a helpful and healing stream into the earthly nature of the microcosmic mortal man.

Then the depth psychologist continues in showing that the *lapis*, the stone, and the alchemical gold, the goals of the *opus* are identical with the *salvator macrocosmi*.

In the above, Jung describes how Paracelsus imagined the creation of the subtle or vegetative body. The idea consists in the identity of the microcosm (the human body), with the macrocosm (the universe), reached through the (Hermetic) alchemical *opus*. The result is a sustainable influence of the *salvator* or *homo maximus* upon the mortal body, which has a constructive and healing effect. Since the macrocosm and the microcosm (the universe and the human body)

---

[88] *CW 13, § 163*
[89] *CW 13, § 384*
[90] *CW 13, § 390; CW 14, § 419*
[91] *CW 13, §§ 145-238*
[92] *CW 13, § 203*

are identical, such a procedure has also a healing and redeeming effect on the whole universe.

We realize further that *the process of redeeming the saviour of the world, which, as we have seen, is equivalent to the world soul, is identical with the creation of the vegetative body out of the mortal body.* Also, here the terms *salvator macrocosmi*, the saviour of the universe, the world soul and the subtle or vegetative body become identical. All of them are further '*incorruptibile*, that is [they consist of] an indissoluble substance[93].' This is confirmed in CW 13, where Jung writes[94]:

> Union with the *homo maximus* produces a new life, which Paracelsus calls 'vita cosmographica' [and vita longa; RFR]. In this life 'time appears as well as the body Jesahach' (*cum locus tum corpus Jesahach*). *Locus* can mean 'time' as well as 'space'…The *corpus Jesahach* may thus be the *corpus glorificationis,* the resurrected body of the alchemists, and would coincide with the *corpus astrale.*

All these terms mean the same, namely the deified body, the subtle body or as I call it, the vegetative body. As Paracelsus shows in *De vita longa*, the effect of such a procedure is twofold: first, it serves as the cure of bodily disease and leads to a long life in this world, and second, it is the creation of an individual eternal life in the Beyond.

In a commentary Gerardus Dorneus (a follower of Paracelsus) describes further the process of the creation of the vegetative body[95]:

> From [the astral man, the manifestation of the macrocosm in the microcosm] comes the 'mental vision' of that great Aquaster, which is born supernaturally. That is to say, from the…mother…and through the power of the imagination, comes the great vision, which impregnates the supernatural matrix so that it gives birth to the invisible foetus of longevity.

Aquaster is a symbol for the watery principle, and corresponds to the world soul. The idea is therefore that the transformation of the mortal body into the subtle or vegetative body happens in visions created by the 'power of imagination.' These visions 'impregnate' the 'supernatural matrix,' the world soul. This way she can give birth to an invisible foetus,' which is nothing else than the *elixir vitae*, the healing life essence, the Alexipharmakum (the counter-poison),

---

[93] *CW 16, § 220*
[94] *CW 13, § 205*
[95] *CW 13, § 204*

the *medicina catholica* (the all-healing substance), symbolically also described as the red tincture and the quintessence as the last goal of the *opus*[96]:

> The 'son of the great world' (*filius macrocosmi*, the lapis) is correlated with Christ, who is the *filius microcosmi*, and his blood is the quintessence, the red tincture.

It is obvious that the process described above corresponds to the Hermetic alchemical *coniunctio* as well as to the myth of the creation of the sun child out of the apocalyptic sun woman. This is why in the next section I will delineate once again its essence. Though Jung talks of a correlation, we should realize that what is meant is not the redemption of man by Jesus Christ, but a contrary process, in which the human being redeems the *filius macrocosmi* out of matter and/or of the human body so that the saviour or salvator can begin rescuing the world and the universe[97]:

> Since it is not man but matter that must be redeemed, the spirit that manifests itself in the transformation is not the 'Son of Man' [Jesus Christ; RFR] but, as Khunrath very properly puts it, the *filius macrocosmi*. Therefore, what comes out of the transformation is not Christ but an ineffable material being named the 'stone,' which displays the most paradoxical qualities apart from possessing *corpus, anima, spiritus,* and supernatural powers.

Below I will show the almost incredible fact that this 'ineffable material being' is nothing else than Wolfgang Pauli's antineutrino, if we look at it on a psychophysical level, since it is 'possessing *corpus, anima, spiritus,* and supernatural powers,' i.e., magic, as shown in the Pauli effect, for example.

Also the *Rosarium Philosophorum*, a Hermetic alchemical text published in 1550[98] talks of the *coniunctio*. Its result is the so-called *denarius* (see figure 6.5):

---

[96] *CW 13, § 384*

[97] *CW 12, § 420*

[98] Rosarium philosophorum, Frankfurt, 1550; Jung's interpretation in CW 16 as The Psychology of the Transference. *The interpretation of this text, differing from Jung's in CW 16, is the main content of Chapter 4 of my digital publication* Holy Wedding —C.G. Jung's and Wolfgang Pauli's Inner Development and the Creation of a New Hermetic science, http://paulijungunusmundus.eu/hknw/holy_wedding_alchemy_modern_man_contents.htm

PHILOSOPHORVM.

hie ist geboren die edele Keyserin reich/
Die meister nennen sie ihrer Tochter gleich.
Die vermeret sich/gebiert Kinder ohn zal/
Sein vnd ötlich rain/vnnd ohn alles mahl.

Figure 6.5:
The hermaphrodite (denarius) as the goal of the opus[99]

It is a hermaphrodite with two heads, who holds in one of his/her hands three snakes, and one snake in the other. This immediately reminds us of Pauli's dream of the dancing Chinese woman (the world soul), where a six-fold and a four-fold structure is presented (which I will interpret at the end of the book). As the following quote shows, the six-fold structure is an attribute of the *salvator macrocosmi*, the world soul or the subtle or vegetative body[100]:

> [The *filius macrocosmi* is the] true and authentic duplex Mercurius or Giant [the *homo maximus* above; RFR] of twofold substance...the sole and perfect Healer of all imperfect bodies and men, the true and heavenly physician of the soul...the triune universal essence.

Here we see clearly that the saviour must have a bipolar and a triadic structure, as the *Rosarium* also states. In an abstract presentation the saviour of the universe becomes therefore the Seal of Solomon or the Star of David.

It is this magical liberation of the *salvator macrocosmi* the Hermetic alchemists tried to realize in their *opus*. Their failure laid in the fact that when working with their retorts and phials they were not yet able to distinguish the acausal inner process from the causal outer one and thought that the outer was also acausal, magical. Then, science overcame this misunderstanding of the pre-scientific

---

[99] Rosarium philosophorum, *Frankfurt, 1550; also in Jung, CW 16, p. 307*
[100] *CW 13, § 384*

researchers. It defined the world as completely causal. But then radioactivity was discovered and the physicists had to revise their worldview. Besides the causal there exist also acausal processes—the radioactive decays. Since the singular radioactive decay is however not observable and thus not manipulable, physics invented statistical causality. This way it became possible to manipulate radioactive matter—the nuclear bomb and the nuclear power plants. What the modern researchers do not realize, however, is that radioactive beta decay is an event happening on the *psychophysical* level. It becomes an 'inner-outer' process, which I will define below on the basis of psychophysical nonlocality. The latter is nothing else than a modern formulation of Isaak Luria's *tikkun* mentioned above: when one or several human beings can enter deeply enough this process of the liberation of the saviour in their body and mind, the world and the whole universe can also be redeemed. It is this myth which is constellated today, and in my opinion the survival of the world and mankind depends decisively on the question whether enough people can become conscious of this myth and its implications.

6.8 The elements and processes of the Hermetic alchemical *coniunctio* as the basis of a psychophysical theory

The second meaning of Pauli's Fludd/flood synchronicity has shown that for the development of a psychophysical theory we have to go back to Hermetic alchemy, of course not in a regressive way, but while including the epistemology of Pauli and quantum physics in general as well as the experiences of C.G. Jung's depth psychology. This means that we have to describe the elements and processes of the *coniunctio*. I will do this first in the mythological language of the medieval *opus*, and then compare it with C.G. Jung's depth psychological theory and Pauli's epistemological thoughts. Then I will include the Nobel laureate's demand for the creation of a neutral language and give an overview of my psychophysical theory and the related empirically observable phenomena.

CONIVNCTIO SIVE
Coitus.

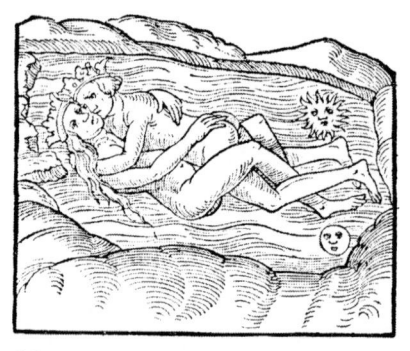

⊙ Luna durch meyn vmbgeben/vnd suffe mynne/
Wirstu schön/starck/vnd gewaltig als ich byn·
☉ Sol/ du bist vber alle liecht zu erkennen/
So bedarffstu doch mein als der han der hennen.

ARISLEVS IN VISIONE.
Coniunge ergo filium tuum Gabricum dilectiorem tibi in omnibus filijs tuis cum sua sorore
Beya

Figure 6.6:
The coniunctio as shown in the Rosarium Philosophorum[101]

The *coniunctio*, the core process of Hermetic alchemy, consists in the sexual intercourse of the divine pair (see figure 6.6). Mostly these are the king and the queen, which mask nothing else than the god and the goddess of Hermetics. A famous example for this divine sexual intercourse is the *Rosarium Philosophorum*, C.G. Jung also dealt with intensely as I mentioned above[102]. The divine sexual act happens in an intermediary realm between the principles of spirit and matter, which has to be created first. This first goal, the intermediary realm, is represented by different symbols: the philosophical gold, the *lapis* (the stone), or the Seal of Solomon. Since it contains the masculine as well as the feminine principle, the *lapis* and its synonyms are androgynous or hermaphroditic. Gerardus Dorneus used the term *unus mundus*, the one world, for this realm, and he postulated that

---

[101] Rosarium philosophorum, *Frankfurt, 1550; also reprinted in Jung, CW 16, p. 249*
[102] *In CW 16, §§ 353-539. However, I do not agree with his interpretation, because he reduces the Hermetic alchemical myth to a Neoplatonic one. This way he uses it as a model for the depth psychological process, especially for the transference/countertransference problem. As I show in my digital publicaton Holy Wedding, http://paulijungunusmundus. eu/hknw/holy_wedding_alchemy_modern_man_contents.htm the* Rosarium *is however deeply Hermetic.*

it has to be regarded as a potential world before the Genesis. It is the pre-big bang of physics, so to speak.

The product and thus the second goal of the Hermetic *opus* is the child of the divine couple. In Robert Fludd's *opus* it is the *infans solaris*, the sun child, which because of its birth out of the intermediary realm is however much more of a sun-moon child. In fact, this product is also looked at as hermaphroditic. Synonymous to this last goal of the Hermetic process are the distillation of the red tincture out of the *lapis* in Gerardus Dorneus' work, and the extraction of the quintessence out of the Seal of Solomon (in Fludd's *opus*, and in others).

In contrast to human sexuality, during the divine sexual intercourse three very distinctive events happen. The first one is the exchange of attributes, which means that the king becomes the queen and vice versa. This process corresponds to the above mentioned development in Taoism, where in the moment of the Tao the masculine yang becomes yin, and the feminine yin becomes yang. Further, the process corresponds to *creatio continua*, the acausal creation and incarnation act discussed above.

A very decisive attribute of the second goal, of the red tincture (the quintessence or the *infans solaris*) is the process of *multiplicatio*, the multiplication. In the instance of the philosophical gold it is meant as gilding the whole surroundings, in the case of the red tincture as possessing an intense radiation which changes the neighbourhood and even the whole universe in an irrevocable way. Of course the quintessence is also thought as having similar attributes.

The third peculiarity of the Hermetic *opus* is that in the moment of *coniunctio* the macrocosm and the microcosm become identical for a short moment. This means that in exactly this decisive moment what happens in the microcosm also happens in the macrocosm, and vice versa. However, such a process should not be looked at as cause and effect. On the contrary, we have to imagine that microcosm and macrocosm are unified by the principle of psychophysical nonlocality. This is only possible when neither corresponds to a metric space.

The reader may think that *coniunctio* is just an old-fashioned myth, which does not have any relevance in our enlightened scientific world and time. We will however realize that it is the basis for a deep revolution of our modern worldview. Before I can continue with the description of the latter, we have to have a look at how Jung's and Pauli's epistemological results fit into the medieval myth.

6.9 C.G. Jung's depth psychology and the Hermetic alchemical myth

Before his big life crisis, the so-called night-sea journey Jung redefined Sigmund Freud's libido term. In his early work *Wandlungen und Symbole der Libido, Beiträge zur Entwicklungsgeschichte des Denkens*[103] (*Psychology of the Unconscious. A Study of the Transformations and Symbolisms of the Libido*[104]), published in two parts in 1911 and 1912, he abandons Freud's exclusively sexual interpretation, and introduces the hunger drive as a second basis for the libido. However—and this is decisive—he defines libido qualitatively as a unipolar masculine principle[105]. He will never change this definition of libido, which he later calls the objective psychic energy.

Thus, C.G. Jung's depth psychology does not fit into the model of Hermetic alchemy, where a bipolar energy term is symbolically represented as the king and the queen, or in Taoism as the yang and the yin principle. It is obvious that because of this crucial limitation C.G. Jung's depth psychology cannot describe the exchange of attributes. Thus, in this very important aspect of the Hermetic worldview his theory fails. It is therefore very understandable that the depth psychologist, as we remember, confessed to Pauli in 1953 that he did not reach the *coniunctio*.

Further, as we have seen, C.G. Jung created a contradiction between a causal and an acausal theory of the archetypes. The causal theory is for example verified in his book *Aion*, in which he describes a deterministic development of the archetype of the Self. On the contrary, the theory of synchronicity is acausal. It was Wolfgang Pauli who realized that synchronicity contains implicitly *multiplicatio*, since when an individual acausally unfolds a new meaning, this meaning has the tendency to spread all over the world in a relatively synchronous manner. We can thus hypothetically conclude that in synchronicity the process of the unification of the microcosm with the macrocosm takes place. Since the meaning of a synchronicity is psychical, such a unification is however restricted to the spiritual/mental level of the universe. Extracting the meaning of a synchronicity is therefore not a creation act in matter itself. Hermetic alchemy, however, was

---

[103] Jung, C.G., Wandlungen und Symbole der Libido, Beiträge zur Entwicklungsgeschichte des Denkens, *1911/12*
[104] *New York, 1916*
[105] *I show this fact in my digital publication* Holy Wedding, *http://paulijungunusmundus.eu/hknw/holy_wedding_alchemy_modern_man_contents.htm*

convinced that the observation of exactly such (magical) creation and incarnation events in matter was possible.

C.G. Jung is not able to distinguish between his metaphysical causal theory of archetypes and the empirically observable acausal processes, synchronicities, since he does not understand Pauli's argument of the transformation of *potential being* into *actual being*. Thus he remains in the conflict of these two theories.

It is therefore the definition of the archetype as *being* in the Neoplatonic sense, together with his unipolar definition of objective psychic energy, as opposed to the Hermetic worldview, that prevented Jung from developing a psychophysical theory, based on the medieval Hermetic process.

6.10 Quantum physics and Wolfgang Pauli's epistemological insights compared to the Hermetic alchemical myth

We have now to ask ourselves whether quantum physical theory as well as Pauli's epistemological conclusions follow the Hermetic alchemical model. To do so we have first to go back to the year 1928 in which Paul A. M. Dirac published his ground-breaking article that determined the further development of quantum physical theory. Dirac was the first to combine Einstein's special relativity theory, a causal theory, with acausal quantum physical concepts. This is how he found an equation that is named after him, the relativistic Dirac equation that describes the electron, he published in 1928. The equation is quadratic; therefore it possesses two solutions like every quadratic equation, a positive and a negative one. The positive solution fits exactly the characteristics of the physical electron.

In classical physics one would simply neglect the second solution as non-physical and/or postulate that the mathematical formalism is too rich. In quantum physics, however, this reduction does not work anymore, because the energy term is not continuous. Thus, quantum leaps that jump over the zero point become possible. This way also the transformation of positive into negative energy is allowed.

The quantization of energy in quantum physics (one of the great differences from the continuous energy term of classical physics), is thus the reason why one has to find in negative energy the physical equivalent to the negative solution of Dirac's equation.

Since, however, negative *energy* has completely non-physical attributes (M. Stöckler), Dirac postulated that the second solution must also describe a physical elementary *particle* that he called positron. It corresponds to the electron, possesses however a positive electrical charge. Therefore it cannot be a usual elementary particle. Thus Dirac invented the concept of antimatter, a special kind of matter, which is produced particularly in accelerators and bubble chambers. In our universe it can survive only very briefly because when it contacts with normal matter it is, together with the material particle, immediately destroyed, i.e., converted into photons or pure energy.

The concept of antimatter however has an important weak point: to explain the creation of antimatter, Dirac had to postulate a daring hypothesis: these particles of antimatter, the positrons, are created out of an infinite 'sea' of electrons with negative energy, which are however *physically unobservable*. Further, because they are transformed into positrons, they leave behind a hole in this 'sea' of unobservable electrons with negative energy.

Since the particles with negative energy are defined as physically unobservable, i.e., metaphysical, such a theory is pure metaphysics, and so is the hypothesis that in such a metaphysical 'sea' there should also exist holes.

The quantum physical hypothesis of antimatter is therefore based on a metaphysical axiom, the principle of negative energy, which is itself defined with the properties of physical unobservability and the concept of 'invisible holes' in an infinite continuum. Infinity and unobservability are however specific characteristics of many archaic God-images.

The professed atheist Dirac departed from the empiricism of physical science with this metaphysical definition. Thus unable to offer a physical explanation he fell into a religious-psychological speculation. This is why during a discussion, Wolfgang Pauli spontaneously created the *bon mot*: 'There is no god, and [Paul] Dirac is his prophet![106]'

We realize then that because of the redefinition of the negative energy term into antimatter, quantum physics also possesses a unipolar energy term. And we can conclude that this hypothesis cannot serve as a basis for a psychophysical theory on the background of the Hermetic process. Of course without a bipolar energy term we cannot describe the exchange of attributes happening in the twin process on the basis of the psychophysical reality either, since this would mean that physical energy would be able to transform into a qualitatively altered form,

---

[106] *Quotation see for example in* Fischer, E. P., An den Grenzen des Denkens, Wolfgang Pauli, Ein Nobelpreisträger über die Nachtseiten der Wissenschaft, *Herder, Freiburg, Basel, Wien,* 2000, *p.* 66.

and that this other sort of energy would retransform. Further, such a double transformation is not possible since mathematics cannot describe qualitative processes.

Radioactive radiation however fits into a Hermetic alchemical model and also into a modern psychophysical theory. We remember that Pauli compared it with the red tincture and its *multiplicatio*, i.e., with the 'radiation' of the philosophical gold, one of the goals of the *opus*. He could not realize however that with the dogmatic defence of the energy conservation law he excluded the idea of a qualitative energy transformation, and this way could not approach the Taoist and the Hermetic bipolar energy definition. Thus he had no idea that some sort of a 'radioactivity' could be also possible on the psychophysical level of the *unus mundus*.

The advantage of Pauli's limitation is however that it becomes crystal clear that physics and depth psychology have to be complementary ways of describing nature, and that depth psychology thus cannot be included into physics, which would also mean a mathematical quantification of objective psychic energy, an idea that Marie-Louise von Franz passionately rejected[107].

This restriction paved the way for Pauli's decisive insight that instead of depth psychology parapsychology should be integrated into an expanded physics. This way, the physicist approached Hermetic alchemy and the psychophysical theory rooted in it, based on the principle of a magical energy beyond physical and objective psychic energy. However, he was not able to really formulate it because of his assumption of the unipolarity of energy.

Though the Nobel laureate is not able to define a psychophysical theory of the *unus mundus*, he prepares its formulation with a brilliant idea. He assumes that the nonascertainable X—the metaphysical realm which we can call matter, psyche, spirit, the psychophysical reality or *unus mundus*—consists neither in *nonbeing* as science argues nor in *being* as C.G. Jung assumes, but in *potential being*. This way the definition of the process

{potential being → actual being},

becomes possible, i.e. the possibility of a creation and incarnation process out of a potential reality into our world. This is the deepest philosophical and quantum physical background of my hypothesis about the core process of a new Hermetic science. It concerns the psychophysical reality and the unique collapse of the wave function or the singular (acausal) quantum leap. As opposed to the quantum physical collapse, the quantum leap is not initialized by the conscious will but is involuntary, i.e. spontaneously observed in the inner as well as in the outer world.

---

[107] See especially Pauli's letters [1598] from July, 11, 1953 and [1667] from Oct 30, 1953 in WB 4/II. The latter also contains the Klavierstunde (The Piano Lesson). Von Franz' letters had been destroyed by Pauli's wife Franca Bertram.

6.11 An overview on the necessary elements and processes of a new psychophysical theory

I hope that my comments and conclusions above clarified what elements and processes are needed for the formulation of a psychophysical theory on the one hand, and on the other the missing aspects of quantum physics and Wolfgang Pauli's epistemological conclusions as well as of C.G. Jung's depth psychology. As an introduction to the concepts I will present, I would like to sum up these necessities and deficiencies.

After the insight that alchemy was split into two completely different branches, Pauli demanded a return to Hermetic alchemy on a higher level. In other words, he postulated that we have to include parapsychology and paraphysics based on the magic of Hermetic alchemy into an expanded physics, as expressed in his *bon mot*: 'What is still older is always the newer[108].'

The physicist's Fludd/flood synchronicity has further shown what elements and processes should be included in such a new psychophysical theory. The first and most important process that should be included and explained is in Taoist terms the transformation of yang into yin and a simultaneous change of yin into yang, the 'Chinese fluidity,' and its result, the Tao, symbolizing a state of increased order, be it in the world of the spirit/mind, or in matter.

Hermetic alchemy symbolically demonstrated such a process with the *coniunctio*, the sexual intercourse of the king and the queen, in which an exchange of attributes happens. The godlike masculine principle—in a neutral language I call it spirit-psyche—transforms into the divine feminine, matter-psyche, and vice versa. Together with Pauli's epistemological insight we have to accept that the first yang is metaphysical and thus unobservable, the process of the creation of higher order (the second of the twin process), is however observable. This way we can consider the process as a transformation of *potential being* into *actual being*. Further, we assume that such processes are singular and acausal.

Using the Hermetic alchemical symbols we can postulate that with this procedure the *infans solaris* in the intermediary realm is created or the red tincture or the quintessence are extracted from the *lapis*, the alchemical stone. This product of *coniunctio* is hermaphroditic, masculine as well as feminine, which means that

---

[108] *Translation quoted according to* Miller, Arthur, I., Deciphering The Cosmic Number, The Strange Relationship of Wolfgang Pauli and C.G. Jung, W. W. Norton & Company, New York, London, 2009, p. 217. Original in Wolfgang Pauli, WB 4/1, p. 386

it symbolizes the reunion of the greatest opposites. This union is the goal of the individuation process. We remember that Pauli interpreted it differently than C.G. Jung. Jung described with this term what he called the integration of the Anima, i.e., symbolic thinking, Pauli however anticipated a different process deeply rooted in Jewish mysticism: the creation of the so-called *homunculus*[109].

Jung's interpretation leads to the inclusion of synchronicity, since only with symbolic thinking can we find its meaning and thus unify the inner and the outer event. Pauli's assumption, however, leads to the observation of singular magical processes, be it in the outside (UFOs; Pauli effect), or in one's inside (BCI; SST).

It is obvious that the description of such processes needs an energetic point of view. One could therefore suppose that what is meant is the transformation of physical energy into objective psychic energy, and vice versa. The discussion between Pauli and Jung has shown us however that because of the complementary relationship between physics and depth psychology such a transformation from outer spirit-psyche into inner spirit-psyche (from the 'particle' to the 'wave,' so to speak), is impossible. Further, we can conclude that we cannot integrate depth psychology into physics, as the Nobel laureate first intended to.

We realized further that Hermetic alchemy as well as Taoism included the real feminine energetic principle. This means that in contrast to physics and depth psychology a psychophysical theory must contain a bipolar energy term, yang *and* yin, the masculine energetic principle as well as the feminine. In a neutral language I call these qualitatively different principles spirit-psyche (split into physical and objective psychic energy: outer and inner spirit-psyche), and matter-psyche (a 'supernatural,' i.e. a magical principle repressed in the 17th century, when mathematics reduced natural science to causal science).

With the inclusion of bipolar magical processes we have fulfilled the most important demand of Pauli's Fludd/flood synchronicity. The energy term is expanded with the reintegration of the feminine energetic principle. This makes possible the above double transformation with its result, a state of increased order (or as the physicist would say: with increased negentropy).

Increased order, a higher quality, is mathematically non-describable, since mathematics is completely quantitative. Further, increased order means a creation and even an incarnation process, a singular acausal event, which is symbolically represented in Wolfgang Pauli's incarnation synchronicity in 1952 and in fact

---

[109] The homunculus *is synonymous to the* lapis, *the stone [CW 12, § 243], which C.G. Jung interprets as the Self, as the center of the collective unconscious. However, in the same paragraph (243) the depth psychologist states that 'the* lapis *is not just a "stone" since it is expressly stated to be composed "de re animali, vegetabili et minerali," and to consist of body, soul, and spirit; moreover, it grows from flesh and blood.' Thus, what is meant is the creation of the vegetative or subtle body, the resurrected body, the diamond body of Chinese alchemy out of the mortal body.*

contradicts the energy conservation law of physics. Since in such processes at the background of the psychophysical reality yang transforms into yin, and vice versa, the psychophysical theory has to consider that the complementarity between physics and depth psychology stated by Pauli—where no such transformation is possible—has to be overcome.

As we have further seen, such processes can be manifested on the one hand as creation by cognition, on the other as creation by observation. A psychophysical theory should therefore include both creation principles. We will realize that synchronicity can be described as a combination of these two principles, which leads to a creation in the spirit/mind aspect of our world. However, this principle has to be expanded by a magical process triggered by mere observation leading to an incarnation in matter.

Based on the *coniunctio* archetype the new worldview should also include its first goal: the creation of the *lapis*, the gold or the Seal of Solomon. This first product we can translate as the creation of an 'intermediary realm,' 'an invisible, potential reality only indirectly inferable by its effects' (W. Pauli). As we know, C.G. Jung used Gerardus Dorneus' term *unus mundus* for this intermediate world and Pauli called it the unified psychophysical reality. The second goal of the Hermetic alchemical *coniunctio* is the observation of the effects radiating from this world. It is called the red tincture, the quintessence or the gilding ability of the alchemical gold. Pauli compared physical radioactivity with the radiation of the red tincture or the quintessence, the so-called *multiplicatio*, which is of course symbolically equivalent to the gilding of the surroundings (and the whole universe) by the alchemical gold. The Nobel laureate did not yet realize however that with this comparison he implicitly stated that radioactivity is not only a process on the physical level, but reaches deep down into the 'invisible, potential reality,' into the background of matter and the body, as well as of spirit and mind, into the *unus mundus*.

Since Pauli talks of a reality, as a quantum physicist he implies that this world is observable through its effects. My hypothesis will therefore be that the effects of psychophysical radioactivity are on the one hand observable in UFO encounter and abduction and in psychokinetic events like the Pauli effect, and on the other hand in events consciously experienced in Body-Centered Imagination and Symptom-Symbol Transformation. This is why the psychophysical theory should also explain these paranormal aspects.

What Robert Fludd and other Hermetic alchemists called *coniunctio* was for Gerardus Dorneus *unio corporalis*. It is the reunification of spirit-psyche and dead matter in the intermediary realm into some sort of spirit-psyche-matter. This way the body is revived. This resurrected matter (or the resurrected body) is however not of the same consistency as the mortal body. It consists of subtle matter and is also called the deified body, the glorification body, the subtle body, or—as in Taoist alchemy—the diamond body. The latter term shows that such a vegetative body observed with the help of the vegetative nervous system is 'incorruptibile,' undissolvable and this is why it is the vehicle for Paracelsus' *vita longa*, long life in this world on the one hand, on the other an *individual* existence in the Beyond. The liberation of the vegetative body is equivalent to the liberation of the *salvator macrocosmi*, the saviour of the universe. Such liberation obtained in a deeply introverted meditation or imagination is the only possible way for the (now released) saviour to save and release mankind and the universe.

In contrast to all other alchemists Dorneus adds a further phase, where the ego unites with the *unus mundus*. This means that man, the microcosm, unifies with the macrocosm. Thus our theory should also include such a process. As we will see, this union is only possible if the scientific consciousness (the Logos ego), is able to transform into the Eros ego. The latter is in a position to observe singular quantum leaps on the psychophysical level—unique acausal events that correspond to the above mentioned transformation of yang into yin, and vice versa—, the twin process.

Since the observed layer (the psychophysical reality or Eros Self), is in fact 'inner-outer,' the process of observation overcomes the subject-object boundary and becomes psychophysically nonlocal. As we have seen, with the example of his Point A situation, C.G. Jung anticipated the psychophysical nonlocality as early as 1929, without however being able to include the processes that belong to it into his theory. Much later, in 1954, he comes back to this intuition. He writes in a letter[110] concerning Luria's *tikkun* (the restoration of the universe by mystical human contemplation)[111]:

> Here the thought emerges for the first time that man must help God to repair the damage wrought by the Creation. For the first time man's cosmic responsibility is acknowledged.

As I have shown above, neither the depth psychologist nor the quantum physicist were able to solve this problem, mainly because both defined the energy term as unipolar and were not able to realize that the psychophysical reality has to overcome the complementarity of depth psychology and physics. This challenge of solving the psychophysical problem becomes our urgent task at the beginning of the 21st century.

---

[110] Letters, *Volume 2, p. 155*
[111] *Isaak Luria (1534 - 1572) was a Cabbalist contemporary of Paracelsus*

6.12 Solving the psychophysical problem: the psychophysical theory and its application for the understanding of paranormal phenomena

6.12.1 The task: explaining the Hermetic alchemical twin process with the help of a neutral language

The presentation of the *coniunctio* archetype at work on the different levels of Hermetic alchemy, physics, and C.G. Jung's depth psychology and its description in a new, neutral language might be confusing. It was however necessary to proceed along these lines, since in the above disciplines the elements and processes necessary for the development of a new theory are not all defined. For example the expression 'exchange of attributes' does not have a meaning either in physics or in depth psychology, since both define energy as unipolar and thus exclude the possibility of its qualitative transformation. This is why the language of Hermetic alchemy was the only one available to describe this possibility.

The situation will become much clearer when we can describe all these elements and processes in a neutral language that uses as few physical and depth psychological terms as possible. Therefore this section will be dedicated to the development of this language as demanded by Wolfgang Pauli.

As I have shown at the beginning of this chapter, a new interpretation of the age-old Axiom of Maria Prophetissa pointed out that the energy term must be regarded as bipolar. In a neutral language the energy term consists in spirit-psyche on the one hand and matter-psyche on the other. Further I assume that spirit-psyche is itself divided into two, an outer and an inner energetic principle. Outer spirit-psyche expresses the energy principle of (classical) physics, and inner spirit-psyche C.G. Jung's objective psychic energy. We can represent it as follows:

```
                          ┌─→ Outer Spirit-Psyche (physical energy)
              ┌─ Spirit-Psyche ─┤
              │           └─→ Inner Spirit-Psyche (objective psychic energy)
Energy Term ──┤
              └─ Matter-Psyche (paranormal energy)
```

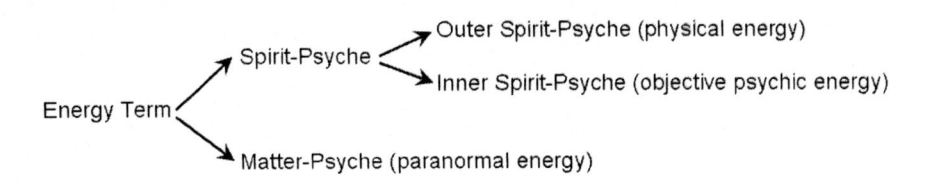

Figure 6.7:
Spirit-Psyche and Matter-Psyche

Since the matter-psyche principle is defined on a psychophysical level, it cannot be split into a physical and a psychic part. This means that in every process in which matter-psyche energy is produced, the physical as well as the psychical level can be affected.

I will show below that with the above hypothesis all possible processes that happen on the physical, on the depth psychological and on the psychophysical level can be described: the collapse of the wave function or quantum physical quantum leap in the moment of the observation, the radioactive beta decay and the production of the antineutrino, the radioactive decay on a psychophysical level, the observation and interpretation of dreams and other products of the unconscious, synchronicity, the Hermetic magical process, UFO encounter and abduction, the Pauli effect and psychokinetic processes in general, and eventually Body-Centered Imagination and Symptom-Symbol Transformation.

The difference between these processes is that some of them lead to a creation in the mind/spirit dimension of our world, others to a creation in the material dimension. There is even a third possibility of an incarnation in the *unus mundus* itself.

Using the neutral language we can define the double transformation as follows:

{X = *unobservable* matter/psyche/spirit[112] → matter-psyche}

And its parallel process:

{Matter-psyche → *observable* spirit-psyche of an altered quality}

corresponding to a hypothetical process, where the unobservable X transforms into matter-psyche and re-transforms into spirit-psyche with a completely new quality.

---

[112] *The reader should remember here the epistemological conclusion derived from quantum physics that reality is only created in the moment of the observation of the quantum leap.*

Using this hypothesis we can define our task as follows:

To solve the psychophysical problem we have to find a neutral language with which we can formulate a theory that describes the elements and the energetic exchange processes happening in the unified psychophysical reality (matter-psyche), as well as in the physical reality (outer spirit-psyche) and on the level of C.G. Jung's objective psyche (inner spirit-psyche). The theory has to be based on the *coniunctio* archetype of Hermetic alchemy and has to be able to describe the background of synchronicity as well as of paranormal processes like UFOs, the Pauli effect and psychokinetic events in general.

The theory has further to include the epistemological conclusions drawn from the fact that psychophysical reality as *potential being,* in the act of observation transforms into *actual being,* into observable incarnation processes. *Since the background of this theory is the coniunctio archetype, it also has to include (1) the bipolar energy term, (2) the duality of spirit-psyche and matter-psyche, (3) the exchange of attributes and (4) multiplicatio. As a modern theory it has further to be based on (5) the quantum physical epistemological insight of the acausal collapse of the wave function (which corresponds to the creatio continua of medieval Theology) during the act of observation. It also has to contain (6) the idea that in the moment of coniunctio the microcosm and the macrocosm become for a short moment identical* (which is the modern way to interpret Luria's *tikkun,* as well as the appearance of the saviour of the universe and the Taoist rainmaker[113]).

---

[113] Actually the term is wrong since he does not 'make' rain, but rather his deeply introverted state leads to inner balance. Since in the moment of perfect inner balance the singular acausal quantum leap is observed (where the microcosm and the macrocosm become for a short moment identical), nature also attains a new balance—it begins to rain.

6.12.2 The translation into a modern language of the Hermetic alchemical exchange of attributes happening during *coniunctio*

6.12.2.1 The collapse of the wave function or (acausal) quantum leap in the act of measurement and in the radioactive beta decay

With the above definition of the qualitative energy transformation in the twin process we can now describe the quantum physical collapse of the wave function during the act of measurement and in the singular radioactive beta decay.

Quantum physics describes what happens during the act of observation as follows:

The collapse of the wave function during the act of observation:

**{X = (wave function = unobservable 'object')
→ observable physical matter}**

As we realized in section 5.2.2.1, the wave function as a mere potentiality describes all the possibilities it can collapse into. This means that (as a linear combination) it delineates for example ten different particles. These particles are mutually exclusive and only one is created during measuring when the collapse takes place. As no one knows which of the ten possibilities becomes real, the process is acausal.

The wave function is unobservable, the spontaneously created particle however is observable: this process corresponds exactly to what Wolfgang Pauli described in a philosophical language: *potential being* transforms into *actual being*:

The transformation of *potential being* into *actual being*:

{Potential being → actual being}

During this process a new reality is created (which is an incarnation), since out of nothing something real, physically observable is created.

Physics uses the same idea to describe the acausal beta decay of a single radioactive atom. A neutron of the radioactive nuclear core *spontaneously* decays into a proton and an electron. Since in this decisive process the energy conservation law is violated Wolfgang Pauli invented a hypothetical particle, the electron-antineutrino, in 1930. As in physics energy and matter are equivalent, with the help of this new particle the energy on the left side of the equation was again equal to the one on the right side—the most imperturbable dogma of physics was saved.

Physics describes this process in the following formula:

The radioactive beta decay:

Neutron → proton + electron + electron-antineutrino

This means that in an energetic process the neutron transforms into a proton, an electron and an electron-antineutrino.

In fact, we do not know what the neutron of this specific atomic core really is before the decay. We call it matter, but in fact we do not know what the matter of the core per se could be, since according to the Copenhagen interpretation of quantum physics reality is created in the observation of the energetic process. Thus, talking of the neutron of the core is a metaphysical statement: we deal with it as if it was *being* in the Aristotelian sense. Therefore, the epistemological conclusion is that the neutron of this specific core is nonascertainable *potential being* before the decay. Only the result of the energetic process, of the spontaneous change, is ascertainable *being*.

Though both processes, the collapse of the wave function during the act of measurement and the radioactive beta decay can be written the same way, there are two decisive differences: 1, the former process is triggered by an act of will of the observer, whereas the latter is spontaneous, acausal and can therefore not be influenced by will; no one knows which atom will decay next; and 2, the collapse of the wave function is observable, since the physicist is able to observe the acausally produced particle. In the case of the radioactive decay we do not know however when such a particle decays—it could be in the next second, or in an infinitely long span of time. Therefore, the decay of a single atom is physically unobservable.

In the course of my comments in this book the first difference will become very important because there are people who are forced to observe such spontaneous events, even against their will. They are compelled into the altered consciousness I call the Eros ego, and in this way they become able to look directly into the *unus mundus* beyond physical reality.

Further, as we have realized in section 6.1.4, we have to define 'observability' in physics. The term means that the observation is a will-based act of the Logos ego. That is we observe when and where we decide to. This way it is only possible to observe a mass of radioactive atoms and their decays. Though the decay of a single atom is still acausal and thus unobservable—the singular decay can happen at any time and in any atom—the mass decay is describable by statistical causality, i.e. by a likelihood distribution. The mean of this distribution is the so-called radioactive half-life, the period in which half of the atoms decay.

In contrast to this observational method we will become acquainted with an observation without will. We just enter the altered state, the Eros ego, and possibly observe something. This way we become able to observe singular quantum leaps. We will further see that especially in UFO encounter humans are forced into this way of observing.

6.12.2.2 The psychophysical radioactive beta decay, the acausal production of the matter-psyche, and the twin process

As we have seen, Wolfgang Pauli compared the radioactive (beta) decay with the Hermetic red tincture, the last product of *coniunctio*. He realized that both are determined by *multiplicatio*. Thus, the Nobel laureate compared *physical* radioactivity with the red tincture. He was however not yet able to reach the idea that *the radioactive beta decay could be an event happening on the psychophysical level, producing matter-psyche and creating energy or matter of an altered quality.*

I postulate that the process on the psychophysical level corresponds to the above defined twin process. Also, the missing energy, interpreted by Pauli as the antineutrino, first disappears, and thus first enters the psychophysical reality, the *unus mundus*, where it is transformed into matter-psyche energy. This means that the energy gains an altered quality, which is however only potential. In the moment of the observation this qualitatively altered energy incarnates. On the psychophysical level this incarnation does not correspond however to an antineutrino, but to *qualitatively altered* spirit-psyche energy. Thus the result of this process does not have the same quality of energy as the original neutron.

Applying the above generalization of the wave function's collapse in the case of the production of the antineutrino we can formulate the physical beta decay as follows:

The physical radioactive beta decay described in the neutral language:

{X = unobservable matter/psyche/spirit → observable *outer* spirit-psyche without any change in its quality}

With the help of the extraverted Logos ego and its observation tool the physicist is not able to observe the transmutation into matter-psyche. Thus he cannot realize that the new particle could have a different quality than the original neutron, and believes that it consists of antimatter. However, since radioactivity belongs to *multiplicatio*, we can assume that like the production of the red tincture radioactivity is in fact a psychophysical process, rooted in the *unus mundus* beyond the artificial split into the physical and the psychical world. Thus, on a psychophysical level the radioactive beta decay becomes the twin process, where as an intermediate result matter-psyche is produced:

The psychophysical radioactive beta decay described in the neutral language:

{X = unobservable matter/psyche/spirit → matter-psyche with potentially altered quality}

And

{Matter-psyche with potentially altered quality → observable *outer* spirit-psyche with realized altered quality}

The difference to the physical beta decay is that we accept consciously that a qualitative change, a transmutation has taken place, which results in the second process, creating spirit-psyche having different qualitative attributes compared with common matter/antimatter.

In agreement with Wolfgang Pauli's definition we assume that the first of the twin process is potential and the second process happens only in the case of the observation, and an incarnation takes place. Therefore, to fulfill the process of {potential being → actual being} both of the above processes, the physical and the psychophysical, must be observable.

In the physical process the antineutrino is an observable elementary particle[114]. However, since with physical observational means one cannot measure qualities, physics is unable to observe any qualitative alteration. Thus, it treats the antineutrino in the same manner as the other three particles. It just adds the energies at the right side of the equation and receives the same quantity as on the left side.

Further, we have seen that the physical observation of the singular creation of an antineutrino during the radioactive decay of a specific atom is not

---

[114] Though experimental physics needed 26 years to do so after Pauli postulated its theoretical existence.

possible[115]. Since the radioactive decay is acausal, a radioactive atom can decay anytime. Thus, in some cases the observer would have to live eternally to record it.

This is why physics has to observe a mass of radioactive atoms. This way it can create statistical mathematical equations, which describe the mass decay. However, the original acausal event is excluded and replaced by statistical causality, which can state nothing about the radioactive decay of a single atom.

In the case of the *psychophysical* radioactive decay I assume that the unknown X first transforms into matter-psyche with potentially altered quality. This means that I replace the antineutrino, i.e., antimatter, by matter-psyche, equivalent to negative energy. In the second of the twin processes matter-psyche then re-transforms into outer spirit-psyche, however qualitatively altered.

Radioactivity belongs to *multiplicatio*, contaminating the whole surroundings and making it also radioactive. This is an indication that the radioactive beta decay is in fact a psychophysical process that obeys the twin process of the *coniunctio* archetype leading to the production of the psychophysical red tincture (or the psychophysical quintessence). In contrast to the red tincture and the quintessence of the Hermetic *coniunctio*, the artificial radioactive beta decay has nothing to do with unification, but is produced as a result of fission, the split of the atom. Since it is a process enforced by the conscious will, artificial radioactivity has effects opposite to the products of *coniunctio*: it does not heal but destroys.

I postulated above that the world of psychophysical radioactivity and of matter-psyche, the *unus mundus*, has the attribute of psychophysical nonlocality: what happens in one point also happens in other parts of the world or even in the whole universe. If radioactivity is a psychophysical phenomenon, *there should exist also observable events that happen parallel to the artificial fission of the atom.* Further, since in such processes matter-psyche with non-physical attributes (M. Stöckler) is produced, it is likely that such events do not obey the known physical laws. This counterpart to the artificial production of radioactivity would be like some sort of Siamese twin that necessarily accompanies every decay.

Here the question arises as to whether the idea to split the atom artificially and to produce artificial radiation could not be the result of a projection of a psychophysical fact into the matter of physics. To discuss this question we have to remember that the singular radioactive beta decay is no topic for the physicist because it is not observable with physical means, which all are constructed by the concretizing Logos ego. However, there could exist a different ego, *the Eros*

---

[115] *The reader would perhaps argue that the decay of any radioactive substance is observable. This is however only the case since a mass of atoms is observed. Would we observe only 10 atoms or so, we could perhaps wait an infinitely long time for the first decay to happen. The same is true when the radioactive half-life is long. Radium has a half-life of 162.2 years. Thus, on average, one of 10 atoms would decay every 324.4 years, which is already too long for a single observer.*

ego that is not based on thinking, extraverted sensation and will, but on *vegetative sensation and feeling*, which is completely without will. Expressed in Pauli's physical-symbolic terminology, the ability to observe accidentally makes such an ego behave as some sort of a radioactive nucleus. Such a 'conscious radioactive nucleus' could observe singular quantum leaps spontaneously happening in the *unus mundus*, and incarnating into our world. In the next sub-sections I will describe such processes.

/ / /

Before we can deal with the transformation of the Logos ego into the Eros ego—the transformation of the observer—we have to differentiate between the ways of observation. Since human consciousness can behave in an extraverted and in an introverted way, there are two different possibilities to observe the 'psychophysical collapse of the wave function,' i.e. the 'psychophysical quantum leap' or the 'psychophysical radioactive decay.'

One way of observation is comparable with the physical observational act, i.e., one looks for outer quantum leaps. One observes the twin process and thus the transformation of spirit-psyche into matter-psyche and the re-transformation of the latter into qualitatively altered spirit-psyche *in the outside world*. One observes the collective matter-psyche corresponding to the medieval *anima mundi*, the world soul. Using these terms we can define the following observable twin process:

A: The psychophysical collapse of the wave function on the collective/material level:

{X = unobservable matter/psyche/spirit → 'collective' matter-psyche with potentially altered quality}

And

{'Collective' matter-psyche with potentially altered quality → observable *outer* spirit-psyche with altered quality}

We can hypothetically define a process in a neutral language, in which an extraverted ego observes the transmutation of what we call physical matter or energy into matter or energy with altered quality *in the outside world*. This process is equivalent to the one that I call the collective/material twin process, in which first a transmutation into the *vegetative aspect* of so-called inanimate matter—into the world soul—takes place, and then is followed by a re-transformation of the world soul aspect into physical matter or energy with altered quality. As we will see, this type of event happens to UFO encounter experiencers, who however are not conscious of this fact.

Since human consciousness can also be introspective, there is also another possibility: the introverted ego observes the (acausal) twin process *in the vegetative body*. In a deeply introverted state, in the above defined Eros consciousness, the ego is open to singular inner quantum leaps, in which an individual twin process takes place: corporeal energy or matter transforms into an aspect of the vegetative body, and the latter re-transforms into spirit-psyche with altered quality. Thus we can define the following observable twin process:

B: The psychophysical collapse of the wave function on the individual/corporeal level:

{X = unobservable matter/psyche/spirit → 'corporeal' matter-psyche with potentially altered quality}

And

{'Corporeal' matter-psyche with potentially altered quality → observable *corporeal* spirit-psyche with altered quality}

Experience shows that this process is constellated in those who experience UFO abduction. Such experiences would therefore mean for them that they have to transform corporeal matter or energy into the vegetative aspect of the body, into subtle body. We will later realize that Body-Centered Imagination and Symptom-Symbol Transformation are based on this deeply introverted process. However, in contrast to UFO abduction one is conscious of being in the Eros ego.

According to my definition, matter-psyche is psychophysically nonlocal. Thus, the above distinction between collective matter-psyche and individual/corporeal matter-psyche is not correct. However, we live in a world of the Logos ego and distinguish between subject and object. We can only differentiate between individual/corporeal and collective processes this way. This is why in connection with matter-psyche I write the terms 'collective' and 'corporeal' in quotation marks.

As we remember, the old alchemists identified the *salvator macrocosmi*, the savior of the universe, with the world soul, a collective principle, as well as with the subtle body defined on the individual level. We realize now that they unconsciously applied the idea of the psychophysical nonlocality of matter-psyche. We, however, can now distinguish much more: the Logos ego differentiates between the subject and the object, thus also between individual/corporeal processes and collective ones, whereas the Eros ego because of its ability to merge with the Eros Self overcomes the subject-object boundary of Western philosophy and also the distinction between individual/corporeal and collective/material. For the Eros ego the world soul and the subtle or vegetative body are thus one and the same, which includes the phenomenon of psychophysical nonlocality.

The above differentiation is very important when we try to see whether the alchemists projected something into the matter in their phials, and also whether those who experience UFO encounter also project—as C.G. Jung thought. We will see that in the case of the alchemists there existed indeed a projection, as opposed to UFO encounter. This means that Jung's statement that UFOs are projections of the Self into the sky is not valid anymore; they have observable outer reality, i.e. spirit-psyche with altered quality, which is however non-sustainable because of the unconsciousness of the people involved.

/ / /

In the above we discussed the radioactive decay on a psychophysical level according to the hypothesis that outer spirit-psyche, physical energy with altered order is produced. Besides this process, which is itself possible on the individual/corporeal as well as on the collective/material level, there is a third process that is theoretically conceivable:

C: The psychophysical collapse of the wave function on the level of the mind:

{X = unobservable matter/psyche/spirit → 'collective' matter-psyche with potentially altered quality}

And

{'Collective' matter-psyche with potentially altered quality → observable *inner* spirit-psyche with realized altered quality}

We will later see that the result of this process, the *inner* spirit-psyche with realized altered quality, is nothing other than the understanding of the meaning of a synchronicity. We remember[116] that Wolfgang Pauli compared the *multiplicatio* of physical radioactivity with the collective spreading of ideas, which were first realized as the result of an individually interpreted synchronicity. Further, he

---

[116] See section 5.4.12 in Part 1

concluded that with such historical synchronicities the Self becomes more conscious. I translated this metaphysical statement into the idea that the collective consciousness is expanded. This is why in Pauli's case the magician/stranger always replaced the term synchronicity with radioactivity: he meant the *psychophysical* radioactive decay, which can be interpreted on three different levels:

a: Psychophysical radioactivity on the 'collective/material' level

b: Psychophysical radioactivity on the 'individual/corporeal' level, and

c: Psychophysical radioactivity on the level of the individual/collective mind.

UFO encounter witnesses experience a mixture of *a* and *b*, since they live unconsciously in the extraverted and in the introverted Eros state. UFO abduction victims realize process *b*, and people who experience and interpret synchronicity live process *c*. We will see that somebody who realizes consciously the introverted Eros ego is able to experience Symptom-Symbol Transformation, i.e. process *b*, or Body-Centered Imagination, i.e. process *a*. Further, consciousness of the process leads to its sustainability.

///

What I define as the observable process of psychophysical radioactivity helps us understand one of the most enigmatic phenomena in Pauli's inner life. In letter [37P] from 28 June, 1949 he writes to Jung about a specific statement of the magician/stranger that came to him. He described it as a thought experiment[117]:

> Please imagine that on the evening after the incident with the scarab that you have described [Jung's scarab synchronicity mentioned in CW 8, § 843; RFR], a stranger visits you and says something on the lines of: 'Congratulations, doctor, in having finally succeeded in producing a *radioactive substance*. It will be most beneficial to the health of your patient'.

It is obvious that the magician/stanger would like to convince the physicist that one creates a radioactive substance by the observation of synchronicities. With the above differentiation we can now understand this statement: the 'radioactive substance' is the 'psychophysical radioactive core,' which can 'decay'

---

[117] *AaA*, p. 39; *PJB*, p. 43; [*not yet published in WB*]

on the collective/material level, on the individual/corporeal or on the level of the mind/spirit. If this 'radioactive substance' 'decays' on the level of the mind/spirit, synchronicities happen. If it 'decays' on the collective/material level, there will be creation acts in matter, while if it does so on the individual/corporeal level, there will be creation acts in the body. *Pauli, however, did not realize these two additional cases of 'psychophysical radioactivity,' thus the magician/stranger wanted the physicist to become conscious of the possibility of 'synchronicities' on the material or corporeal level.* As we know, Pauli did not succeed in this task.

Fate forced me to continue Pauli's unfinished lifework. This is why I had a very enigmatic dream already in 1984, in which I was given the task to find the 'synchronous synchronicity.' Of course first I did not understand at all what this expression could mean. Only when writing this book I suddenly realized the meaning of this dream. I will describe and interpret it in the context of the Pauli effect in section 6.12.3.2 below.

6.12.2.3 The observation of dreams and visions out of the unconscious

Before we can continue to explain the specific paranormal phenomena with the help of the twin process, we have first to formulate depth psychological dream observation and interpretation in a neutral language. In my definition I will include C.G Jung's above mentioned supposition about the location of altered consciousness. The inclusion of this hypothesis allows us to define the general process of the perception of dreams in a new way. Following this definition we can use this general process to clear the phenomenology of some paranormal phenomena.

I define the process leading to the observation of a dream as follows:

Observation of a dream as the result of the twin process formulated in the neutral language:

{X = ('Psyche' = unobservable spirit/psyche/matter = unobservable unconscious) → matter-psyche with potentially higher order}

And

{Matter-psyche with potentially higher order → *inner* spirit-psyche with realized higher order}

I define the dream or more generally a content of the unconscious as unobservable *potential being* consisting in matter-psyche energy that transforms into *actual being* in a spontaneous process, i.e., it becomes an object with realized higher order. This transformation process happens if and only if it is observed by the (introverted) Eros ego.

A closer look at the observational process shows that dreams and visions are at first perceived mostly as spontaneous images, and only then translated into words. Thus, during the observation of a dream consciousness is first in the introverted Eros state—which can only observe inner objects—and then to memorize the dream transforms into Logos (words). Such a definition of the observational process would also explain why many people do not dream: they directly wake up into the Logos state, which is unable to observe the dream. This interpretation is backed by my observation that people who consciously enter the Eros state before falling asleep start to remember their dreams. They do not wake up into the Logos ego anymore, but into the Eros.

In the perception of dreams, where images are observed in the Eros state and verbalized and memorized in the Logos, the ego is located somewhere between Eros and Logos, or rather, unites these two different kinds of consciousness. We can thus also describe this specific state of the ego as an intermediary state. We are immediately reminded of the intermediary state of the Hermetic alchemical *coniunctio*. I also call such a consciousness the Hermetic ego, differentiating it from the Neoplatonic Logos ego. It is exactly the Hermetic consciousness, which will allow us to explain paranormal phenomena like UFO encounter and abduction in new ways.

Since the emergence of dreams and other products of the unconscious is spontaneous and independent of the conscious will, as is also their observation by the Eros ego, *the observed process as well as the observational act are acausal*. Such a process is thus different from the above defined two ways of the collapse of the wave function, the physical observational act, and the singular physical radioactive decay. The process differs from the physical act of measurement insofar as the moment of 'measurement' is accidental. It differs from the physically defined radioactive decay insofar as the inner observational process is a twin process, where matter-psyche energy is created as the first step, and retransforms into inner spirit-psyche energy with higher order. Further, since the Eros ego, in contrast to the Logos ego, observes the psychophysical radioactive decay in an acausal way, the former itself becomes some sort of a 'radioactive core,' which is able to observe singular acausal radioactive decays, i.e., unique incarnation phenomena. Thus, the mere observation of dreams even without their interpretation changes the conscious standpoint slowly but surely in a constructive way, because the quality of the conscious inner spirit-psyche (i.e., the qualitative energy of consciousness) is increased.

However, for C.G. Jung the (spontaneous, i.e., accidental) observation of the acausal emergence of a dream is not yet sufficient. According to him, the ego has further to associate to the elements of the dream. In accompanying and leading this process the dream interpreter has to remain conscious that the patient's associations have to become acausal. Experience shows that the best way to get acausal associations is to select some of the main elements of the dream with the help of the feeling function, and to present them to the dreamer as in Jung's association test. It seems this is the only way to break the verbal connection with the dream and produce real acausal associations.

As we remember, singular acausal processes lead to spirit-psyche with increased order, because they are real creation acts. Increased order is obtained with the acausal association process, since this one reunifies contents that were separated by the Logos ego and at least partly repressed. Therefore, the association process also leads to *coniunctio*, the reunion of conscious aspects and 'emotional complexes' (C.G. Jung). Experience shows further that mostly when acausally associating, the interpretation and its goal spontaneously enter the conscious ego bringing increased meaning: the dream interprets itself. This Aha experience (the acausal creation of higher order in the ego connected with the feeling of increased meaning) leads to a state of happiness or even bliss.

However nowadays this procedure C.G. Jung and Marie-Louise von Franz insisted upon is more and more replaced by an 'interpretation' without the intermediate step of asking for *acausal* associations in Jungian circles. Further, as analysts take money for their service and believe that they always have to supply the patient with an 'interpretation,' most of them do not wait for the creative 'self-interpretation' out of the preconscious knowledge of the collective unconscious, but 'interpret' with the help of their conscious thinking: they just know the (wrong!) meaning. This way the acausal observation of the spontaneous idea coming out of the unconscious and with it the creative interpretation is prevented. The dream interpreter just presents their prejudices about the dream, and no real meaning is extracted. On the contrary, they project their wrong idea of the meaning of the dream, and rape the dreamer.

/ / /

Differentiating between the two different egos that participate in the observation of a dream is very important for my research. We will realize that in Body-Centered Imagination and Symptom-Symbol Transformation the goal is to train the ego to enter and to remain in the Eros state. The ego can observe and memorize the corporeal images coming from the body, especially the belly. Since it does not transform them into words, we can say that the Eros ego memorizes these images with the gut brain. This differentiation also includes C.G. Jung's above quoted supposition that[118] 'the perceptions taking place in such a second psychic system [are] carried over into [the Logos] ego-consciousness.' This, ac-

---

[118] CW 8, § 369

cording to his second hypothesis, would allow us to realize 'the possibility of enormously extending the bounds of our mental horizon.' In contrast to the depth psychologist's statement I would postulate that it is not only our mental horizon which is expanded, but that the ego also becomes able to observe acausal creation and incarnation events in the body and/or matter. Body-Centered Imagination and Symptom-Symbol Transformation allow for such a possibility, as one consciously enters or remains in the Eros ego.

6.12.2.4 Synchronicity described in the neutral language

After the definition of the unique radioactive decay or singular quantum leap on the psychophysical level and the description of dream observation with a neutral language, we can now describe synchronicity. As we know, it consists of two relatively synchronous events with similar meaning, the first being a dream or another inner observation of events out of the unconscious, the second the observation of an outer event. Further, according to Jung and especially Marie-Louise von Franz, the exchange of energy between the inner and the outer event is impossible. This is exactly the reason why Jung calls the synchronistic connection acausal: the dream does not cause the outer phenomenon. As we will see below, there are however other types of events, especially psychokinetic ones, in which an acausal energy exchange must take place, as for example in the famous Pauli effect. I would therefore like to state here explicitly that the Pauli effect cannot be explained with the synchronicity principle, but is a magical phenomenon in the sense of Hermetic alchemy.

In a neutral language we can define synchronicity as follows:

The observation of a synchronicity described in the neutral language:

1 The inner process of synchronicity, the observation of a dream:

1a: {X = 'Psyche' = (unobservable spirit/psyche/ matter = unobservable unconscious) → 'inner' matter-psyche with potentially increased order}

And

1b: {'Inner' matter-psyche with potentially increased order → *inner* spirit-psyche with realized increased order}

2. The outer process of synchronicity:

2a: {X = 'matter' = unobservable spirit/psyche/matter → 'outer' matter-psyche with potentially increased order}

And

2b: {'Outer' matter-psyche with potentially increased order → *outer* spirit-psyche with realized increased order}

As we know, I use the terms 'inner' and 'outer' in relation to matter-psyche between quotation marks, since, as we have seen, matter-psyche is in fact 'inner-outer,' i.e., psychophysically nonlocal. Therefore the Eros ego and the Eros Self become one, and the subject-object boundary is, at least partly, broken through. However, since Logos consciousness does not realize this specific attribute of matter-psyche, 'inner' and 'outer' still have some meaning.

The inner process, the dream etc., can be described with the twin process as presented above, and one can symbolically treat its emergence and interpretation like the radioactive beta decay on the psychophysical level. According to my hypothesis the outer process also follows the process of the singular radioactive beta decay described earlier. Since it also occurs spontaneously, we can also treat the outer process as a singular quantum leap on the psychophysical level.

To realize and interpret a synchronicity we have to include the outer event. Since synchronicity happens spontaneously, and not by will, it is only observable when the ego transforms into the Eros state. Further, this transformation into the Eros state can happen consciously or unconsciously. Usually it happens unconsciously and the person concerned does not realize the change. As we will see, there is also a possibility of a conscious transformation, which leads to what I call the synchronicity quest.

With the help of the above conclusion we obtain the further insight that for the perception of synchronicities the ego must be split: one part, which observes the inner process is living in the introverted Eros, the other, which spontaneously finds the outer process, is living in the extraverted Eros.

It is possible that at the precise moment when the outer event is acausally noticed the meaning of a synchronicity is also understood. This is what happens in the two examples from Jung we will study later. It is also possible that it takes a shorter or longer time to understand the meaning of two synchronistically connected events. Such an example I will explain in the next section.

Exactly when we get the meaning common to both events (in the *kairos*), when the inner and the outer phenomenon spontaneously 'match' their meaning in our consciousness, *inner* spirit-psyche with increased order, the result of process *1b* (see above), is created. The spontaneous character of this creation process shows that the Eros ego not only experiences but also interprets the synchronicity, as it is the only means to realize acausal incarnations. Further, accepting the reality of synchronicities, calls for the development of the feeling function, the valuation function[119]. This function tells us that such relatively synchronous inner and outer events must contain *mana*, i.e. a potentially increased meaning.

To demonstrate the above, let us briefly return to the two synchronicities that Jung describes in his work. In the scarab synchronicity Jung was in fact unconsciously in the Eros ego. This is why he was able to hear the noise at the window—to feel it as an important event and give worth to it—and to catch the rose chafer. We can express the process in Pauli's physical-symbolic terminology: in this spontaneous, i.e. acausal act, Jung's ego unconsciously transformed into the 'psychophysical radioactive core,' the Eros·ego, and enabled this one to realize its own 'psychophysical radioactive decay.' This way the patient's dream was completed with the outer event. Then, when the depth psychologist showed the rose chafer to his patient, the inner and the outer event also 'matched' in her ego, and she realized the meaning of the synchronicity, its inner spirit-psyche aspect with increased order: the demand for a transformation of the Logos into the Eros ego that happened to her spontaneously in this moment.

In the second synchronicity, the realization of the 'match' happened exactly in the moment when the fox crossed their path in the woods, and supplemented the patient's dream. Here, again, it was Jung who lived unconsciously in the Eros ego—he felt the value of a walk with his patient—and decided spontaneously to ask for it. The outer and the inner event could only come together this way, and the spontaneous increase of meaning in spirit-psyche, (in their consciousness), could happen. As we remember, I stated that this was the insight that Jung's patient should return to her instinctive intelligence.

/ / /

What in an archaic language is called *mana*—divine spiritual power—we can translate into the modern term matter-psyche energy with potentially increased quality. Since it possesses the attribute of being inner and outer or of obeying psychophysical nonlocality, it *is exactly the matter-psyche aspect of energy that unifies the dream and the outer event in a synchronicity. The transformation into matter-psyche in both events, in the inner as well as in the outer, is thus the reason why the outer event seems to 'know' of the inner, and vice versa.* This way synchronicity relativizes the subject-object boundary. Further, we can conclude that there must be an 'instance' in the 'unconscious,' which has telepathic and/or precognitive abilities. Spatial and temporal distances are relative for this

---

[119] See CW 6, § 724

instance. Thus it is able to perceive large distances and time spans[120]. We have therefore to answer the question, how such ability to perceive large distances and time spans is possible.

If we include Jung's and Pauli's hypothesis of the relativity of space and time in the collective unconscious[121], we can formulate this insight in a slightly different way: such an instance would be able to dilate the time and the space measure. As regards time this means symbolically that the tic toc of the clock becomes a tiiiiiiiiiiiiiiiiiiiiiiiiiiiiiiiiic tooooooooooooooooooooooooc. However, if the time measure dilates, time itself contracts. The instant can even become eternal, thus timeless; the *kairos* corresponds to eternity. If now the (Eros) ego becomes able to feel and perceive this qualitative moment of the *kairos*, it is in a position to perceive much longer time spans. This means that for it such events appear synchronous. The usual ego, the Logos consciousness, would allocate them to different locations in time. Since for such an ego events that are separated for the Logos ego happen simultaneously it is able to realize precognitive insights, i.e., present and future events together, as one event.

I became conscious of the above phenomenon—and what together with the insights about the relativity of psychic space (see below) I would call the psychic or psychophysical application of Albert Einstein's Special Relativity Theory— about 18 years ago in the following circumstances. My son, Simon, was 8 years old. He came back from school very hungry. His mother was cooking. He kept asking: 'when do we eat?' An incident happened in the kitchen and all the cooking was burnt. My wife had to go to the store to buy food again. She came back and started to cook. Our son was of course very angry. I told him to play with his Lego. After a short time he was completely absorbed in it. He 'forgot time.' After about an hour and a half, when dinner was ready, I called him and ironically remarked: 'Simon, it's one and a half hours late, you can eat now.' He was very surprised because for him it seemed that only five minutes had passed.

In his second year at school my son was still half in what I call today the Eros ego. After school he was still able to let himself fall into the altered consciousness. In this state one still feels very intensely the 'will of the unconscious'. This means that one does not follow one's conscious will but allows oneself to 'flow' with the unconscious, the Tao. There seems to exist what C.G. Jung called the counter-will, which follows its natural slope. Thus, if consciousness is able to follow this slope, conscious time also becomes dilated—the tiiiiiiiiiiiiiiiiiiiiiiiiiiiiiiic tooooooooooooooooooooooooc.

---

[120] *This is of course a metaphysical statement which is transformed into an empirical fact by observation.*

[121] *See sections 6.1.3 and 6.1.5; respectively AaA, letters [29], [30] and [7]; Letters [29] and [30] are wrongly dated and thus belong to letter [7] from 1934: [29] from April 28, 1934, [30] from May, 24, 1934 and [7] from October 26, 1934.*

As regards synchronicity we can postulate that the Eros ego with its conscious introverted feeling, the valuation function, can measure the 'real interest' of a higher instance in oneself. This way, the behaviour of my son deprived of will lead him to creative playing. An adult, however, can use their developed feeling function to observe synchronistic events, which leads to new conscious knowledge.

In telepathy not the time measure but the space measure is dilated. Space itself becomes compressed; in the extreme case the 'point space' becomes the 'all space,' the whole universe. Thus, the person concerned can 'survey' a much wider space than he can during 'normal' states of Logos consciousness. He perceives remote places. For Eros this remote place is identical with the place where the person is, it is just the 'right place,' which for Logos however is completely arbitrary and accidental.

In the early 1980s I realized that the amount of synchronicities dramatically increases when one consciously remains in the Eros ego, i.e. one approaches the telepathic and precognitive ability of the altered consciousness. I began to have the following habit: in the morning, after a dream, still half asleep, I went outside to town. Many times synchronicities happened, for example I came across the same person I dreamed of during the night. Such experiences confirmed my anticipation that it is only Logos that separates us from a more or less permanently synchronistic life.

If one follows this change in one's conscious life, one enters the above mentioned synchronicity quest slowly but surely. In this way of life, one remains more or less permanently in the Eros ego and spontaneously 'catches' outer events whose meaning is related to (dream contents, constellated ideas, etc). Thus spontaneously, the common meaning of both inner and outer events breaks through to consciousness, and a new creative idea is born. This behavior helps me very much in my creative life.

During these years I recognized further (first half consciously), that the Eros ego, and especially its vegetative sensation and introverted feeling function existed. They perceive the vegetative aspect of the body and its surroundings, and are also related to the *kairos*, the 'right time.' Thus, it seems that these specific functions of the Eros ego are the medium of perception of telepathy and precognition. With the possibility of a psychophysically nonlocal perception of the vegetative nervous system (inner-outer) we also acknowledge that telepathy and precognition are the mode of perception of the 'gut brain,' because it is the seat of the Eros ego.

Let us briefly return to my extension of the definition of the Eros ego in section 6.1.3. As I mentioned there, it is determined by the vegetative sensation function, rooted in the vegetative nervous system. There, I also compared this new ego with Jung's hypothesis[122] of the 'subject of the unconscious', 'a sort of ego…a sec-

---

[122] CW 8, § 369

ond psychic system coexisting with consciousness,' the existence of which could 'radically alter our view of the world,' if its perceptions could be realized and carried over into [Logos] ego-consciousness, which would 'enormously extend the bound of our mental horizon.' We can now hypothetically state that the Eros ego is the instance necessary for the conscious realization of synchronicities, and that the observation and interpretation of synchronicities leads to the enormous extension of our mental horizon Jung mentioned.

We will later see that in UFO encounter and abduction people are forced into this state and unconsciously observe with the help of the VNS. In Symptom-Symbol Transformation and Body-Centered Imagination the Eros state is consciously achieved. Therefore, in contrast to the UFO phenomena the observed incarnation becomes sustainable.

When a synchronicity is not immediately recognized in the moment of observation, the outer event has to be realized, i.e., incarnated. This happens as in dream interpretation where the ego associates with and amplifies the elements of the dream and the outer event. Patiently dealing with the synchronicity in this manner leads to the sudden realization of the potential meaning and its incarnation (see example below). This shows that the interpretation of a synchronicity is also acausal; it is a spontaneous process happening on the basis of the spontaneous inner quantum leap. The increased order, the inherent meaning becomes conscious and thus *actual being*, which is always experienced as deep bliss. This seems to be the main reason why in such moments of spontaneous creative insights the concerning individual has an Aha experience.

I would also like to stress here that the spontaneous interpretation of a synchronicity out of the preconscious knowledge of the collective unconscious leads to a creation act on the level of the conscious inner spirit-psyche, i.e., the human mind, the Logos. *Thus, the observation and the spontaneous interpretation of a synchronicity is the way incarnations on the Logos level become observable* in the meaning of quantum physics. As we will see later, there are however also creation or even incarnation phenomena experienced on the level of outer matter and/or of the physical body—and even incarnation events on the level of matter-psyche itself, i.e., in the *unus mundus*. We will deal with them in section 6.12.3.

6.12.2.5 The Kappa synchronicity—an example of a spontaneously realized meaning of a synchronicity

To illustrate how one can find the meaning of a synchronicity I will share a personal experience. This established how I started to deal with the bipolarity of the energy term and lead to my eventual definition of matter-psyche, i.e. negative energy, as a complementary principle to spirit-psyche (the latter representing physical energy on the one hand and objective psychic energy (Jung) on the other).

In my book *I Cercatori di Dio*[123] (The Quest for God) a question remained open. I was not yet able to interpret in a depth psychological or even psychophysical language the concept of quantum physical antimatter derived from the so-called negative energy. As we know from physicists[124], negative energy possesses very strange physical characteristics. For example, it slows down the velocity of a particle in motion when supplied to it—(an absolutely absurd idea in the terms of physics), or it must be defined as the quality of particles that move faster than light. Already these show the impossibility of describing the concept of negative energy within the boundaries of physics.

A. The first event of the Kappa synchronicity

About two years after the completion of the above mentioned manuscript in April 1986, I experienced an impressive synchronicity.

The first event was a dream on March 7, 1988, and the second was an external event that took place on May 17, 1988.

Since more and more socially marginalized people were seeking my assistance, (i.e., the unemployed, the poor, the physically sick and drug addicts), I decided in 1986 to work in a social institution, in order to study the depth psychological background of social marginalization. My intensive involvement with these people, which was also an extremely extraverted work, exhausted me. After about one and a half years I was drained out and had no energy left for any creative activity.

In this context I had the following dream:

I am looking for a new job. The problem with my present occupation seems to be that my small horse ran away. It joined a herd of wild horses, threatened by lions. It is a very dangerous situation for my 'helpful animal.' I am looking for my horse in this wild herd, calling its name. To my great astonishment it is called 'Kappa' (the Greek letter K.)

As an association it occurred to me that 'Kappa'—I mean the Greek letter K, which is in German differentiated from K ('Ka'; English 'Kay')—, as much as I

---

[123] Roth, Remo F.: I Cercatori di Dio-Una riunificatione della mistica cristiana e della fisica dei quanti nella sincronicità die C.G. Jung, Di Renzo, Roma, 1994. *Revised Italian translation of* Die Gottsucher, Frankfurt, 1992.
[124] See for example Stöckler, M.: Philosophische Probleme der relativistischen Quantenmechanik, Berlin, 1984, p. 91. He writes: 'The occurance of negative energy involves fundamental problems...The energy of a particle with negative energy decreases with increasing velocity...The acceleration is opposed to the force.' [Translation mine]

knew, was the only letter of the Greek alphabet, which is not used for the description of quantum physical elementary particles. It is true that the letter K is used for higher energetic mesons, i.e., the Kaons, the Greek letter *K* ('Kappa') however I never found in the physical studies I had done for my manuscript.

At first I was very disappointed about this, because in the previous years I had derived some important physical-symbolic statements (W. Pauli)[125] about some elementary particles, especially about the Kaons, which could be described in the context of C.G. Jung's synchronicity concept. Therefore I hoped to find further properties of elementary particles, which can be used as the common archetypal background of physical and depth psychological phenomena.

My amplification about the letter Kappa resulted in the following: Kappa is the 11th letter of the Greek alphabet, it has the numerical value of 20 and comes from the Phoenician expression for '.' (point). I knew that number 11 was also the symbol of the union of yin and yang, i.e., the Tao, in Taoism.

I was already preoccupied with the symbolism of the point as a thirteen-year-old boy. Already at the time, I was fascinated with an idea explained by our geometry teacher: the point does not have extension. (At least this is common in older philosophical texts, e.g. Bergson) Therefore our teacher never drew points on the blackboard, but small circles, whose centers marked these points without mass, space or time.

Many years later I discovered in the writings of Marie-Louise von Franz that the circle around an empty center represents the most original God-image we know of. Already before this conscious insight, in 1974, I drew a series of mandalas which culminated in the one called 'Herr Roth hat Frau Weiss geheiratet' ('Mr. Red has married Mrs. White'; see figure 6.8).

It also has an empty center, and it was obviously the expression of my still unconscious fascination with the God-image of my youth, which was activated out of the collective unconscious during my great life-crisis of the time.

---

[125] *AaA, p. 9: 'The fantasies often assumed their own peculiar character by using physical terminology…to express analogies with psychich facts,' and p. 11: '(symbolically interpreted) physical expressions;' PJB, p. 13, p. 15 [not yet published in WB]*

Figure 6.8:
The Mandala

B. Interpretation of the dream

My helpful horse, *Kappa*, seems to be connected to a world without mass, space or time on the one hand and on the other hand with the *original God-image*, preconsciously constellated in me[126]. Further, this God-image has something to do with *the Taoist yin/yang, the bipolar energy concept.*

I began to describe this God-image in my manuscript *I Cercatori di Dio*, finished in 1986. But due to my work, I finally lost the contact with this natural God-image and its synchronistic and psychophysical manifestations. Obviously a very dangerous situation developed, because in fairy tales the hero must never lose the helpful animal, otherwise he dies.

With the help of my associations and amplifications I understood the dream, but did not know how I could have lost this God-image. Also, a question remained open: why should my helpful animal be called Kappa, when this letter is not used in quantum physics to describe any elementary particle (while this was my preoccupation in the previous seven years)? The meaning of the outer event of the synchronicity will answer these questions.

---

[126] *And as I have realized since then, in the West in general.*

C. The second event of the Kappa synchronicity

The day before the outer event of the synchronicity, I preoccupied myself intensely with the phenomenon of the so-called negative energy in connection with a very enigmatic dream of the 'blessing of time.' In physics, the terms 'energy' and 'time' are so-called conjugated variables, thus negative energy and negative time belong together. However, as we realized above, Dirac replaced negative energy by antimatter, which was a metaphysical assumption, since antimatter is based on the properties of physical unobservability and on the concept of 'invisible holes' in an infinite continuum. Infinity and unobservability are however specific characteristics of many ancient God-images and the invisible hole is, as I mentioned above, even the attribute of the oldest one[127].

On 17 May 1988 on the tramway to my daily work I was musing over this phenomenon of the negative energy of physics and its strange metaphysical background. It surprised me that *physics transforms negative energy with the help of a metaphysical hypothesis into antimatter.* I asked myself, whether it would not be better to stay with negative energy and the associated negative time.

When the term 'negative energy' came to my mind, I spontaneously looked up. This shows that *I was still in the Eros ego. At this crucial moment, however, this vegetative state transformed into extraversion.* My eyes fell on a man outside. He was dressed in a jogging suit, and on the trousers, from above downward, as largely as possible the word *Kappa* was written twice[128].

I was immediately reminded of the dream about my lost Kappa horse I had to find again, and at the same time I remembered that I did not have any other associations, except that the Greek letter Kappa is not used in quantum physics.

D. The spontaneous interpretation of the Kappa synchronicity

Then, out of the blue, I was overwhelmed by an idea: Kappa is the symbol of negative energy, i.e., what I call today matter-psyche, and it has nothing to do with physics, it transcends it. Thus, we have to realize that negative energy must

---

[127] When I experienced the *Kappa synchronicity* in 1988, I did not know yet that Wolfgang Pauli had some decades after Dirac's antimatter axiom stated the hypothesis of the unified psychophysical reality, which he defined as *'an invisible, potential form of reality that is only indirectly inferable through its effects.'* This realm is of course exactly the world Paul Dirac talked about when defining the physically unobservable, infinite 'sea' of negative energy with its holes. As we have seen, the difference is that Dirac regarded the 'sea' as being, *Pauli however as* potential being *and therefore avoided the inadmissible metaphysical hypothesis.*

[128] *The clothes of this company were not well known at this time in Switzerland, therefore I did not know that this was the name of an Italian sportswear company.*

consist in psychophysical energy. Since it was connected with the subtle body, i.e., psychophysical energy, the term 'Kappa' appeared on the body of a sportsman.

With this realization about the outer event of the synchronicity in a singular inner quantum leap the potentially increased meaning of the synchronicity broke through, and the potentiality transformed into reality in my mind. The transformation of *potential being* into *actual being* had taken place triggered by a spontaneous creation by mere observation. Since then I know that the loss of the God-image that was at the centre of the dream was caused by the repression of the matter-psyche aspect of the energy term.

Though I did not see this so consciously at the time, with this illumination I started to realize the bipolarity of the energy term, matter-psyche and spirit-psyche split into outer spirit-psyche, physical energy, and inner spirit-psyche, C.G. Jung's objective psychic energy. Matter-psyche is however, as we will see, unified in an 'inner-outer,' magical parapsychological and nonlocal energy, and it can transform into inner spirit-psyche with altered order, i.e., into the conscious meaning of a synchronicity, as well as into outer spirit-psyche, into physical energy with altered order, expressed in psychokinetic events. The Kappa synchronicity also showed me that beyond C.G. Jung's concept of synchronicity, there is a principle even deeper that has to do with an incarnation process in living matter, the creation of the 'Kappa body,' the subtle body or Paracelsus' astral body, and the Taoist diamond body. I will describe in the next sub-section this magical principle.

6.12.3 Description of the paranormal magic processes in the neutral language

6.12.3.1 The twin process of Hermetic magic and the crucial role of the individual

The Kappa synchronicity is an example of the process that in section 6.12.2.2 I called the psychophysical radioactivity on the level of the mind or the creation of inner spirit-psyche with increased order. After this description of the fertilizing role of the preconscious knowledge of the collective unconscious I would like to present the main process I will discuss here: Hermetic magic, in its archaic occurrence as well as in my modern formulation.

As we have seen with the inclusion of mathematics and empiricism into the philosophy of nature Logos took over Western science emphasizing thinking and extraverted sensation. Alchemy was at its best when Eros in the most general sense prevailed. Collective consciousness was much more receptive towards vegetative sensation, feeling, and intuition. Thus, it is very difficult for us moderns educated in the Logos to imagine the situation of the alchemists and their archaic worldview some four hundred years ago, before the scientific revolution of the 17th century.

Living in Eros means observing the world with the help of the altered consciousness in the way I described above. Thus, unconsciously, the alchemists performed the twin process: when observing outer matter, they believed to experience a transformation into matter-psyche and its re-transformation into spirit-psyche with increased order. In physical-symbolic terms we could say that they experienced singular acausal quantum leaps or psychophysical radioactive decays. In the neutral language we can describe this process as follows:

The (illusionary) twin process of Hermetic magic:

{X = unobservable matter/psyche/spirit → matter-psyche with potentially increased order}

And

{Matter-psyche with potentially increased order → observable *outer* spirit-psyche (physical energy) with realized increased order}

As we remember, in synchronicity the end product was inner spirit-psyche with increased order, the increased meaning of a creative idea. Here, however, since the alchemists do 'research' in their laboratory, the product is outer spirit-psyche, thus physical energy of higher order or with increased quality. Of course, this formulation in the neutral language in the archaic terminology of alchemy means the transformation of the less valuable into the more valuable thus exactly what alchemists interpreted as the transmutation of lead into gold, for example.

As we know further, none of these archaic scientists ever produced gold. However, on a psychophysical level they experienced this transformation. This means that, in the formulation of their archaic language, they experienced the *mana* of the substances they experimented with. Formulated in the neutral language we can say that this fascination with the *mana* was the result of the first process, the transformation into matter-psyche with potentially increased order. Then, they observed the processes in their phials and *potential being* transformed into *actual being*—the singular quantum leap happened.

Since the alchemists however completely unconsciously identified with the Eros ego, they were not able to distinguish the outer from the inner processes. Thus, in experiencing with outer matter they underwent the illusion of inner processes—as we will see, exactly the 'gilding of corporeal matter'—as visionary images emerging out of the psychophysical reality in their phials. Since the root of these psychophysical images was the *coniunctio* archetype, most of these images were symbols of this process and its goal. As an example I show in figure 6.9 the vision of the creation of the hermaphroditic *homunculus*, symbolically equivalent with the red tincture and the quintessence, in the retort:

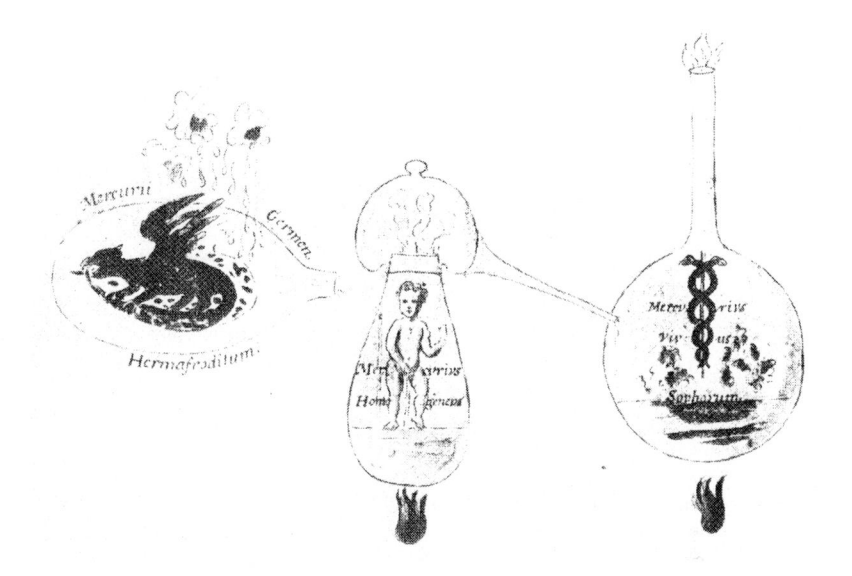

Figure 6.9:
The transformation of Mercurius in the Hermetic vessel.
The homunculus shown as a 'pissing manikin'[129]

On the other hand, since the alchemists experienced with concrete outer matter, they also observed causal physical processes, as for example the evaporation of a liquid in their phials. *Still living unconsciously in the Eros ego and thus unable to distinguish inner from outer processes, they were under the illusion that these causal processes were also magical.* In a modern language we would say that the alchemists were convinced that they experienced in outer matter the acausal twin process with its singular quantum leap, in fact happening in their belly brain. In a physical-symbolic language we can say that they thought to observe psychophysical radioactivity in outer matter, but in fact these processes

---

[129] *Source:* Jung, CW 12, figure 121

were mere causal physical transformation processes. With the help of the neutral language we can thus write:

Hermetic observation of the *transformation* processes in matter in the alchemical retort described in the neutral language:

{X = unobservable matter/psyche/spirit → causal transformations of *outer* spirit-psyche (of physical energy) without increased order}

Had they however been conscious of their being in the state of the Eros ego, they would not have projected these processes into the outer world of the alchemical experiment but would have experienced the introverted process: with the belly brain they would have observed singular acausal quantum leaps transforming matter into the vegetative body *in their own* physical body. As we will see, this spontaneous process is the basis of the modern Hermetic alchemical *opus*, of Body-Centered Imagination and Symptom-Symbol Transformation. We can describe the process in the case of the alchemists' unconscious identification with the Eros ego as follows:

Hermetic observation of the *transmutation* process in the body described in the neutral language:

{X = unobservable matter/psyche/spirit → 'individual corporeal' *matter-psyche* with potentially increased quality}

And

{'Individual corporeal' *matter-psyche* with potentially increased quality → observable 'individual corporeal' spirit-psyche with realized increased quality}

Which was however projected into outer matter because they were unconscious of being in the Eros ego state.

The alchemists never realized this contradiction between the outer causal process in matter and the acausal 'individual corporeal' process. They were not able to distinguish the causal energetic transformation processes in their retorts from inner acausal transmutation processes in their body (or in the case of the alchemical physicians, in the body of their patients) because they unconsciously identified with the Eros ego. In a modern language we would say that the alchemists projected the 'individual corporeal' transmutation process onto the energetic processes in outer matter and thus took the outer causal process as acausal. Further, because of this projection they confused the inner images expressing the first product of the twin process, with projections into their retorts and phials. Thus, the belief in the observation of acausal processes in their experiments was of course completely erroneous. However, we will see later that in the case of UFO encounter witnesses realize—though completely unconsciously - this original alchemical idea of acausal transmutation in the outer world as an effect of the artificial fission of the atom. In contrast to C.G. Jung's opinion, I postulate therefore that these phenomena are not at all projections, but real (although non-sustainable) events, however only observable with the help of the Eros ego.

Since the processes the alchemists observed in outer reality were causal energy transformations, and only those in the introspective reality of their body were acausal, *we have to limit the above Hermetic process to the phenomena of the human body. Seen from a psychophysical point of view, these twin processes happen between the outer aspect of the physical body (the X), and the inner aspect, matter-psyche or the vegetative body (by which bodily matter receives increased order, i.e., new 'life essence').* Thus, without being conscious of the modern terminology, the Hermetic physicians, Paracelsus, Gerardus Dorneus, Michael Mayer, Robert Fludd and others, tried to experience exactly such magical processes in their body and/or in the body of their patients. We know of Paracelsus especially that he cured and healed this way. During the 17th century, when mathematical science developed and magic was more and more repressed, this way of healing disappeared into the unconscious[130]. Today, however, we have to come back to these Hermetic practices—as we know, on a more differentiated level. Below I will thus mention an example of the magical healing method I have applied in my practice.

In contrast to alchemy contemporary physics is able to distinguish the causal processes of classical physics (Newton/Einstein) from the statistical causal processes of quantum physics in matter. As it does not accept matter-psyche, the twin process, and the corresponding Eros ego, *science is not able to observe singular acausal processes in the matter of nature. Since modern medicine does alike, it is also unable to observe singular acausal events in the human body. The modern Hermetic alchemical procedures, Body-Centered Imagination and Symptom-Symbol Transformation, fill this gap and can cure physical and certain psychological diseases in a completely new way.*

The observation of the twin process with its singular acausal quantum leap is only possible with the Eros ego. We have therefore to ask ourselves whether such processes exist, where human beings observe anew with the Eros ego and are able to experience such singular acausal quantum leaps, in their own body, and

---

[130] *Exactly at this time, between the second half of the 16th century and the first half of the 17th, when the modern scientific worldview fought its war against the magical view of alchemy, we notice also the culmination of the delusion of healers being witches and of their prosecution. Johannes Kepler had to defend his mother many times, who was accused of being a witch.*

in outer matter. As we will see, Eros ego observation of matter happens unconsciously in UFO encounter and UFO abduction, whereas the *conscious* observation of singular quantum leaps happens in Symptom-Symbol Transformation as well as in Body-Centered Imagination. This is why in a symbolic language I call such processes the observation of 'the UFOs emerging from the belly.'

For scientists the existence of such processes seems completely impossible; they are even more unbelievable than synchronistic phenomena, since scientists consider the background of such phenomena, the *unus mundus* as *nonbeing*. For someone witnessing such events, for example a UFO encounter victim, such processes are however real, i.e., the result is *actual being* created out of *potential being*. Thus, accepting my hypothesis of the *unus mundus* as *potential being* includes the acceptance that for these specific individuals such events are reality. They experience nothing less than incarnations out of the *unus mundus*, and thus also out of the Beyond, into our world.

We understand now how important is Pauli's replacement of matter, psyche and spirit as metaphysical being by an unobservable psychophysical reality as potential being, (which becomes observable in what I call the singular (acausal) quantum leap). In such singular quantum leaps the metaphysical or transcendent world, the 'invisible, potential form of reality [becomes] indirectly inferable' (W. Pauli).

The above insights based on quantum physical epistemology allow us further to extend our worldview from a Neoplatonic or materialistic to a modern Hermetic and magical one. However, we have to accept that such phenomena are only observable by some individuals who possess specific capacities of observation. As the reader remembers, I described these attributes in section 6.1.4.

/ / /

Before we continue with the description of other paranormal phenomena I would like to point out another aspect of the inclusion of the Hermetic magical process, the necessary revolution of our worldview[131] in the 21st century. It is what C.G. Jung anticipated as the point A situation, mentioned above: when one person gets in contact with the *unus mundus* the whole universe can change. *Now we can sustain Jung's intuitive hypothesis with the results of my research: such point A events adhere to the psychophysical nonlocality principle and correspond to the observation of the Hermetic magical twin process, the singular (acausal) quantum leap in one's own body as well as in outer matter.*

This way Jung's intuition is formulated in accordance with quantum physical epistemology, especially Wolfgang Pauli's clarification concerning the *potential*

---

[131] Closer description see in section 5.4.14 in Part I

being of the *unus mundus,* and C.G. Jung's empirical discovery of the collective unconscious; and I follow the Nobel laureate's statement that I had chosen as the motto of Part I of my book: 'What is still older is always the newer.' This is why I had to go back to Hermetic alchemy since we can only find there the necessary hypotheses, especially the magical nexus, for an all-embracing theory.

Another formulation of the point A idea we find in the *tikkun* by Isaac Luria (1534-1572). He lived in a world where Hermetic alchemy was still very alive[132]. The main (and heretic) idea of the *tikkun* is the redemption of God. Expressed in modern terms this redemption is based on an archetypal transformation of the God-image, which in fact also means a New Genesis: when God created the ten-fold tree of the Sephiroth—a Gnostic and Cabbalist image of the Anthropos (god-man)—only the first three Sephiroth were strong enough to absorb the Divine Light. The rest of the Sephiroth were too weak, they broke and were swallowed by the demonic forces. With this disintegration of the Anthropos a state of non-redemption of man *and* God was created. Therefore, certain human beings have the challenge of the *tikkun,* the restitution of the Anthropos in his wholeness. In this way they assist the godhead in reversing the destruction of the creation of the world.

As we remember, a similar motif is the liberation of the *salvator macrocosmi,* as a result of the alchemical *opus.* Further, we have seen that we can equate the symbol of the saviour with the vegetative body and with the world soul, which, on the other hand, is equivalent to the *homunculus,* the hermaphroditic end product of the alchemical work.

When we consider the current state of the world, we can be tempted to think that such a method to liberate the *salvator macrocosmi* (who by its own release can liberate the world and the universe), could be the crucial and perhaps very last attempt at rescuing humankind and the world. As we have seen above[133], it was C.G. Jung, who was excited about this idea of Luria's Cabbalah. He realized a mystical correspondence to the individuation process, discovered through empirical experience.

The above shows that the depth psychologist anticipated not only new creation on the level of the spirit and mind, in the Logos Self, but also an incarnation into the material world. Implicitly he talks of the creation and liberation of the salvator macrocosmi, the world soul, the vegetative body or the homunculus. However, as we remember[134], *C.G. Jung defined the individuation process as happening in the mind and spirit. Thus, his conception of the goal of the individuation process began to change. At the age of 80, he got closer to Wolfgang Pauli's view and began to think that an incarnation in the material part of our world*

---

[132] Also the Hermetic Rosarium Philosophorum *was published in 1550, and it was the time of Gerardus Dorneus (second half of the 16th century).*

[133] See section 6.11

[134] See section 3.3.3 in Part 1

was to be considered. However, because of his unipolar definition of the energy term he was never able to grasp the twin process, the transformation into matter-psyche and its re-transformation into spirit-psyche with altered quality. He was not able either to distinguish incarnation processes in the Logos Self from similar processes in the Eros Self; thus he confused synchronicity (i.e., the telepathic/precognitive observation of outer events similar to the content of a dream), with Hermetic magical processes (psychokinesis and Pauli effect; BCI/SST).

In fact, also contemporary Jungians believe that psychokinesis can be explained by the synchronicity principle, though Jung and Marie-Louise von Franz always underlined that in this case no physical energy exchange is allowed. Psychokinesis is however impossible without an exchange between a magical and physical energy. As an example we can take the above mentioned psychokinetic Pauli effect at Princeton[135]: when Pauli was close to it, the accelerator as a result of the transmutation of magic into physical energy caught fire. The Nobel laureate was convinced that this explosion was an effect of his presence, and he interpreted it as a Pauli effect—a destructive magical phenomenon. It was destructive because he was not yet able to realize that by adhering to the classical account of the conservation law of energy he could not see the transmutation of magical energy into physical energy and the altered quality accompanying it.

We can state here a further implication: since both principles, synchronicity and the magical process are only observable by an individual, their inclusion leads to an almost incredible change in our worldview. *The individual is at the centre of the observation of singular quantum leaps in synchronicity and in psychokinetic events, and this way he co-creates by his observation new spiritual and new material reality during this introverted process. A crucial change happens as the importance of the observation of the individual in the Eros state enters the history of science.*

6.12.3.2 The Pauli effect as a psychokinetic phenomenon and the 'synchronous synchronicity'

A. The destructive Pauli effect versus constructive Hermetic magic ('synchronous synchronicity')

a. Some of Pauli's and Jung's Pauli effects and the death of the king in the Hermetic *coniunctio*

---

[135] WB 4/I, p. 37; letter [1085] from February 26, 1950 to C.A. Meier

After the examination of the archaic Hermetic *opus* we are ready to deal with some psychokinetic effects. The first is the famous Pauli effect. I opened Part I of the book with the incident that happened at the inauguration ceremony of the C.G. Jung Institute in 1948. I also mentioned the episode of the burning accelerator in Princeton which happened in Pauli's presence as another instance of a Pauli effect. This seems likely because the real reason for the destruction of the accelerator was never found[136]. We know further that the physicist was deeply convinced that he was able to cause such psychokinetic effects.

There were many other Pauli effects. One of them shows that they must belong to an unconscious emotional complex on the psychophysical level[137]: Pauli was sitting in the famous Café Odeon at Bellevue Place in Zurich and was musing about his feeling and emotional problems. He knew that in Jung's psychology red is the color of the feeling function. Spontaneously, he glanced outside just when a large red car caught fire. Also the following event shows that something in Pauli was able to cause such effects, where a transformation from a nonphysical to a physical energy took place: his colleague in experimental physics, Otto Stern, forbade him to enter his laboratory because he always caused destructive Pauli effects[138].

Of course one should examine more effects of the kind to learn about the specific characteristic of these paranormal phenomena. However, these few examples already show that the effect happened exactly when Pauli entered the scene (Princeton, Fludd/flood synchronicity, Stern's laboratory) or spontaneously paid attention to the outer phenomenon (Odeon). This pattern differs from that of synchronicity: in it, the outer, physical effect happened exactly simultaneously to the inner, psychic; and not just more or less simultaneously, as in the two twin processes of synchronicity. Thus, events must be simultaneous to become psychokinetic (and not telepathic or precognitive as in synchronicity).

There are other psychokinetic events that on the one hand are centered around one specific person and on the other manifest when this person enters the scene. Hans Bender, former professor of parapsychology at the University of Freiburg im Breisgau (Germany) shares a story of multiple, incredible, almost impossible psychokinetic events in the office of a lawyer[139]. As long as a young

---

[136] *WB 4/I, p. 37; see also note 19, p. 38. Further Fischer, E.P., An den Grenzen des Denkens, Wolfgang Pauli—ein Nobelpreisträger über die Nachtseiten der Wissenschaft, Herder, Freiburg, Basel, Wien, 2000, p. 132.*

[137] *For the following see for example Fischer, E.P., An den Grenzen des Denkens, Wolfgang Pauli—ein Nobelpreisträger über die Nachtseiten der Wissenschaft, Herder, Freiburg, Basel, Wien, 2000, p. 132*

[138] *Enz, Ch,P., No Time to be Brief, A Scientific Biography of Wolfgang Pauli, Oxford University Press, Oxford, 2002, p. 149*

[139] *Bender, H., Unser sechster Sinn, Hellsehen, Telepathie, Spuk, Rowohlt, Reinbeck b. Hamburg, 1972, p. 123-128.*

girl worked in his office, incredible mechanical and electrical abnormalities happened there. The phone bills reached astronomical amounts, as if someone had phoned day and night with the whole world. The hanging lamps began to swing in increasing amplitudes. All this happened only during the office hours; and these paranormal phenomena spontaneously began when the young lady entered the office. The researchers concluded that the reason for these paranormal phenomena, 'whose description was not possible with the established principles of physics,' was this 19-year-old girl. When she left the office for another job, the psychokinetic events immediately ceased.

Of course we are also reminded of the psychokinetic events in Jung's household at the end of the 19th century[140]: in August or September 1898, something occurred[141], which we would call today a psychokinetic Pauli effect. During these years Jung held mediumistic séances with his cousin Helly Preiswerk and other family members. At the beginning of his clinical semesters he stopped attending these séances because he lost interest in parapsychology, as his attention was drawn to causal medicine and Nietzsche's philosophy. Then, the seventy-year-old walnut dining table used for the séances split from center to rim, and a few weeks later a bread knife in Jung's household exploded, shattering into four pieces with a loud bang. All members of the circle felt that these parapsychological events were a call from the spirits to go on with the mediumistic sessions.

Further, the reader perhaps remembers another psychokinetic event in Jung's life, described in *Memories, Dreams, Reflections*. It was at the end of March 1909 when he visited Freud in Vienna for the second time. During their talk a famous psychokinetic event happened[142]:

> While Freud was going on [rejecting parapsychology], I had a curious sensation. It was as if my diaphragm were made of iron and were becoming red-hot—a glowing vault. And at that moment there was such a loud report in the bookcase, which stood right next to us, that we both started up in alarm, fearing the thing was going to topple over on us.

And then Jung stated this hypothesis: 'there, that is an example of a so-called catalytic exteriorization phenomenon,' a psychokinetic event. As I have shown in *Holy Wedding*[143], these psychokinetic events happened in the context of Jung's rejection of parapsychology in 1898 on the one hand, and on the other in the context of the constellation of psychosynthesis complementary to psychoanalysis in Jung, and the rejection of parapsychology related to psychosynthesis

---

[140] Details see in my digital publication Holy Wedding, http://paulijungunusmundus.eu/bknw/holy_wedding_alchemy_modern_man_contents.htm

[141] Zumstein-Preiswerk, p. 80 and note 44, p. 124; Bair, p. 42 & p. 51

[142] MDR, p 178

[143] Digital publication

by Freud in 1909. For our concern it is very important that Jung felt 'a glowing vault' in his guts. It shows us that together with the parapsychological complex a sensation in the gut brain was present[144]. We know, however, that the conscious relationship with the belly brain and the Eros ego is only possible if one is able to give up will- and power-possession that belongs to the Logos ego. Therefore, five years after the 'catalytic exteriorisation phenomenon,' at the beginning of his dramatic mental breakdown in 1913, Jung was forced to follow what he called the counter-will 'thwarting our conscious will[145].'

As I have further shown in Holy Wedding, the archetype of Hermetic alchemy, the Holy Wedding, the *coniunctio* was constellated in a specific form in C.G. Jung. It is the myth of the king entering the womb of the queen, wherein he dies. Then however this *deus absconditus* (the hidden god) becomes the phallus of the queen, the latter herself the *dea abscondita*. In a *vegetative* myth then she begets the new king out of herself alone, with the seeds of *her* phallus. I interpret the death of the king as the 'death' of the Logos ego and its *causal* attitude. This is how one can enter the Eros ego, which is able to observe the creations of 'the phallus of the queen,' the singular *acausal* creation acts. It is this myth that was at the background of C.G. Jung's fascination with Sabina Spielrein, and also behind her fascination with Siegfried, the fatherless child, i.e., the acausal event. The necessary condition for the observation of such phenomena is however the renunciation of the will- and power-possessed consciousness, the other aspect of Siegfried, which was constellated in Jung.

As I mentioned above, it is impossible to interpret such psychokinetic events with the synchronicity hypothesis because in the latter no physical energy is exchanged between the inner event, the dream, and the outer phenomenon. We can therefore conclude that the Pauli effect and psychokinetic events in general must be explained in a manner other than the synchronicity hypothesis.

b. My dream of the 'synchronous synchronicity'

On July 14, 1984 I had a very odd dream, which I only understood when I began to deal with the content of this book. It shows that the key to the understanding of these psychokinetic events seems to be what the dream called 'synchronous synchronicities.' Since it sheds some light on the difference between common and 'synchronous' synchronicities, I will share this dream:

---

[144] See also the description of Pauli's sensation of being liberated and lightened after a Pauli effect, below.
[145] CW 14, § 151

DREAM OF THE 'SYNCHRONOUS SYNCHRONICITY':

The government of England (or perhaps the Queen of England; I am not sure) decided to do some research on the question whether consciously experienced 'synchronicities'[146] could have an influence on the state of the world and on the fate of humankind. The government or the Queen also asked Marie-Louise von Franz to give a statement on this topic. She decided however to send the letter to me to answer.

From somewhere (I do not know where and I also wonder if there was anything about the subject in the letter) I got some details about such 'synchronicities.' Of course, when I woke up I forgot most of these details. However, I remember one tiny but important piece of information: the 'synchronicities' had to be of the type of 'synchronous synchronicities,' i.e., 'synchronicities,' in which the inner and the outer phenomena happen exactly simultaneously (and not more or less simultaneously as in common synchronicities).

In the dream such a decisive event that creates a 'synchronous synchronicity' is also described: I am the passenger in a car and am reading the work of C.G. Jung. He describes this sort of 'synchronicity' as a bridge between two natural landscapes. They are however separated by exactly this highway where we drive. The piers of the bridge are in place, the bridge, however, is missing (see image 6.10).

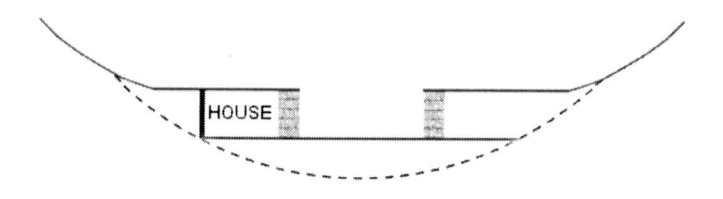

Figure 6.10:
Synchronous synchronicity as the missing bridge

In the moment, when I read this passage in Jung's work, I spontaneously looked up and realized that precisely in this moment we passed exactly

---

[146] I write the term in quotation marks since these phenomena are not really synchronicities. It seems that the preconscious knowledge of the unconscious did not have a suitable term at its disposal.

this scene in the outside. Further there was a detail which I did not notice in Jung's description: in the left pier there was a built-in house.

I get further the information from somewhere that the landscapes were once connected by a natural hollow, but were then separated by a 'cultural effort.' It is exactly this separation why we are now in need of constructing the bridge of 'synchronous synchronicity.' The latter corresponds to the construction of the bridge, which connects the two landscapes again.

Of course already immediately after the dream I associated with some elements. Since I had the dream more than 25 years ago and did not really understand it, I went on looking for spontaneous associations later. I would like to add them here.

The beginning of the dream exposes the constellated problem. I associated earlier dreams with it, in which Marie-Louise von Franz was presented as the Queen of England. Thus, if we put these together, we realize that the motif is the constellation of the queen—which means of course the *anima mundi*, the partner of equal worth to the king in Hermetic alchemy, with whom she consummates the *coniunctio*. The problem to solve in the dream is thus the subject of this book.

We know further that the *coniunctio* takes place on the background of Eros in its most comprehensive meaning. Together with the motif in the dream that consciously experienced 'synchronous synchronicities' could have an influence on the state of the world and on the fate of humankind, the Eros motif reminds us of Wolfgang Pauli's unpublished dreams of 1934/35 and 1936[147]. In these dreams 'the dark anima [the Chinese *anima mundi*; RFR] asserts with a certain persistence that there is a 'magical' connection between sexuality and eroticism [the Eros principle in general; RFR] on the one hand, and political or historical events on the other.' This was 'extremely surprising and unexpected for [Pauli].' Further, as we have seen, these dreams happened in a period when Pauli also began to have dreams and fantasies that contained[148] 'close links with…parapsychological areas that are not easily accessible.' They also used a physical-symbolic terminology, talking for example of 'fine structure' [obviously the fine structure constant; RFR] and 'radioactive nucleus[149].'

When, in 1996, I read these passages for the first time in the German original of *Atom and Archetype*, I was immediately reminded of my above dream. Of course I had not the slightest idea about its meaning. I just saw the similar content. Later, however, I realized that my dream gave a decisive hint: *the connection*

---

[147] See section 5.2.2.5 in Part 1
[148] AaA, p. 9, letter [9P] from June 22nd, 1935; PJB, p. 13
[149] AaA, p. 9, letter [9P] from June 22nd, 1935; PJB, p. 13. See also section 6.16.7 of this book, in which I interpret Pauli's fine structure constant and death room synchronicity.

between the Eros principle and contemporary history seems to be what the dream calls *'synchronous synchronicities'* constellated in myself and likely in Pauli as well.

Already when I had the dream I had a very interesting association with the symbol 'car.' 'Car,' in German 'Auto,' symbolizes a spontaneously beginning *automatism* in the vegetative nervous system (VNS)[150]. Thus I concluded that there was *a spontaneous observation mode* beyond my spontaneous looking up, behind the motion of my head. Today I see the same beyond Pauli's spontaneous glance through the windows of the Café Odeon. *In this observation mode, time and space are 'chosen' accidentally thus it is the observational mode of the Eros ego*[151].

With the government of England I associated also Margaret Thatcher, the Prime Minister at that time. On July 16, 1984, two days after my dream, she declared a state of emergency because of the strike of the dockers. I concluded that such a behavior is exactly the above mentioned will-possessed attitude which according to Jung is compensated by the counter-will of the unconscious. Thus, we can also give a second interpretation of the beginning of the dream: the problem is not only the constellation of the *anima mundi*, the ruler of the Eros Self, but it is also connected to the contrast between the will-dominated state of the Logos ego and the state without will of the Eros ego. Of course this was also exactly the situation in which C.G. Jung was when his big life crisis began in 1913. It was heralded four years earlier by the psychokinetic events at Freud's place, and even 15 years earlier, when he decided to break off the mediumistic, i.e., parapsychological experiments with Helly, and began to study causal medicine and philosophy instead.

c. Physical-symbolic uncertainty relation and 'synchronous synchronicity' on the psychophysical level

To continue my interpretation, I will use physical-symbolic terms as in Pauli's dreams of 1934/35 and 1936[152] and define statements about psychophysical processes. Werner Heisenberg's uncertainty relation defines the acausality of the quantum leap in a specific way that can be described mathematically. To define a causal physical process we need on the one hand Newton's differential equations, and on the other hand the initial conditions of four variables; of time, of

---

[150] *Today I see in this mode an automatism of the VNS, which begins however in an acausal way as soon as somebody is able to abandon the Logos ego and the CNS and enters the Eros ego and the VNS, the gut brain. As we will see in sections 6.13 and 6.14, this process is the background of Symptom-Symbol Transformation and Body-Centered Imagination.*

[151] *See section 6.1.4*

[152] *AaA, letters [9P], p. 9, [11P], p. 10, and [13P], p. 10-12; PJB, p. 13-17*

the position in space, of the momentum of the physical object observed, and of the amount of energy it contains. Energy and time are conjugated variables according to physics, and so are position (space) and momentum. The uncertainty relation tells us that the exact measurement of energy and time as well as position and momentum are impossible. If we measure energy as accurately as possible, time measurement becomes proportionately inaccurate and vice versa. The same is true for the other two conjugated variables: an exact measurement of the momentum (mass multiplied with velocity) of an object would cause an infinitely uncertain position of the same object in space.

Already at the time of my dream I was dealing with the uncertainty relation and asked myself whether it could not be used in a depth psychological way. With the discovery of matter-psyche I realized that we have to use Heisenberg's idea on the psychophysical level. This means that beyond Heisenberg's mathematical equation there can be an archetype of uncertainty, which causes a similar situation as in physics: if we let the time and the position in space of the observation of psychophysical events infinitely blur, the energy and the momentum of the object would become exactly observable.

Such an event happens in my dream, in the spontaneous glance at the outer world, and also in the Odeon Pauli effect mentioned above. It is exactly the acausal observation mode happening out of the VNS in the state of the Eros ego, the spontaneously beginning *auto*-matism above, in which time and place (space) of the observation are 'chosen' accidentally, i.e., acausally. Thus, the 'psychophysical momentum' and the 'psychophysical energy' of the acausally observed event should become exactly 'measurable.'

In German the physical term for momentum is 'Impuls,' impulse. We also use the same term for a spontaneous impulse out of the 'unconscious,' or out of the psychophysical reality of the VNS. Thus, if the place of the observation is accidental, according to the psychophysical uncertainty relation we become able to observe the spontaneous impulse out of the psychophysical reality (out of the *unus mundus*), which is not observable by the will-based ego. This spontaneous, acausal impulse out of the Eros Self corresponds to the parallel phenomenon in the inner world, the acausal observation in the state of the Eros ego. This is the 'synchronous synchronicity' between the Eros ego and the Eros Self, which in a physical-symbolic language I defined above as the radioactive core observing its own decay.

Further, if the time of the observation is infinitely uncertain, what occurs, if we accept the *kairos*, is that the spontaneous, i.e. acausal change of energy becomes precisely observable. Such a process is not observable by the Logos ego and its will-based observation mode. *I call this energetic phenomenon the acausal twin process that becomes observable exactly in the kairos and in an accidental place*, the latter symbolized in my dream as the accidental position of the car in the moment of the acausal observation. The transformation of the unobservable X into matter-psyche with potentially increased order in the psychophysical reality or *unus mundus*, and the simultaneous re-transformation of matter-psyche with potentially increased order into spirit-psyche with realized increased order have taken place. The incarnation has happened into our world of spirit-psyche by the spontaneous observation in the moment of the *kairos*.

With the above, the bridge of the dream is also interpreted. It symbolizes on the one hand the spontaneous observation of the twin process—the 'synchronous synchronicity' in consciousness—on the other hand it is the 'synchronous synchronicity' between the *unus mundus* and our world, in which *observable* higher order, or increased 'life essence' is created[153]. The observation of such processes was repressed by a 'cultural effort,' the development of the Logos ego. The 'highway,' the subject-object boundary, splits the one world into two, and such observation by the Eros ego is not subsequently possible. This is why we have to re-construct 'the bridge.' The 'conscious bridge' corresponds to the transformation of the Logos ego into the Eros ego, the altered state. The latter is then, in a process of acausal observation, able to observe the twin process, the bridge reuniting the 'two landscapes,' our world and the *unus mundus*.

As we will see[154], there are two different manifestations of this process: the acausal observation of the twin process between one's own body and the individual vegetative body (subtle body), the outer and the inner aspect of the body, on the one hand, and on the other the acausal observation of the twin process between the 'body of our world' and of its collective vegetative body (subtle body), the world soul in the *unus mundus*. The former process I call Symptom-Symbol Transformation and apply it in the case of somatic, psychosomatic and specific psychological diseases, the latter is Body-Centered Imagination to cure the collective disease of our world.

d. The bridge of the dream as the body/subtle body relationship

There is a further motif in the dream, which we have to interpret: the house built in the left pier of the bridge. The day before this decisive dream I read in the *book Der Mensch und seine Symbole*[155] (*Man and his Symbols*) by C.G. Jung et al. Obviously this is the book I read in my dream the following night. I was fascinated by an image, in which the human body is compared to a house (see image below).

---

[153] If such processes are constellated in an individual and he remains unconscious of it, the creation becomes destructive, as in Pauli's case.

[154] See sections 6.13 to 6.15

[155] Jung, C.G., Von Franz, M.-L., Henderson, J.L. , Jacobi, J., Jaffé, A., Der Mensch und seine Symbole, Walter Verlag, Olten, 1968, p. 78

Figure 6.11:
The human body as a house[156]

Only in 1997, when I came back to this dream, I realized that the built-in house in the pier of the bridge is a symbol of the relationship between the body and the vegetative body. This interpretation is backed by my experience as a dream interpreter and healer, as in dreams the house is mostly a symbol of the body and/or the vegetative body. For example the house is destroyed and must be reconstructed, however in a different way. We will see at the end of Chapter 6, that Wolfgang Pauli's new house dreams in 1954 can be also interpreted in this way.

Since here the house is on the left, the 'unconscious side,' (in the *unus mundus)*, it is a symbol of the vegetative body, the subtle body, observable by the Eros ego and the gut brain (VNS). I began slowly to realize that my dream from 1984 expressed symbolically the method I had been developing since 1987, Body-Centered Imagination, in which the energy of the physical body, the X, is first transformed into intermediate matter-psyche and then re-transformed into outer spirit-psyche with realized increased 'life essence' (see below). As we will see, the dream also symbolically talks about the background of UFO encounter and abduction, and also of what I call the radioactive beta decay on a psychophysical level. Further, it also explains the Pauli effect and psychokinetic phenomena in general.

---

[156] *Source: Wikimedia Commons*

B. The Pauli effect formulated in the neutral language:

After the clarification concerning the energetics of the twin process, the 'synchronous synchronicity,' with the help of my dream, we can now formulate the Pauli effect in the neutral language, as a double twin process:

A. The inner process:

A1: {X = unobservable spirit/psyche/matter → *unconscious* 'individual corporeal' matter-psyche with potentially destructive altered quality}

And

A2: {'Individual corporeal' matter-psyche with potentially altered quality → *unconscious* 'individual corporeal' spirit-psyche with realized destructive altered quality}

B. The outer process:

B1: {X = unobservable spirit/psyche/matter → 'collective' matter-psyche with potentially destructive altered quality}

And

B2: {'Collective' matter-psyche with potentially altered quality → collective outer spirit-psyche with realized destructive altered quality}

As in the case of synchronicity we should remember that the 'individual' and the 'collective' matter-psyche are nonlocally connected. Thus, one can no longer really use these terms to describe the situation. As I have mentioned, I use them in quotation marks, since Logos consciousness needs such a distinction.

The above double twin process explains the Pauli effect in a neutral language. Since the physicist was completely identical with the Logos consciousness, in the VNS, especially in the gut brain, a counter-position was created, which he sensed as a tension in his belly. Using physical-symbolic language I will describe below the situation as the charging of an 'acausal condenser.' Most probably this tension began when, some days after his divorce from the dancer Käthe Deppner, he invented the antineutrino. Instead of consciously acknowledging his disappointment and other negative emotions concerning his broken marriage, he invested himself in his research and repressed the dark side of his emotions. In the neutral language we could say that a creation of matter-psyche took place in the gut brain, however completely unconscious and repressed.

This energetic counter-position corresponds to the above 'individual corporeal' matter-psyche with potentially altered quality (result of process A1), which is however not observable with Logos. Since matter-psyche is psychophysically nonlocal, it was not limited to Pauli's body, but affected the surroundings, as well. This was the creation of 'collective' matter-psyche with potentially altered quality (result of process B1).

When Pauli entered the scene (or spontaneously glanced out of the window as in the Odeon Pauli effect) he became the necessary observer of the constellated acausal transformation process[157]. A psychokinetic energetic process was initialized in him (result of process A2) and psychophysically nonlocally in the surroundings (result of process B2)—the 'synchronous synchronicity' happened spontaneously. Symbolically seen we could say that Pauli became psychophysically radioactive or became the Hermetic red tincture (A1). In the moment of the spontaneous observation (A2) he also 'contaminated' the surroundings. In this moment the 'collective' outer matter-psyche with potentially altered quality, the result of process B1, transformed or better, transmutated into spirit-psyche, physical energy, with altered quality (B2); the incarnation of the destructive energy was triggered.

This process is obvious in the above mentioned Odeon Pauli effect: there was a 'sea' of 'negative energy' in Pauli, made of repressed and thus destructive energy of the 'other world,' of the psychophysical reality, created by the repression of his negative emotions (result of process A1). As long as this process was not observed, the second process, the incarnation also remained latent[158].

On the other hand, in the outside there was the red car filled with gasoline ready to burn and explode. The car was therefore the perfect outer symbol of Pauli's repressed emotions. Because matter-psyche is psychophysically nonlocal, a process parallel to the inner one was constellated in the car (B1). Thus physical matter or energy (the physical energy of the gasoline) also transformed into matter-psyche with potentially altered quality and constellated the second process, the transformation into outer spirit-psyche with altered quality, in this case destructive. However, as long as this process was not observed, it also remained latent.

---

[157] *The process is constellated in the outside, since Pauli is not conscious about the inner process, and because he is not able to observe it with the help of the Eros ego.*

[158] *In fact Pauli was also sometimes overwhelmed by negative emotions, as he shares with Emma Jung in a letter. He writes that these emotions are provoked by an inner figure he calls the magician/stranger. He is an 'anti-scientist,' thus a magician, who, when he feels disregarded sets the places of oppression, the universities afire. [AaA, p. 51; PJB, p. 54; not yet published in WB]*

In the moment of the acausal observation (A2), i.e. when Pauli spontaneously glanced through the window, when he became 'radioactive,' the potential process was released (B2) in an acausal quantum leap in him as well as in the red car (symbolizing the charged emotions). Since matter-psyche possesses the quality of (inner-outer) psychophysical nonlocality, the latent process became real in the outside as well, and the car began to burn.

I would like now to translate the above verbal statement into a physical-symbolic image easy to grasp. We could compare the Pauli effect with some sort of 'acausal condensers.' The situation in Pauli I describe as an 'individual acausal condenser,' the outer situation as a 'collective acausal condenser' in the *unus mundus*. Further I assume that the two condensers, since they both contain matter-psyche energy, are psychophysically nonlocally connected. The charging of Pauli's inner condenser would thus correspond to the situation described in process A1, the charging of the collective condenser to the situation of process B1.

In the course of time the individual condenser in Pauli is charged with matter-psyche with potentially altered quality—in his case because of unconscious negative emotions—and then, in the moment of the spontaneous observation, the inner condenser discharges acausally in time and space. Since the individual condenser is nonlocally connected to the collective condenser, in the moment of the spontaneous observation *both* acausal discharges happen simultaneously—the 'synchronous synchronicity.'

Let me now describe the above process using the physical-symbolic image of the acausal condensers as the double twin process:

C. The Pauli effect formulated in a physical-symbolic language:

A. The inner process:

A1: Unconscious charge of the 'individual corporeal' acausal condenser in Pauli (since he represses the negative emotions and does not know the Eros ego)

And

A2: Acausal discharge of the 'individual corporeal' condenser in Pauli in the moment of the spontaneous observation, producing physical energy with destructive altered quality in himself

B. The outer process:

B1: Charge of the 'collective' acausal condenser

And

B2: Spontaneous discharge of the 'collective' condenser triggered by Pauli's spontaneous observation, producing physical energy with destructive altered quality in the outside world

Since we know that incarnation is only possible when it is observed, I inserted it in the description of the double twin process. In the moment when Pauli spontaneously looked up and glanced through the window (process A2), process B2 was triggered.

The way Pauli himself could sense the effect named after him confirms that we can describe the constellated process using the above double twin process. Markus Fierz, in a comment to *Naturerklärung und Psyche* (the joint book containing Jung's synchronicity article and Pauli's Kepler essay) writes[159]:

> Pauli himself thoroughly believed in his effect. He has told me that he senses the mischief already before as a disagreeable tension, and when the anticipated mischief then hits—another one!—he feels strangely liberated and lightened.

The tension he sensed in his belly is linked to the 'individual charged condenser,' which discharged acausally in the moment of the spontaneous observation with the feeling of liberation and lightening (the relief). Since the Nobel laureate was not conscious of this inner process, which is however psychophysically nonlocal, it was 'projected' into the outside, however, with destructive effects. We can compare this situation with the projection of a complex of the unconscious spirit-psyche (the objective psyche) in C.G. Jung's depth psychology[160]. We know that deeply unconscious complexes can disturb the environment. The Pauli effect would then be some sort of a 'projection,' however on a psychophysical and physical level. Thus, because of his specific ability of 'projecting' the acausal discharge of the condenser, Pauli was never forced to transform the tension (the charged condenser of matter-psyche in his belly), into a conscious and thus constructive discharge in him.

---

[159] *Quoted according to* Enz, No Time to be Brief, *p. 150*
[160] *See Marie-Louise von Franz* Spiegelungen der Seele, *section* Projektion und Projektil *[Projection and Projectile], p. 24-29*

D. The constructive effect formulated in colloquial language:

Let us now compare Pauli's situation with the one in my dream. In contrast to the Pauli effect when I looked up from the book, a positive 'synchronous synchronicity' happened, *the two disconnected landscapes reunified*, i.e. 'our world' of spirit-psyche, and the 'other world' of matter-psyche, the *unus mundus*, melted. *Since the landscape on the left belonged to the 'inner house,' to the realm of the vegetative body or world soul, and the other to the 'outer house,' the gross body, this detail means that in my dream a spontaneous, i.e., acausal process is described, in which matter-psyche with potentially altered quality was consciously observed and thus transmutated into spirit-psyche with incarnated altered quality—the constructive parallel to the destructive consequence of the Pauli effect.* We will later see that the described process, though more differentiated, corresponds exactly to what happens in BCI and SST. We can also observe similar but completely unconscious events in UFO phenomena.

We can now formulate the constructive process analogous to the Pauli effect:

A. The inner process:

A1: *Conscious* **realization of the charge of the 'individual' acausal condenser of matter-psyche in the individual (because of the conscious transformation of the Logos ego into the Eros ego)**

And

A2: Acausal discharge of the 'individual' condenser in the individual in the moment of the spontaneous observation, producing physical energy with constructive altered quality in the individual

B. The outer process:

B1: Charge of the 'collective' acausal condenser of matter-psyche

And

B2: Spontaneous (acausal) discharge of the 'collective' condenser in the individual triggered by his spontaneous observation, producing physical energy with constructive altered quality

This interpretation is verified by a further detail of my dream. I interpreted the car, the 'Auto' as the place of the spontaneously beginning *auto*-matism of the observation without will, in which time and place (space) of the observation are 'chosen' accidentally, i.e., acausally. I was sitting *in* the car, thus where these spontaneous observations happened. The dream showed that I had the ability to consciously identify with the Eros ego in the VNS and this way I could observe the acausally beginning, deeply introverted process in my belly brain. In contrast to the Pauli effect this is a completely inner transformation of the matter-psyche with potentially altered quality into spirit-psyche with realized altered quality. The result of the process is not 'projected' into the outside anymore, and thus is constructive. Further, since matter-psyche is psychophysically nonlocal, it is also possible that the surroundings are magically influenced in a positive way.

Pauli, however, did not sit in the car, the 'Auto,' the place where these spontaneous *auto*-matisms begin, since he was not conscious of the possibility of the transformation of the Logos ego into the Eros ego. On the contrary, he was sitting in the Café Odeon, a place where one eats and drinks, i.e., he was identified with the gross body. We can therefore interpret this detail as identification with the CNS. Thus, he was not able to consciously observe the spontaneously beginning *auto*-matism in himself. This is why the acausal discharge of the condenser happened 'projected' into the outside, into the concrete car. Because of the unconscious 'projection' it was destructive—the car burnt.

E. Comparison of the Pauli effect, synchronicity and the Hermetic magical process ('synchronous synchronicity')

We can now compare the Pauli effect, synchronicity, and 'synchronous synchronicity' or Hermetic magic. Let us first compare the Pauli effect with synchronicity. We immediately realize that the two phenomena can be described in the same way in a neutral language except for the order of the two twin processes. Thus we could argue that they describe the same process. However, there are three very important differences. First, as we know, synchronicity leads to an incarnation in the world of the conscious *inner* spirit-psyche, the human mind (and because of psychophysical nonlocality eventually in the collective consciousness). The result of the Pauli effect is a destructive incarnation in the world of *outer* spirit-psyche, of physical energy. Second, in synchronicity there is no energy exchange between the inner and the outer phenomena—the dream does not cause the outer event—in the Pauli effect, however, the acausal 'discharge' of the condenser in Pauli, the 'individual corporeal' radioactive decay on the psychophysical level causes the outer destructive effect (in our example the burning of the car). Third, in the Pauli effect the inner and the outer processes are completely synchronous, in synchronicity however they are only relatively synchronous. In the Pauli effect we recognize the exact simultaneity of the material incarnation of spirit-psyche with realized altered quality (**B2**) and the 'inner radioactive decay' (**A2**). *We immediately realize that in a physical-symbolic language the discharge of the 'individual corporeal' condenser and the discharge of the 'collective' condenser are synchronous.* Since the ego does not observe by will (which means that it does not specify the time and place of observation as in physical and scientific experiments in general), the observation itself becomes acausal and happens exactly in the moment of the acausal collective quantum leap—perfect simultaneity.

We can find the same difference between the conscious Hermetic magical process (the conscious 'synchronous synchronicity'), and synchronicity: they are distinguished by the simultaneousity of the 'discharge' of the two condensers, of the singular quantum leaps in the 'individual corporeal' and in the 'collective landscape.' *Exactly* in the moment when the world soul acausally incarnates, when she produces the singular psychophysical quantum leap, the 'radioactive ego' observes it: the Eros ego acausally observes exactly in the moment of the *kairos*, the acausal incarnation moment. Further in the magical process (which as we will see corresponds to SST/BCI), both phenomena, the observation of the 'individual' and of the 'collective' event happen in one's own body, in synchronicity, however, the experience is split into an inner and an outer event.

We can also compare the Pauli effect (the unconscious 'synchronous synchronicity') with the Hermetic magical process (the conscious 'synchronous synchronicity'). As we know, the result of the former is always destructive. This is because the physicist was not conscious of the Eros ego and its being a 'radioactive core.' Since he was not able to accept 'psychophysical radioactivity' (observable by the 'radioactive ego') he could not recognize the psychophysical incarnation process. As we know, this incapacity comes from his refusal of the matter-psyche principle that led to the invention of the antineutrino, and thus Pauli never had a chance to discover the Eros ego/Eros Self connection (or rather: fusion).

Pauli was not able to realize that there was an observation tool in himself with which he could observe in a 'radioactive' way, i.e., acausally. Thus, the *automatism* of the VNS forced him to observe unconsciously and extraverted. He was forced to look up and out through the window by a spontaneous i.e. acausal impulse by the VNS exactly in the right moment—and the car burnt down. It is thus his unconsciousness of the 'radioactive Eros ego' that first made Pauli realize the acausal quantum leap in the outer world in a destructive way. Further, we can conclude that in Pauli's Odeon event the process of looking through the *fenestra aeternitatis* (the window into eternity; see next section) was constellated. Since he was identical with the Logos, the Eros ego was yet projected into the physical body; the process was concretized and happened as a spontaneous looking out of the concrete *fenestra*. We will realize in the next sections that a similar attitude, especially the unconsciousness about being in the Eros ego, is also at the background of UFO encounter and abduction; people involved in UFO experiences are unconsciously forced into the Eros ego, be it in an extraverted way as in encounter, or in an introverted way as in abduction.

In the Hermetic magical process described in my dream, the ego is however 'in the car,' which means that I let myself consciously fall into the Eros ego, which is then able to observe the *auto*-matically triggered singular quantum leap. The quantum leap in the 'inner landscape' and the psychophysically nonlocally connected quantum leap in the 'outer landscape' happen synchronous, in exactly the same moment of time, in the *kairos*. In this specific moment the microcosm is nonlocally connected to the macrocosm, and thus the point A situation is reached: what happens in the inner world happens also in the outer world or in one's own body.

This observation mode corresponds also to SST/BCI. When we realize the spontaneously emerging image or vegetative sensation out of the belly brain, the 'inner-outer' i.e., the psychophysically nonlocal 'landscape' is grasped. The epistemology of quantum physics tells us that reality is created by the mere observation of such an acausal process. In my terminology we can express this fact as the observation by the Eros ego of an incarnation act into our world out of the *unus mundus*. As we will see, this is not the only incarnation process which can happen, since also the creation of observable matter-psyche with increased order is possible (a creation process in the *unus mundus* itself). The former incarnation corresponds to UFO encounter, the latter to UFO abduction, as well as to SST and BCI, in which the process is however consciously observed and thus leads to a healing effect in one's own body and in the 'body of the universe.'

6.12.3.3 Marie-Louise von Franz' anticipation of the *fenestra aeternitatis* and the solution of the problem of physical incarnation out of the *unus mundus*

In her book *Number and Time* Marie-Louise von Franz shows[161] that the idea of energy precedes the conception of time, as empirically proven by Jean Piaget's research with children. This is the reason why archetypal personifications of time in mythology and history were gods representing energy. She brings the examples of the Hindu gods Krishna and Shiva and their representations of Maha-Kala, great time and Kala-Rudra, all-consuming time, as the energy of the universe. The name of the goddess Kali is derived from Kala, which is etymologically connected to *kairos*.

In ancient Iran it was Zurvan, who himself split into Ormuzd and Ahriman. In Mithraism Ahriman became the (evil) god of linear time, Zurvan akarana,

---

[161] Number and Time, *p. 254-259*

however, the eternal reality behind clock time. Further, in Mithraism there was Aion[162], eternal time as a world creating principle, in contrast to the Greek god Chronos, linear time. For our concern a further amplification is very important: in the Gnosis of the *Corpus hermeticum*, the predecessor of Hermetic alchemy, the Demiurge created the universe and time as both Chronos and as becoming, Genesis. The Mayas, finally, believed that the god of the ninth world imprinted the vulture 'cuch' on his back, representing an eon of 3.600 years.

Marie-Louise von Franz concludes[163] that behind the personification of time there exist 'the archetypal image of a god in his world-creating energy' and interprets the latter as the objective psychic energy in the meaning of C.G. Jung. In my terminology we would call this principle inner spirit-psyche. In contrast to this interpretation (bearing in mind the bipolarity of the energy term) I call this principle matter-psyche, the energy of the *unus mundus*, symbolically represented by the *anima mundi*.

In some of the above examples the god of time is split into two, into a personification of eternal time, the time of psychophysical reality, and the representation of the chronological time of our world. If we combine these two different times with the idea of the singular acausal quantum leap out of the *unus mundus* (the singular radioactive decay on a psychophysical level in the moment of the *kairos*), we obtain the idea of the singular acausal incarnation act observable by the 'radioactive ego,' the Eros ego.

Marie-Louise von Franz was attracted by the bipolarity of the divine time representations and came very close to the above idea. She showed that ancient Chinese culture realized the union of eternal and chronological time with the so-called fire clock (see figure 6.12):

> This type of clock was constructed by spreading a combustible powder over a labyrinth and igniting it at one end, so that its burning head crept slowly forward like a fuse. Time was marked off according to the progress of the fire. The labyrinths were usually mandala-shaped (see illustration). Such clocks depicted the pattern of a relatively closed system.

Then she mentions that by the gap in the rim—marked as an I—this time mandala was open to human contact, and continues:

---

[162] In C.G. Jung's life Aion came back in his third vision in 1913 that induced his great life crisis, the so-called night-sea journey. Aion also symbolizes coniunctio or unio corporalis; Jung however interpreted it in a Neoplatonic way as the unio mentalis. See my digital publication Holy Wedding, http://paulijungunusmundus.eu/hknw/holy_wedding_alchemy_modern_man_contents.htm

[163] Number and Time, p. 259-260

> Practically speaking, this 'hole' in the mandala of the fire clock signifies the spot at which man relates himself to time, and at which he... can exert an influence on time...Time has a 'hole' at this spot, where it begins and ends. This hole in the time-space continuum figures as an archetypal motif in other contexts. The *fenestra aeternitatis* ('window into eternity') plays an important role in Western alchemy. In the Middle Ages the Virgin Mary was extolled as the 'window of enlightenment' or 'window of escape' (from the world), and in alchemy these attributes were transferred to the philosophers' stone.

Figure 6.12:
Chinese Fire Clock[164]

Marie-Louise von Franz shows further that Paracelsus' student, Gerardus Dorneus, was also fascinated with a similar idea, the *spiraculum aeternitatis*, the air hole into eternity, and continues:

> [Dorneus] recommended a kind of alchemistic exercise in meditation, in which the instinctual aspect of the body was first to be subdued, by separating soul and spirit from it. Then soul and spirit were to be fused into a *unio mentalis* in order to be reunited subsequently with the purified body [consisting in the so-called *unio corporalis*; RFR].

In all that has been shared at this point the reader can imagine that I do not agree with C.G. Jung's and Marie-Louise von Franz' interpretation of the philosophers' stone as the goal of the *unio mentalis*, the Neoplatonic goal of the *opus* and

---

[164] *Zahl und Zeit, p. 228*

the first phase of Dorneus, corresponding to Jung's quaternity in the Heavens[165]. The philosophers' stone, the *lapis* (which stresses the material aspect of the goal and does not belong to the Christian Heaven) is symbolically equivalent to the Seal of Solomon and the philosophical gold with its ability of gilding the surroundings or the whole universe. The *lapis*, the Seal and the gold all represent *the first goal of the second phase* of the alchemical *opus*, the *unio corporalis* or *coniunctio*. Translated into modern terms we can say that these symbols correspond to the bipolarity of the energy term, the necessary background for the twin process, i.e. the transformation of spirit-psyche into matter-psyche and vice versa.

In the first phase, the Neoplatonic *unio mentalis*, such a double transformation is however not included. This part of alchemy corresponds to the liberation of the spirit from matter and its ascent to Heaven, the spiritualization of matter and of the instincts—in modern terms: psychoanalysis. In the second phase, however, the spirit-soul, the result of the *unio mentalis*, has to come down again and re-unify with the body or with matter in general. According to Marie-Louise von Franz[166] this aspect developed by Dorneus is absolutely unique in mediaeval alchemy. As we have just seen, Dorneus called this second phase the *unio corporalis*, and as we have seen its modern form is Body-Centered Imagination. Both correspond to *coniunctio*, to the Holy Wedding of Hermetic alchemy—the main subject of this book. In this second phase not only the spirit-psyche has to come down from the Christian Heavens, but matter also has to transform into matter-psyche and to ascend—though not into the Christian Heaven, as in the dogma of the Assumption. In contrast to it the god and the goddess of equal worth (spirit-psyche and matter-psyche) meet in the middle, in an intermediary realm, which is neither matter nor spirit, but the excluded third; the *tertium non datur*. In this subtle realm best symbolized by the bipolar Seal of Solomon, the god and the goddess, the representatives of spirit-psyche and matter-psyche, have sexual intercourse to create the *infans solaris*, the equivalent to the red tincture and the quintessence. In Paracelsus' words, the second goal of the *unio corporalis* is the *astral body*. As we remember, Wolfgang Pauli was fascinated with this process also anticipated by Robert Fludd. In Paracelsus' *opus* the red tincture, the quintessence, the *infans solaris* and the subtle body lead to the *vita longa*, the long life,

---

[165] As the reader remembers this aspect of Jung's conclusions, especially in Answer to Job (CW 11), provoked Wolfgang Pauli's resistance and sometimes caustic argumentation against the idea of the quaternity.

[166] '[Dorneus] goes one step further, a unique step which you find in no mystical text of the Middle Ages: He feels sorry for this body which has been cast out, and says that it cannot simply be thrown into the rubbish heap, but that it too must be redeemed into the inner unification, into the already existing unio mentalis [with the help of the procedure called unio corporalis; RFR]' [Marie-Louise von Franz, Creation Myths, Spring Publications, University of Dallas, Irving, Texas, US, 3rd ed., 1978, p. 240.

which is the healing and life essence to cure physical disease on the one hand, and on the other it is the necessary vehicle for the individual eternal life in the Beyond.

Let us return to *Number and Time*. To demonstrate the bipolarity of time Marie-Louise von Franz also presents the famous copper engraving[167] *The Spiritual Pilgrim discovering another world*, in which 'the pilgrim leaves ordinary space-time behind and glances through 'the window of eternity'.' (See figure 6.13)

Figure 6.13:
The spiritual pilgrim discovering another world[168]

In the upper left corner there is a double wheel representing Ezekiel's vision from the Old Testament[169]. Von Franz reminds us that the double wheel is a so-called double mandala containing eternal and chronological, linear time. Of course we are immediately reminded of my mandala from 1974, which is made of two times nine sectors of circles; the 'Zweierkreise,' the circles of the two, and the 'Dreierkreise,' the circles of the three. Some years later I read in *Number and Time*[170] that in ancient China number two was the beginning of the feminine

---

[167] *It is not a wood-cut as wrongly translated*
[168] *From CW 10, picture VII after p. 404*
[169] *Ezekiel, 1, 15-16*
[170] *Number and Time, p. 78*

series of even numbers, and number three was the beginning of the masculine series of odd numbers. Thus, my mandala represents the re-unification of the masculine linear time with the feminine eternal time, as does Ezekiel's double wheel.

In the continuation of the argument about the specific content of double mandalas Marie-Louise von Franz wonders whether these two different times are somehow 'interlocked.' She says that 'the manner in which they may contact each other remains obscure.' She cannot answer this crucial question. Let us examine why.

Based on what we saw in the section about the Pauli effect, we can *say that eternal time, the unus mundus together with the beyond, are linked with linear time, the time of our world, exactly by the singular acausal quantum leap in the kairos. The 'accidental' time of the coniunctio is not measurable by the will-dominated Logos ego, but is perceived by the 'radioactive' ego, the Eros consciousness in the moment of the observation of the 'synchronous synchronicity.'* Thus, if we become conscious of the existence of the Eros ego and enter it by abandoning the Logos ego, the observation of creation and incarnation phenomena out of the *unus mundus* becomes possible.

We can also see why C.G. Jung and Marie-Louise von Franz were not able to solve the enigma of *incarnatio*, a decisive topic the depth psychologist began to discuss with Wolfgang Pauli in May 1952[171]. Already in 1911, in his early work *Transformationen und Symbole der Libido*[172], C.G. Jung defined the objective psychic energy as unipolar, and he never changed his opinion. It is true that together with Pauli he was able to realize the complementarity of physics and depth psychology, however (as mentioned in a letter to Pauli[173]) he was not yet able to consciously enter the *unio corporalis*, the *coniunctio* of Hermetic alchemy. As we have seen, this is the case since he avoided the definition and realization of the above defined twin process, in which with the singular acausal quantum leap the unobservable X transforms into matter-psyche, and the latter into spirit-psyche with altered quality. In its core Jung's theory remained therefore Neoplatonic and causal (the liberation of the masculine spirit out of matter). However with the synchronicity concept Jung approached acausal Hermetics, which created a contradiction between a causal and an acausal theory. Pauli was aware of this contradiction, but could not find the way out. Though both Jung and Pauli experienced strange phenomena proper to this reality—the depth psychologist for example in

---

[171] See section 5.4.1 in Part I

[172] *English translation:* Psychology of the Unconscious. A Study of the Transformations and Symbolisms of the Libido. A Contribution of the History of the Evolution of Thought, New York, 1916. *Revised edition with the title* Symbols of Transformation *published in the year 1952; Today in CW 6; further information in my digital publication* Holy Wedding, http://paulijungunusmundus.eu/hknw/holy_wedding_alchemy_modern_man_contents.htm

[173] AaA, p. 101

his visions after his first heart attack[174], the physicist in the psychokinetic effect named after him—neither of them were able to include the necessary structure and processes into a psychophysical theory. As we have seen, the reason is their theoretical limitations, the prejudice of the unipolar energy term, which prevented the discovery of the above defined twin process.

However, during these 50 years that passed by since the death of Jung and Pauli, phenomena began to happen in an accelerated manner, that can be understood neither with the help of Neoplatonic science nor with Jung's depth psychology. I am referring to the UFO phenomenon, which must be explained on a psychophysical level. We will realize that these phenomena cannot be the definite solution of the Hermetic enigma, since the witnesses are not conscious of the possibility of observing with the Eros ego. Since in a physical-symbolic language the latter corresponds to the observation of singular psychophysical radioactive decays by the radioactive consciousness, first we have to return to radioactivity.

The Eros ego, in contrast to the Logos ego is able to observe such incarnation events similar to what all mystical traditions describe as the opening of the ego to infinity, to the Beyond, and to God. Looking back to the above, we can conclude that Wolfgang Pauli by initializing the singular quantum leap in his Odeon Pauli effect unconsciously approached the 'hole in the time-space continuum' (M.-L. von Franz), the *fenestra aeternitatis*[175]. We will see at the end of the book that for a conscious realization of such a union with the *unus mundus* he had had the task to give up the idea of the spin and the neutrino/antineutrino on the psychophysical level.

6.12.3.4 UFO encounter, the artificial fission of the atom and the observation of incarnation into our world by the extraverted Eros ego

Before we can turn towards the above question[176], whether on the psychophysical level there could exist observable events parallel to the artificial fission of the atom in nuclear bombs and power plants, which lead to the production of matter-psyche or negative energy with its completely non-physical attributes (M. Stöckler), we again have to deal with the mentioned possibility of an altered consciousness. As we have seen[177], already in 1946 C.G. Jung assumed the existence of a 'second psychic system' with 'absolutely revolutionary significance,' since it

---

[174] See MDR, chapter X
[175] The same is true for C.G. G. Jung in his out-of-body experience after his heart attack in 1944. See MDR, Chapter X Visions.
[176] See section 6.12.2.2
[177] In section 6.12.2.3

would give us 'the possibility of enormously extending the bounds of our mental horizon.' Further, in 1952 he guessed that such a different psychic system could be related to the VNS.

In section 6.1.3 I defined this second psychic system as the Eros ego or Eros consciousness. With this definition we can hypothesize the possibility of abandoning the Logos ego and entering the Eros ego. This would mean that the replacement of *the observation of the physical radioactive decay (and of the creation of the antineutrino) by an observation of a 'radioactive decay' on a psychophysical level by the altered consciousness* could be a serious ability to discuss.

Regarded from an energetic view such a change would mean that we replace P.A.M. Dirac's antimatter by the original metaphysical 'sea' of negative energy, which I call the matter-psyche. However, in contrast to Dirac's metaphysical hypothesis, we would describe observable events. As we know, if we would be able to describe *observable* acausal energetic changes in or out of this 'sea' of the *unus mundus*, we would indirectly prove its existence. Further, in an extension of C.G. Jung's anticipation that with the help of this 'second psychic system' we could 'enormously extend the bounds of our *mental* horizon,' i.e., realize a creation in the world of the conscious *inner* spirit-psyche, of the mind, we can hypothesize an observable creation and incarnation phenomenon out of the psychophysical reality into the *physical* world, the creation of *outer* spirit-psyche, of physical energy/matter with altered quality.

I have already shown that also during the perception of dreams a transformation of the ego happens. The dream is *potential being* in the *unus mundus*, which is observed with the help of the Eros ego and then memorized by the introverted Logos consciousness. As we have realized, the Eros ego is a combination of the introverted feeling function, (introverted) vegetative sensation and of intuition. Further, we realized that such a consciousness perceives, i.e. feels and senses with the help of the vegetative nervous system (VNS). This means concretely that the Eros ego's perceptions are not based on the Central Nervous System (CNS), which mainstream science believes to be the only organ of consciousness.

If we, first hypothetically, assume that there are in fact humans who could be in possession of such particular abilities and thus be able of experiencing perceptions with the help of the VNS, we can postulate a further hypothesis: There are observable events during which certain humans fall unconsciously into the above altered state, and like this are in a position to observe such processes happening in and out of the psychophysical reality, the *unus mundus,* the 'inner-outer realm' with its attribute of psychophysical nonlocality. However, in contrast to the perception of a dream as well as of a synchronicity, in this case an incarnation into the material world, into the world of the outer spirit-psyche is perceived. This means concretely that the Eros ego, the 'individual' matter-psyche, would be able to observe events concerning the 'collective' matter-psyche, and thus observes inner-outer phenomena happening in as well as out of the *unus mundus,* the Eros Self. Then however, the observation of such a material incarnation is 'carried over into ego-consciousness,' i.e., memorized with the help of the Logos ego and the CNS. As I described, to really fulfil this task the ego has in fact to be in an intermediary state, in which Logos and Eros come together—the conscious *coniunctio* (Point 1 of the Hermetic process defined in section 6.12.1).

We must now ask ourselves, whether there are observable processes, which would empirically prove the hypothetical one. If we approach the problem of an alternate observation's possibility with an open mind, we are actually in the position to describe such phenomena: UFO encounter. In it the consciousness is coerced to transform *unconsciously* and spontaneously into the Eros ego and in this way becomes able to observe, also spontaneously, the UFO. It is this process, which I will describe below with the help of the neutral language.

I hypothesize therefore that the Eros ego is able to observe *coniunctio*. Thus, we must now have a look whether UFO phenomena correspond to *coniunctio*, and especially whether they match the attributes of the final goal of the Hermetic myth, the red tincture or the quintessence. This means that we should be able to show that they correspond to the above defined[178] six preconditions and processes belonging to the Holy Wedding.

Before we can compare the UFOs with the *coniunctio* and its result, we have to remind ourselves that the physical process of the beta decay of the neutron into a proton, an electron and Wolfgang Pauli's physical antineutrino has to be redefined in the psychophysical language. This would especially mean that, as shown above, we have to replace the antineutrino by the original negative energy, which itself corresponds to the matter-psyche. In an alchemical language we would call this product the red tincture or the quintessence. As we further remember, this product of the *coniunctio* possesses the attribute of altered quality. Since UFOs are somehow physical matter/energy, they should thus obey to laws which cannot be explained with today's physical theory, neither with the causal of Newton/Einstein nor with quantum physics.

In fact, UFOs are able to move in strange motions which escape physical laws. This is a severe empirical hint that UFOs are somehow related to the Hermetic alchemical *coniunctio*, which, as we realized, produces as a result the 'alchemical psychophysical radioactivity,' i.e., the (observed) red tincture, i.e., physical energy (outer spirit-psyche) with completely non-physical attributes (M. Stöckler).

To really correspond to the Hermetic alchemical process (on a higher scientific level) of the *coniunctio* (Point 1 above) such a process has to fulfil all six characteristics defined in section 6.12.1. This is in fact the case: Many UFOs possess the attribute of the *multiplicatio* (4), insofar as they are able to split into many different parts. We can also observe the exchange of attributes (3), if we include their ability to move almost instantly from one point in space to another with

---

[178] See section 6.12.1

velocities much higher than physically possible. The obviously acausal splitting in parts we could also interpret as the equivalence of the 'point-space' with the 'all-space,' the identity of the microcosm with the macrocosm (6) in the moment of the incarnation, though perceived in the outside and in the sky. The ability of appearing out of the nothing and of executing very strange movements could also be interpreted as a quantum leap (5), in a Hermetic language as the *creatio continua*, the spontaneous creation and incarnation out of the *unus mundus*. The ability of spontaneous appearance and disappearance shows further that a transformation of (invisible) matter-psyche into (visible) spirit-psyche et vice versa, the twin process (2), is also included. Summarizing, we notice that UFOs fulfill all the six characteristics of the *coniunctio*.

If we assume that the existence of UFOs belongs to processes rooting in the psychophysical reality, and that their appearance is a direct effect of the artificial fission, we can thus also regard their spontaneous appearance and their observation as the acausal double twin process of Hermetic alchemy. As in the Pauli effect there is therefore a 'collective' as well as an 'individual' process. The 'collective' twin process looks like this:

Artificial fission and the constellation of UFO encounter described on a psychophysical level in the neutral language:

'Collective' twin process in the neutral language:

1a: {X = unobservable matter/psyche/spirit → 'collective' matter-psyche with potentially altered quality}

And

1b: {'Collective' matter-psyche with potentially altered quality → *observable outer* spirit-psyche with realized altered quality = observable UFO}

Using the language of the Hermetic alchemists we can write the 'collective' twin process as follows:

'Collective' twin process in Hermetic language:

1a: {X = unobservable matter/psyche/spirit → potential red tincture or quintessence (which is psychophysical and replaces the physical antineutrino)

And

1b: {Potential red tincture → observable incarnated red tincture or quintessence in 'our world' = observable UFO}

Or described in colloquial language:

'Collective' twin process in colloquial language:

1a: Constellation of altered physical energy with potentially destructive influence as an effect of artificial fission

And

1b: Creation of destructive physical energy of altered quality = observable UFO

The first process of the 'collective' twin process would mean the transformation of physical energy into potential magic energy, matter-psyche or negative energy, caused by the artificial radioactive beta decay, i.e., by the artificial fission of the atom in nuclear bombs and nuclear power plants. In the above used physical-symbolic language we could say that the collective acausal condenser in the *unus mundus* is more and more charged.

Of course the physicist would argue that matter is matter. Thus, it would be impossible to distinguish between naturally and artificially produced neutrinos or antineutrinos. However, as I hypothesized in section 5.4.14, a hypothesis that will be empirically confirmed by Wolfgang Pauli's dreams and visions interpreted at the end of the book, on a psychophysical layer the neutrino or antineutrino becomes matter-psyche, i.e., magic energy. In the natural radioactive beta decay the antineutrino is thus produced in the spontaneous moment when 'the *anima mundi* likes to do so.' It is a singular acausal creation and incarnation process of the Goddess independent of human's will. In the case of the artificial production of the antineutrino, in nuclear bombs and in the nuclear power plants, it is however the human will and not the spontaneity of the Goddess, which produces the magic energy. Thus, the will-possessed sorcerer's apprentices ape the *anima mundi*'s efforts, and artificially produce 'children' that she does not want at all. Therefore, the *unus mundus* is charged with what physics calls negative energy, which is in fact destructive.

The second process of the 'collective' twin process above demonstrates in a neutral language the observability of UFOs, the possibility of an acausal incarnation of physical matter/energy with altered quality out of the *unus mundus* into the physical world[179]. Physically-symbolically we could express this fact in the way that the collective acausal condenser discharges from time to time. Since such a singular discharge is acausal, it is however not observable with the help of the Logos ego.

Thus, I state that regarded on the psychophysical level such *singular acausal* actualization of *potential being* created by the artificial fission of the atom (the second process) and its acausal creation of matter-psyche with altered quality (the first process), which Hermetic alchemists would have called the creation of the red tincture or of the quintessence, is potentially observable.

This process is only potentially observable since there must be a consciousness that observes it. Only when such observation is realized the transformation of 'collective' *potential being* into *actual being* has taken place. Thus we must also describe the process of the creation of the observing Eros ego and its spontaneous observation:

The unconscious transformation of the Logos ego into the *extraverted* Eros ego and the observation of UFO encounter described on a psychophysical level in the neutral language:

Individual extraverted twin process and observed UFO:

2a1: {X = unobservable spirit/psyche/matter → unconscious 'individual' matter-psyche with potentially altered quality}

And

2b1: {Unconscious 'individual' matter-psyche with potentially altered quality → observed *outer* spirit-psyche with realized altered quality = observed UFO}

If we replace the terms with the ones of the Logos ego and the Eros ego we obtain:

Individual extraverted twin process in colloquial language:

2a1: {X = Logos ego → unconscious *extraverted* Eros ego}

And

---

[179] *This could result in an increase as well as in a decrease of order. In the first case we would experience positive effects, in the latter however negative ones. Actually, UFO encounter can be experienced in both ways.*

2b1: {Unconscious *extraverted* Eros ego → spontaneous observation realized by the *extraverted* Eros ego = observed UFO}

Let us first deal with the first term. The Logos ego is insofar unobservable as no one knows what (Logos) consciousness is. The reason for this shortcoming is the fact that science does not know singular processes in which *potential being* transforms into *actual being* and in this way creates (Logos) consciousness[180]. What however is observable is the change of the Logos ego into the Eros ego in an acausal act as for example in UFO encounter. Thus, the transformation process obeys the above defined transformation of the unobservable X into the observable result of the spontaneous quantum leap; *potential being* is transformed into *actual being*, the latter being the 'radioactive' ego, the Eros ego, which is able to observe the discharge of the acausal condenser on the psychophysical level.

In colloquial language the first process corresponds thus to the unconscious transformation of the Logos ego into the Eros ego, which happens completely acausally, spontaneously. If this process has taken place, the second process, an instant and acausal observation of the 'individual' transformation of matter-psyche into spirit-psyche with potentially altered quality becomes possible. Since 'individual' and 'collective' matter-psyche are psychophysically nonlocally connected, this observation means the simultaneous observation of the 'collective,' of the 'outer' acausal incarnation out of the *unus mundus* potentially constellated as an effect of the artificial fission. With the help of another physical-symbolic term we could say that a wormhole between the Eros ego and the psychophysical reality, the Eros Self, opened, which is observed as a UFO.

Compared with physical observation we have to consider decisive differences of the UFO observation: First, the UFO experiencer is unconsciously *forced* into the Eros ego and is compelled into such a specific observation, and second, such an observation is completely *involuntary*; UFO encounter happens spontaneously and cannot be controlled by the conscious will. In such moments witnesses do not have any other choice than to observe the strange phenomena in the sky. Since, however, they are forced to abandon the Logos and enter the Eros such events are not perceived with the help of the CNS, but with the VNS.

I stated above that as in the experience of a dream also in UFO encounter the memorization happens afterward with the help of the Logos ego. The first difference to the memorization of a dream formulated in a neutral language is however the *extraverted orientation* of the Eros ego; the second difference is the fact that not an acausal creation in the conscious spirit-psyche, in the mind (the Logos ego) as in the case of a spontaneously interpreted dream or a synchronicity, takes place, but *an incarnation into the material world*.

---

[180] *This fact transforms supposed rational science in fact into metaphysics. As we have seen in section 6.12.2.4, the observation and spontaneous interpretation of synchronicities leads however into observable incarnation phenomena on the Logos level.*

Since with the help of the VNS, the gut brain in the belly, the Eros ego has the ability of 'inner-outer,' of psychophysically nonlocal observation, it experiences in fact such psychophysically nonlocal processes, incarnations out of the psychophysical reality into our world in the outside, in the sky. The hypothetical world behind or even beyond our world in the words of Wolfgang Pauli corresponds, as I mentioned several times, to 'an invisible, potential form of reality that is only indirectly inferable through its effects.' His term 'indirectly inferable' means thus in my translation 'observable in the state of the Eros ego with the help of the VNS or belly brain.' Since the ego of such people is however completely extraverted oriented, they observe these strange phenomena based on the psychophysical nonlocality in the outside.

As a next step let us compare UFO encounter with the archaic Hermetic process as described above: As we remember, the alchemist observed events in the outer physical world with the help of his chemical 'experiments' in the state of the Eros ego, and he interpreted this observation as an acausal event. In the outer experiment, however, in his dealing with the processes in the crucibles and alembics causal transformations of physical/chemical energy took place. The visions the alchemist realized in his phials were thus projections of his inner process into the outside.

There exists therefore a decisive difference between the UFO encounter witness and the alchemist: As a by-product of artificial fission the witness observes *real* singular acausal quantum leaps in the outside, whereas the alchemist projects them. In this way the UFO witness unconsciously returns to the archaic Hermetic process, or more exactly to what the alchemists wrongly believed to be the outer process: Acausal incarnation out of the *unus mundus* into our world.

The difference between the outer observation in the archaic alchemical experiment and in the experience in UFO encounter is further the above mentioned fact that on the one hand the witness of the latter is forced to abandon the Logos ego and enter the Eros ego, whereas the alchemist never realized the Logos, and on the other the impossibility of planning the completely involuntary 'experiment.'

As we remember, I hypothesized that on the psychophysical level the artificial fission causes the UFO phenomenon. If so, we can therefore conclude that the artificial fission of the atom has lead to the fulfilment of the alchemist's dream, of the original idea of the Hermetic alchemical *opus*, the observation of acausal incarnation out of the *unus mundus* into our world.

If artificial radioactivity and the UFO phenomenon are really psychophysical events, the question arises whether they could not only influence matter, but also the spirit-psyche of man, the human mind.

The corresponding twin process would then look like this:

Individual introverted twin process and telepathic communication:

2a2: {X = unobservable matter/psyche/spirit → 'individual' matter-psyche with potentially altered quality}

And

2b2: {'Individual' matter-psyche with potentially altered quality → observable *inner* spirit-psyche with realized altered quality}

Instead of *outer* spirit psyche (physical energy) with altered quality, *inner* spirit-psyche (objective psychic energy) with altered quality is produced. Actually such inner experiences are observable, as we know from many UFO encounters. Witnesses many times feel that they receive messages from the 'aliens.' Further, they are convinced that the respective communication is telepathic and even precognitive. As we have seen, matter-psyche is 'inner-outer,' psychophysically nonlocal, which would explain the relativization of space and time visible in such phenomena. The transmission of the telepathic and precognitive message would then be understandable exactly by the above transformation process: Inner-outer, i.e., psychophysically nonlocal matter-psyche with potentially altered quality transforms into inner spirit-psyche with realized altered quality. Since such a relationship is telepathic or even precognitive, we have to conclude that between the UFO witnesses and the 'aliens' there is a synchronistic relationship.

In colloquial language we can write:

Individual introverted twin process in colloquial language:

2a2: {X = Logos ego → unconscious *introverted* Eros ego}

And

2b2: {Unconscious *introverted* Eros ego → spontaneous telepathic communication with the 'aliens'}

The reader can surely imagine that phenomena like UFO encounter are experienced as somehow otherworldly. This is the reason why in many cases they cause real conversion experiences, which themselves lead into the various UFO cults, especially of the contactees. The destructive aspect of such a spontaneous change in the spirit-psyche of the witnesses is the well known UFO sect's phenomenon. The members believe to be chosen by a new godhead, and thus fall into a big inflation, i.e., megalomania. Further, since their consciousness is so extremely extraverted, they think that they have to tell the world their new 'truth.'

We know further that UFO encounter can also spontaneously heal disease, or on the contrary cause the witnesses to become sick. Thus, it is also possible that the experiencer realizes inner acausal phenomena on the level of his own body. This would correspond to a re-psychification of his body, which is, as we will see below, equivalent to the transformation of bodily matter into the vegetative or subtle body that happens in SST/BCI, in the latter however not unconsciously, but consciously.

I am clearly aware that I present here the scientific reader an almost unbelievable theory. Thus, they may perhaps shake their head because of the above interpretation of UFO encounter. I would however like to remind them again of C.G. Jung's hypothesis concerning a second consciousness connected to the VNS in his synchronicity article already quoted above[181]. There he also presents a case of deep coma of a patient[182] after

---

[181] See section 6.1.2

[182] *A further, more recent example is described by Dr. Michael Sabom: 'Dr. Michael Sabom is a cardiologist whose latest book,* Light and Death, *includes a detailed medical and scientific analysis of an amazing near-death experience of a woman named Pam Reynolds. She underwent a rare operation to remove a giant basilar artery aneurysm in her brain that threatened her life. The size and location of the aneurysm, however, precluded its safe removal using the standard neuro-surgical techniques. She was referred to a doctor who had pioneered a daring surgical procedure known as hypothermic cardiac arrest. It allowed Pam's aneurysm to be excised with a reasonable chance of success. This operation, nicknamed "standstill" by the doctors who perform it, required that Pam's body temperature be lowered to 60 degrees, her heartbeat and breathing stopped, her brain waves flattened, and the blood drained from her head. In everyday terms, she was put to death. After removing the aneurysm, she was restored to life. During the time that Pam was in standstill, she experienced a NDE. Her remarkably detailed veridical out-of-body observations during her surgery were later verified to be very accurate.* This case is considered to be one of the strongest cases of veridical evidence in NDE research *because of her ability to describe the unique surgical instruments and procedures used and her ability to describe in detail these events while she was clinically and brain dead.*
When all of Pam's vital signs were stopped, the doctor turned on a surgical saw and began to cut through Pam's skull. While this was going on, Pam reported that she felt herself 'pop' outside her body and hover above the operating table. Then she watched the doctors working on her lifeless body for awhile. From her out-of-body position, she observed the doctor sawing into her skull with what looked to her like an electric toothbrush. Pam heard and reported later what the nurses in the operating room had said and exactly what was happening during the operation. At this time, every monitor attached to Pam's body registered "no life" whatsoever. At some point, Pam's consciousness floated out of the operating room and traveled down a tunnel which had a light at the end of it where her deceased relatives and friends were waiting including her long-dead grandmother. Pam's NDE ended when her deceased uncle led her back to her body for her to re-entered it. Pam compared the feeling of reentering her dead body to "plunging into a pool of ice."'

a very difficult birth[183]. In this state she had a near death experience. In it she first was lifted up to the ceiling, where she saw herself lying in the bed, deadly pale, with closed eyes. Further, she saw the doctor pacing up and down the room excitedly, as if he had lost his head. Her mother and her husband were frightened and thought that she will die. She, however, knew that she will come back again. Further, she experienced something that I would like to quote literally[184]:

> All this time she knew that behind her was a glorious, park-like landscape shining in the brightest colors, and in particular an emerald green meadow with short grass, which sloped gently upwards beyond a wrought-iron gate leading into the park. It was spring, and little gay flowers such as she had never seen before were scattered about in the grass. The whole demesne sparkled in the sunlight, and all the colors were of an indescribable splendour. The sloping meadow was flanked on both sides by dark green trees. It gave her the impression of a clearing in the forest, never yet trodden by the foot of man. 'I knew that this was the entrance to another world, and that if I turned round to gaze at the picture directly, I should feel tempted to go in at the gate, and thus step out of life.' She did not actually *see* this landscape, as her back was turned to it, but she *knew* it was there. She felt there was nothing to stop her from entering in through the gate. She only knew that she would turn back to her body and would not die. That was why she found the agitation of the doctor and the distress of her relatives stupid and out of place.

After she had awoken from her coma, about fifteen hours later[185], 'she made a remark to the nurse about the incompetent and 'hysteric' behaviour of the doctor during her coma' and 'she described in full detail what had happened.' Thus, 'the nurse [was] obliged to admit that the patient had perceived the events exactly as they happened in reality.'

In this vegetative state of near death experience C.G. Jung's patient experienced however also the 'other reality,' the Beyond, the *unus mundus*. Actually she observed exactly at the border between the concrete outer life and the inner world, which corresponds in its deepest aspect to the Beyond. Further, she did not perceive these worlds with her physical eyes, but with an 'inner eye.' We can therefore conclude that it is the inner eye, the observational organ of the belly brain psychophysically nonlocally connected to the outer world, which has the ability to realize inner-outer phenomena.

[Source: *http://www.near-death.com/experiences/evidence01.html* . *I thank Gregory J. Sova, CA, USA for letting me know about this very interesting case.*]

[183] *For the following see CW 8, §§ 950-955*
[184] *CW 8, § 950*
[185] *For the following see CW 8, § 851*

Jung describes a further example, in which extra sensory perception (ESP) went even much further. He writes[186]:

> During a state of collapse the patient noted the splitting off of an integral consciousness from his bodily consciousness, the latter gradually resolving itself into its organ components. The other consciousness possessed verifiable ESP. [especially telepathy and precognition; RFR]

Then he presents the above quoted idea that[187]

> These experiences seem to show that in swoon states, where by all human standards there is every guarantee that conscious activity and sense perception are suspended, consciousness, reproducible ideas, acts of judgement, and perceptions can still continue to exist.

Further he concludes that there seems to be[188]

> A shift in the localization of consciousness, a sort of separation from the body, or from the cerebral cortex or cerebrum which is conjectured to be the seat of conscious phenomena.

And he postulates that this other consciousness has its seat in the VNS. Extrasensory perception is, however, only possible since the VNS has the ability of inner-outer, psychophysically nonlocal perception. In C.G. Jung's as well as in the case of UFO encounter we have the same nexus. Jung's example shows in this way that the observation mode experienced in UFO phenomena is possible.

As we realized, the goal of the Hermetic *opus* is the production of the red tincture or of the quintessence, which are looked at as being the life elixir. Since they all are produced as a result of the *coniunctio*, of the union or reunion, the product of the Holy Wedding has such a unifying quality. In radioactivity this aspect is however completely absent. On the other hand, compared with radioactivity, in UFO encounter the possibility to multiply is accompanied by the ability to unify. However this is some sort of an oscillating process, since one never knows when the union divides anew.

Such oscillating processes were a frequent theme of Pauli's dreams and visions[189]. They tried to transform the oscillation—in some way an unredeemed state—into a rotation. On the other hand we know that UFOs are especially

---

[186] CW 8, § 954
[187] CW 8, § 955
[188] CW 8, § 955
[189] See for example the manuscript Background Physics, in AaA, where we find a whole chapter about this phenomenon.

stamped by exactly these two attributes: Oscillation and rotation. However, one gets the impression that there is no solution with a lasting effect, i.e., no real transformation or transmutation.

Since UFO encounter remains somehow in a potential state, the vehicles of the 'aliens' do not have any sustainable existence in our world; they occur and disappear spontaneously, acausally. Only the UFO witness can see them and sometimes also sensate physical effects of a higher order. Also, these peculiarities show that the UFO phenomenon remains in the state of a mere potentiality, and no sustained end product is created.

Therefore we have to conclude that UFO encounter is not yet the complete transmutation process, and thus does not really lead into the definite goal of alchemy: The creation of the healing life essence, the Alexipharmakum, the counter-poison, the *medicina catholica*, the all-healing substance symbolically described as the red tincture or the quintessence as the last goal.

We will see at the end of this Chapter that the 'production' of sustainability is symbolically represented in Pauli's visual-auditive experience of the dancing Chinese woman, the Seal of Solomon, the quintessence and the square already presented in section 4.3.3.

/ / /

In the above twin process describing in a neutral language UFO encounter as an effect of the artificial radioactive decay completely unconscious to today's mankind, I provided the incarnated spirit-psyche with the attribute of an altered quality. This is an intentional choice of terms, since I did not want to qualitatively judge the end product. Now, however we have to have a look at the effects of radioactivity as well as of UFOs. As I already mentioned, the radioactive decay causes in any case destructive consequences. In UFO encounter there is a different situation: On the one hand, UFOs show a *higher* quality of their energetic behavior. Such observable effects are mostly interpreted as higher physical laws the 'aliens' visiting us from other places of the universe or even of parallel universes are in possession of. On the background of Wolfgang Pauli's and my research results we realize immediately that such a diction is metaphysical, since we cannot say anything about unobservable parallel universes. Thus, the hypothesis has more relevance that in processes obeying to singular acausal quantum leaps, i.e., in this case the creation of UFOs, out of the *unus mundus* outer spirit-psyche, physical energy with altered quality, is produced. As we know, according to my hypothesis in exactly such processes 'contents' of the unobservable *unus mundus* are incarnated into our world, and become like this observable. Whether these incarnations follow higher physical laws only the future can tell.

Besides the physical aspect there are also psychic and depth psychological phenomena: telepathy and precognition. Since the contamination with artificial radioactivity increases more and more—the psychophysical condenser is charged more and more—it is to be expected that in more and more humans such abilities will develop. In the positive case this means that such people become psychic and in this way can more and more see through the negative intentions of their fellow beings. In the negative case—and because of the unconsciousness of most people about the background of such phenomena, this case is much more likely—many more humans than today will become psychotic and/or sociopathic. They will only be able to survive in their sect, which means that the world becomes more and more dissociated, and a war between these different sects begins.

As I mentioned above, it is further a matter of fact that UFO encounters can have constructive as well as destructive effects. It seems that the quality of these effects depends in some way on the attitude of the individual; if they believe in UFOs and their good intentions, they seem to be positive, if they however believe in the prejudice that the 'aliens' come with a hostile intention, the effects are destructive. The most important difference to radioactivity is however the possibility of an increased quality of the effects.

We can also ask ourselves, if the above mentioned depth psychological effects are not already real today. Fanatic religious belief, in which people also believe to be chosen by God, could be such a phenomenon. Since the members of these sects identify with the principle of the absolute Good, they split off their evil shadow and live it unconsciously. Thus the question arises if it could not also be possible that the increase of moral hypocrisy, of cruelty, of political irresponsibility, of terrorism, of today's greed in the business world, etc., is not a result of a destructive, poisoning effect of the artificial fission of the atom on the mind/spirit level of mankind. If we can answer this question with yes, we are confronted with the further question: Does there exist an Alexipharmakum, a counter-poison to this acceleration of evil in our world? I will answer this question later.

6.12.3.5 UFO abduction and the observation of incarnation in the *unus mundus* by the introverted Eros ego

More than 50 years ago, in 1961, Betty and Barney Hill had an experience which later was designated as the first UFO abduction by 'aliens.' Since then thousands of humans tell us such stories. They only differ in details, thus the suspicion arises that somehow these abduction experiences are, at least subjectively, true. Since these stories belong to the phenomenology of UFO experiences, I am trying to integrate the general process behind them into my considerations.

The difference between UFO encounter and abduction consists in the fact that the latter is not experienced as a phenomenon in the outer world, but in one's inside. Usually the witnesses are asleep in their bed and 'wake up' into a state of sleep paralysis. In this altered state of consciousness they see first a bright light coming from nowhere and anywhere. Strange-looking 'aliens' enter the bedroom through the wall or the closed door, and lead the abductees out, also crossing the wall. Then they are lead to a UFO waiting in the sky, where mostly very cruel breeding experiments are performed on them. These experiments seem to have the goal to extract ova and sperm, but sometimes even culminate in a rape of the human. The objective of these cruel experiments seems to be the fertilization and birth of hybrid beings, half man and half 'alien'[190].

I guess that the reader has already realized that with this sexual symbolism UFO abduction is a modern expression of the Hermetic *coniunctio* archetype. Thus, it seems that at the end of the 20th century and the beginning of the 21st Hermetic alchemy comes unconsciously back. What was repressed in the 17th century showed first in the Pauli effect and now in UFO phenomena—both being magic phenomena.

UFO abduction phenomenology does not follow the original Hermetic *opus* in one decisive aspect: It is not the queen and the king, the goddess and the god, who have sexual intercourse, but the experiencers and the 'aliens.' Further, the abductees are compelled into the sexual act. We have therefore to ask ourselves, what these differences could mean.

In dreams the emergence of powerful beings which threaten and force us always means that the consciousness has a wrong attitude towards the unconscious, and therefore has to change. The 'alien's' application of power thus means that a necessary transformation of the ego is constellated. As much as we know up until today this means concretely first that the ego of the abductee has to transform consciously from the Logos to the Eros, as described above. Second, this indicates that the experiencers have to live the Eros completely introverted. Third, this shows that they have to accept and actively to try to receive a *conscious* relationship with the gut brain in their own belly, since only in this way can the Logos ego be abandoned. Fourth, this means the acceptance of the possibility and the conscious looking for singular vegetative quantum leaps in a meditative state, the appearance of which would then show that the abductee has entered the *unus mundus* and can consciously realize its energetic principle, the *anima mundi*[191], and the singular acausal transformations she triggers.

---

[190] For a detailed description of the abduction phenomenon see Mack, John, E.: Passport to the Cosmos, Human Transformation and Alien Encounters, *Crown Publishers, New York, 1999*

[191] Which in the case of a feminine abductee is some sort of an animus mundus. As Jung shows in CW 13, §§ 239, this figure is represented by Mercury. Mercury itself corresponds to the above mentioned Logos Spermatikos, *the acausal principle. Thus in the feminine as well as in the masculine case eventually the same archetype is constellated: the singular inner quantum leap.*

With the fulfilment of these four conditions the first question is answered: *The sexual intercourse of the abductee with the 'alien' in contrast to the original Hermetic opus but in accordance to Luria's Cabbalah shows that the human being has to participate consciously in the process of the incarnation.* 'Man must help God to repair the damage wrought by the Creation. For the first time man's cosmic responsibility is acknowledged[192]' (C.G. Jung about Luria's *tikkun*).

The differences between the original Hermetic *opus* and its modern form, UFO abduction, the fact that now the individual human is included in the *coniunctio*, shows that in the Middle Ages and in the Renaissance the incarnation process was still completely projected into the 'realm of God,' into the Beyond and into the life after death, but now it should develop during this life on earth and include the (Eros) consciousness. This also means of course the acceptance of the reality of the unconscious; of the Logos aspect, the collective unconscious, on the one hand as well as of the Eros aspect, the *unus mundus* or the psychophysical reality on the other. In this way one realizes the necessary consciousness about the structure of the Beyond and its relationship with the ego: The Logos ego deals with the Logos Self, which means dream observation and interpretation, Active Imagination and the observation and interpretation—synchronicities; the Eros ego, however, deals with the Eros Self—thus, enters the *unus mundus* or even melds with it, and consciously observes the *coniunctio*. We can call such a challenge modern mysticism independent of any religious belief. By the acceptance of the possibility of the observation of the singular quantum leap on the level of the Logos Self, i.e., synchronicity, as well as on the Eros Self, i.e., Hermetic magic, the insights of quantum physics and of C.G. Jung's depth psychology are integrated into the modern Hermetic *opus*, and one of the most important demands of Pauli's Fludd/flood synchronicity[193] is fulfilled.

It was the *coniunctio* motif, which already many years ago let me suppose that UFO abduction could have to do with the twin process. Thus, in the following I write the abduction procedure first in the terminology of the double twin process formulated in the neutral language, as well as in Hermetic and colloquial language. Then I will look for concrete elements in abduction, which fit into the twin process.

The 'collective' event of the constellation of the *coniunctio* I describe as follows:

---

[192] Letters, *volume 2, p. 155*
[193] See Chapter 2 in the first volume

Artificial fission and the constellation of UFO abduction described on a psychophysical level in the neutral language:

'Collective' twin process in the neutral language:

1a: {X = unobservable matter/psyche/spirit → 'collective' matter-psyche with potentially altered quality}

And

1b: {'Collective' matter-psyche with potentially altered quality → observable 'collective' *matter-psyche* with realized altered quality}

As the reader realizes, here too I write the term collective in quotation marks. As we have seen, the reason is that in the realm of the matter-psyche, in the psychophysical reality, because of its attribute of psychophysical nonlocality no separation of individual and collective phenomena exists anymore. Thus, events which change the quality of the collective matter-psyche in the *unus mundus* simultaneously change also the quality of the individual matter-psyche, of the Eros ego. On the other hand we must somehow distinguish the 'collective' and the 'individual' twin process, since the Eros ego is nevertheless a consciousness, which can observe, though in these moments of the identity with the gut brain it becomes identical with the world soul/body soul[194].

We can now also write the collective twin process of the abduction phenomenon in the Hermetic language as follows:

'Collective' twin process in the Hermetic language:

1a: {X = unobservable matter/psyche/spirit → 'collective' red tincture or quintessence with potentially altered quality (replacing the antineutrino)}

And

1b: {'Collective' red tincture or quintessence with potentially altered quality → observable 'collective' red tincture with realized altered quality in the *unus mundus*}

---

[194] *Further we realize that here the possibility of expressing these phenomena in our colloquial language comes to its limits. Language is itself causal and based on the subject-object boundary. As Marie-Louise von Franz told me, she knows only one language which is different: The language of the Hopis, which thus consequently does neither distinguish between the past, the present and the future.*

Or in colloquial language:

'Collective' twin process in colloquial language:

1a: Constellation of 'otherworldly' energy of altered quality with potentially destructive influence as an effect of artificial fission

And

1b: Spontaneous (acausal) creation of destructive 'otherworldly' energy

The first part of the twin process corresponds to the first in UFO encounter and means the charge of the 'collective acausal condenser' in the *unus mundus* because of the artificial fission. The second part means the production of energy with destructive quality. There is however one absolutely crucial difference to UFO encounter: Not spirit-psyche, but *matter-psyche with destructive quality is constellated*. This is insofar a very decisive difference, since in this way not energy with destructive quality in the physical and/or psychic world, i.e., spirit-psyche, but *energy with destructive quality in the unus mundus itself, i.e. matter-psyche with a completely new quality is created*. The 'acausal condenser' discharges not into 'our world,' but into the *unus mundus* itself. In colloquial language this would mean that *a destructive transformation in the background of 'our world,' the physical as well as the psychic, is incarnated*. The destructive quality of this energetic process is experienced by the victims as raping 'aliens' in their UFOs and as the coerced fertilization and birth of the hybrid children.

As in UFO encounter we must also describe the process of the creation of the Eros ego and its simultaneous observation of the above process. With the terminology of the neutral language we can thus write:

The *unconscious* transformation of the Logos ego into the *introverted* Eros and the observation of UFO abduction described on a psychophysical level:

Unconscious 'individual' twin process in the neutral language:

2a: {X = unobservable matter/psyche/spirit → (unconscious) 'individual' matter-psyche with potentially destructive quality}

And

2b: {Unconscious 'individual' matter-psyche with potentially altered quality → unconscious observed 'individual' matter-psyche with realized destructive quality}

We can now describe the 'individual' aspect of abduction with the help of the twin process and the neutral language using the Hermetic alchemical terms:

Unconscious 'individual' twin process in Hermetic alchemical terms:

2a: {X = (unobservable world = *unus mundus*) → *coniunctio* of the human in the Eros ego with the 'alien' = potential hybrid child = potential *infans solaris* = potential red tincture = potential quintessence in the *unus mundus*}

And

2b: {Potential hybrid child = potential *infans solaris*, red tincture or quintessence → observed hybrid child incarnated in the *unus mundus* = observed *infans solaris*, red tincture or quintessence, incarnated in the *unus mundus*}

This formulation of the twin process in the case of abduction, which, as we will see, corresponds to the goal of Pauli's dancing Chinese vision/audition, leads again into the conclusion of above that it is nothing less than a modern expression of the Hermetic *opus* with its result of the red tincture or its synonym, the quintessence: The abductees have the task to help to create the subtle body during this life. The vegetative body or diamond body in Taoist alchemy serves then on the one hand as the vehicle of an individual afterlife, on the other for the relationship with the deceased. It is an open question whether in this way the latter are reincarnated in the human concerned. However, we begin to understand why the Nobel laureate was so intensely occupied with the question of reincarnation. Since he dealt with this crucial question only on the Logos level, he was however not yet able to solve the problem.

In colloquial language we can describe the process as follows:

Unconscious 'individual' twin process in colloquial language:

2a: {X = Logos ego → unconscious *introverted* Eros ego}

And

2b: {Unconscious introverted Eros ego → spontaneous experience of the rape in abduction}

In colloquial language the first process describes the fact that the abductee falls asleep in the Logos ego, but spontaneously wakes then up into the state of the (unconscious) *introverted* Eros ego. The second process shows the spontaneous observation of the abduction consisting in the rape and cruel experiments, in the fertilization against the will of the abductee and of the coerced giving birth to hybrid children. However, as I mentioned already above, the whole process happens completely unconsciously[195].

If we compare this process with the general description of the 'individual' process in encounter, we realize the same very important difference as in the 'collective' process: The observed product consists of 'individual' *matter-psyche* with altered quality, and not as in encounter of outer or inner spirit-psyche with altered quality. Thus the result owns the quality of 'inner-outer:' it possesses the attribute of psychophysical nonlocality. This means that a product is created which overcomes the subject-object boundary.

It is the abolition of the subject-object boundary, the entrance into a world of psychophysical nonlocality, which the abductee experiences as the forced sexual union with the 'alien' with its result of the creation of the hybrid child. In the latter the Eros ego and the Eros Self unconsciously merge and become one and the same. Surely this reminds the reader of C.G. Jung's point A hypothesis: When something happens in one human that is deep enough and thus touches the *unus mundus*, it simultaneously happens everywhere in the world—psychophysical nonlocality.

As we remember, unconsciousness creates hostile monsters in the psychophysical reality. This is why the *coniunctio* is presented as such an absolutely traumatizing rape. What is meant is however the creation of the androgyne *homunculus*, of the vegetative body/world soul equivalent to the liberation of the *salvator macrocosmi*, the savior of the universe. The latter happens now not in the phial of the alchemist anymore, but in the uterus of the woman experiencing UFO abduction.

It was exactly in C.G. Jung's year of death that the Hill couple experienced the first documented abduction of mankind. Thus the depth psychologist was not able to deal with it. However, he already had a deep anticipation to which archetype (besides the *coniunctio*) such events belong: The archetype of the apocalyptic

---

[195] *I am conscious about the fact that with the definition of an 'unconscious Eros ego' I create a contradiction in itself. There is however no other way to express the fact that the abductees observe with the help of the completely vegetative Eros ego, are however not conscious about this fact. In BCI the introverted Eros ego is reached consciously.*

Revelation described in the New Testament. In it, after the opening of the seventh seal[196]

> there appeared in heaven, after the destruction of Jerusalem, a vision of the *sun-woman*...She was in the pangs of birth, and before her stood a great red dragon that wanted to devour her child.

Jung then continues[197]:

> The vision...is probably a prelude to the descent of the heavenly bride, Jerusalem, and equivalent of Sophia, for it is all part of the heavenly *hieros gamos,* whose fruit is a divine man-child.

We realize that the depth psychologist combines here this scene of the apocalyptic Revelation with the *hieros gamos,* the *coniunctio* archetype. Then, however, he notes a decisive difference as he writes[198]:

> We must dwell for a moment on the figure of the mother. She is 'a woman clothed with the sun.' Note the simple statement 'a woman'—an ordinary woman, not a goddess and not an eternal virgin immaculately conceived. No special precautions exempting her from complete womanhood are noticeable, except the cosmic and naturalistic attributes which mark her as an *anima mundi* and peer of the primordial cosmic man, or Anthropos. She is the feminine Anthropos, the counterpart of the masculine principle.

This means nothing less than that the 'ordinary woman' is deified and that she gives birth to the Anthropos, the God-man that we can equate with the *salvator macrocosmi.* As we further know, the latter is symbolically equivalent to the vegetative body and the world soul. Since, however, this apocalyptic event is constellated but the abductees remain unconscious about what really happens with them, the conception and the birth of the androgyne *homunculus,* the savior of the universe, becomes a destructive and frightening event. Thus, what is urgently needed is becoming conscious of this apocalyptic event, which is itself the effect of the invention of the artificial fission of the atom.

/ / /

---

[196] *CW 11, § 710*
[197] *CW 11, § 710*
[198] *CW 11, § 711*

Let us return to the twin process described in the neutral language. *How could we express the event of the twin process with the help of quantum physical epistemology?* As we know, because of the artificial fission the *unus mundus*, the acausal condenser is charged. A Hermetic alchemist would say that the first goal of the *coniunctio*, the creation of the intermediary realm symbolized by the Seal of Solomon, the *lapis* (the stone), or the philosophical gold has been created, and like this the preparation for the spontaneous *coniunctio* of god and the goddess has taken place. Then, in the moment of the supremely introverted, spontaneous observation the quality of the 'personal' matter-psyche is altered. Since the latter is nonlocally connected to the 'collective,' also a content of the *unus mundus*, of the 'other world' or the Beyond instantly changes its quality—the 'collective' acausal condenser discharges. In contrast to encounter this incarnation act happens not only in our world, but corresponds to an incarnation act happening in the totality of the psychophysical reality. This means that a content of the *unus mundus* consisting in 'non-physical negative energy' (W. Stöckler) or matter-psyche obtains an altered quality, a different order. In the language of Hermetic alchemy we can express this spontaneous change as the second goal of the *coniunctio*, the creation of the red tincture, or the quintessence, of the 'radiation' of the *lapis* (the stone) or of the gilding of the whole universe by the gold, or of the birth of the *infans solaris*, the sun's child.

The attribute of psychophysical nonlocality of the 'other world' as well as of the Eros ego leads to a further implication: Since 'point-space' and 'all-space' are one and the same, no metric space in the meaning of physics exists anymore—the spaceless space[199]. Further, since in this moment of the *kairos*, the spontaneous qualitative moment becomes equal to eternity, neither time in the sense of physics is defined anymore. In addition, the subtlety of this world leads to the abolishment of physical mass. Together with the annihilation of space and time this fact leads to the secret identity of the subtle body/vegetative body and the world soul, which Hermetic alchemy expressed as the red tincture, the quintessence or as the liberated *salvator macrocosmi*. As we will see at the end of my book, exactly the quintessence is also the end product in Pauli's visual-auditive experience of the dancing Chinese woman of the year 1953.

If there is no space in the physical definition anymore, the Pauli principle, the idea that matter distinguishes from force insofar as the former needs physical space and the latter does not, is abolished. This is the deepest reason why in abduction the vegetative body, the one of the abductee as well as the one of the 'alien,' is able to penetrate walls and closed doors. The subtlety of the vegetative

---

[199] Though I am conscious about the fact that I present like this metaphysical terms about the *unus mundus*, I use them to show the reader the qualitatively different aspect of it.

body on the other hand allows it to abandon the body of the sleeping abductee and to hover over it or even to fly to the waiting UFOs in the sky[200].

Besides this difference of the *coniunctio* in encounter and abduction, we find however many accordances: Since abduction can be formulated with the help of the (double) twin process it implicitly contains the other motifs, processes and goals of the Hermetic *opus* as described in section 6.12.1: The bipolar energy term (2), the collapse of the wave function (5) with its exchange of attributes (3), the *multiplicatio* in the motif of the hybrid children to be created (4), as also the identity of microcosm and macrocosm (6) in the moment of the collapse.

A further accordance is the fact that also abduction happens completely unconsciously. Since only a conscious observation leads to a sustained incarnation, the process must become conscious. The great progress of finding such a procedure of a *conscious* transformation into the Eros ego, the task and challenge the preconscious knowledge of the collective unconscious demands of abductees, would therefore be that *the Eros ego becomes able to consciously observe transmutations of matter-psyche with potentially altered quality into matter-psyche with incarnated altered quality, i.e., the realization of the singular quantum leap happening completely in the unus mundus or psychophysical reality itself.* Thus, *not only a creation out of the psychophysical reality into our world as in UFO encounter, but an incarnation happening completely in the unus mundus would become consciously observable and thus real.* Such a change in the ubiquitous and eternal *unus mundus*, in the 'always-everywhere,' indicates however that in deepest contrast to the Neoplatonic world view even the background of physical space-time, the allegedly eternal frame of physical life in this world, has spontaneously, i.e., acausally changed. Neoplatonic infertility is overcome and replaced by Hermetic fertility—a revolutionary alteration of the background of the physical as well as of the world of the mind. Thus we can hypothetically conclude that in the near future completely novel organic life could be created as well as drastic changes in the world of the mind could happen.

---

[200] How much the process of the abolition of the spin and of the distinction between matter and force is also constellated today in physics, shows the example of K. Alex Müller, the Swiss Nobel laureate of physics of 1986 (together with G. Bednorz) and former student of Wolfgang Pauli: They received the Nobel price for their discovery of high temperature superconductivity, in which the electrons begin to move in a specific order and in this way create some sort of matter/force. When K. Alex Mueller together with Georg Bednorz presented their results in the American Society's March Meeting of 1987, 'later named the Woodstock of Physics,' this was 'an impromptu crash course...an insane physics demonstration...Suddenly, over three and a half thousand physicists (with twice as many elbows) seemed hell-bent on proving that two bodies could occupy the same place at the same time.' [Emphasis mine][Holton, G., et al., How a Scientific Discovery is Made: A Case History, American Scientist, Volume 84, July-August, 1996, p. 367. I thank K. Alex Müller of being aware of this article.]

Comparing abduction with encounter leads to a further result: In encounter the outer and the inner experience are still separated; on the one hand the 'aliens' with their UFOs in the outside are experienced, on the other telepathic and/or precognitive communication with them. In abduction, however, the experiencers enter the *unus mundus* and abolish the subject-object boundary completely. They even become unconsciously identical with the psychophysical reality, which fact we can interpret in the way that the abductees unconsciously enter the Beyond during this life. Unconsciously the Eros ego melds with the Eros Self. Thus, without knowing of it, abductees follow the process which the Cabbalist Isaak Luria described many centuries ago as the *tikkun*[201]. This process we have to realize consciously. We will see that exactly such a *conscious* realization of the Eros ego and its psychophysically nonlocal connection with the Eros Self happens in Body-Centered Imagination.

Let us return to the abductees. Both parts of the above 'individual' twin process are characterized by the fact that they happen completely unconsciously, which means, as mentioned above, especially *without any conscious observation tool* (which, as we will realize later, is created in SST/BCI). In medieval times' and Renaissance Hermetic's alchemy this was the case since the alchemists of those times still lived unconsciously in the Eros ego, the abductees of today, however, fall *unconsciously* out of the Logos into the altered state of the introverted Eros. We therefore have to find a consciously applicable procedure which leads the people concerned into the introverted Eros, in which they are able to consciously observe the *coniunctio*.

---

[201] *See section 6.12.1*

6.13 Symptom-Symbol Transformation—conscious 'UFO abduction' for the cure of disease

All the above considerations and conclusions had as the only goal to become able to describe Body-Centered Imagination as well as Symptom-Symbol Transformation with the help of the neutral language on the background of empirically observed paranormal events like the Pauli effect, UFO encounter and abduction. Since the reader can understand my argument better, and since chronologically seen I discovered SST before BCI I would like to begin with the practical application of SST in my daily work of healing. Actually it is the success of this method which provides the necessary empirical proof of my theory.

Concretely the application of SST means that one tries to observe the spontaneous transformation of the symptom of a disease, for example the pains, into an inner image or a vegetative sensation, into a (corporeal) symbol. Experience shows that such inner images are always connected to deep emotions and are experienced very intensely corporeally. It is, besides the spontaneity of the process, exactly this fact which always shows me whether the imagining human has a real relationship with the vegetative symbol aspect of his symptom. If there is no such side effect, I am mostly almost sure that the patient just fantasizes in his head. The old alchemists called the latter process the *imaginatio phantastica*, the former however the *imaginatio vera*.

My practice showed me further—and this is one of my most decisive experiences—that in the case of disease, and especially severe disease, on the psychophysical level compensatory corporeal symbols in the form of 'images out of the belly' are constellated. Therefore, if we can liberate the symbol or symbols connected to the disease—the matter-psyche aspect of the symptom—we can use such compensating contents of the psychophysical reality as a means of healing. I will present the reader an example in section 6.15.

The description of the processes happening in SST using the neutral language looks as follows:

The twin process in the physical body/vegetative body:

The symptom of the disease and the transformation into the symbol on a psychophysical level described in the neutral language:

1a: {X = unobservable matter/psyche/spirit → 'corporeal' matter-psyche with potentially increased order}

And

1b: {'Corporeal' matter-psyche with potentially increased order → 'corporeal' *matter-psyche* **with realized increased order}**

The twin process in the ego:

The conscious transformation of the Logos ego into the *introverted* **Eros and the observation of incarnation phenomena in one's own body described on a psychophysical level in a neutral language:**

2a: {X = unobservable matter/psyche/spirit (Logos ego) → conscious 'individual' *matter-psyche* **with potentially increased order (Eros ego)}**

And

2b: {Conscious 'individual' matter-psyche with potentially increased order (Eros ego) → consciously observed 'individual' *matter-psyche* **with realized increased order (Observed corporeal image}**

Since, however, only the observation leads into an incarnation, process 1b happens only in the moment of the observation of the vegetative image by the Eros ego (process 2b). Otherwise, it remains potential.

As we realized, for example in the description of UFO encounter, there is actually no difference between 'individual' and 'collective' matter-psyche. We can now transfer this attribute of the matter-psyche to the processes, which happen in SST. This means that we cannot really distinguish between the 'individual' and the 'corporeal' process, since between the two the relation of the psychophysical nonlocality is at work. This means that the Eros ego and its observation of the inner quantum leap, of the corporeal image's appearance, are one and the same. As the Logos ego identifies with its thoughts, with the conscious inner spirit-psyche, the Eros ego is identical with the view of the corporeal image, with the matter-psyche. In contrast to the Logos the Eros ego has however overcome the subject-object boundary.

There is a decisive difference between UFO encounter and abduction on the one hand and SST/BCI on the other. As we remember, in the former case *the ego unconsciously falls into the state of the Eros; it is coerced to do so, since it seems that the world soul would like these witnesses to observe the incarnation processes in the unus mundus constellated in our time, and only with the help of the human observation in the state of the Eros ego such an incarnation can happen.* In SST (as well as in BCI), however, the ego is conscious of being in the state of the Eros. It realizes that it has become identical with the vegetative body, the subtle body or diamond body.

In this way it acknowledges that the physical symptom and the vegetative image, the psychophysical symbol, are nonlocally connected to each other. We can express this fact also in the manner that we postulate that *corporeal matter possesses a psychophysical component, the vegetative body*. Since also the vegetative body and the world soul, the ruler of the universe, are psychophysically nonlocally connected, the same is true for (so-called) inorganic matter. Thus, we can conclude that inorganic matter also possesses a psychophysical component. The latter is exactly the world soul, and we will later see that this insight is confirmed by the message of Wolfgang Pauli's dream of the brass tones engraved in a metal plate.

There is a further difference between SST and UFO encounter: We realize that as a result of the conscious realization of the Eros ego not 'collective/corporeal' *spirit-psyche* with altered quality is created, but *matter-psyche* with altered, even higher order. Thus, SST corresponds to UFO abduction; in contrast to the latter there is however a conscious observation. I will come back to this decisive, even crucial difference below.

As in the case of the Pauli effect above, we can now describe SST in the physical-symbolic language:

The twin process in the sick body:

The symptom of the disease and the constellation of the potential transformation into the vegetative symbol:

1a: Charge of the acausal condenser in the psychophysical layer of the body as an effect of the disease

And

1b: Spontaneous discharge of the acausal condenser in the *psychophysical* world, in the world of the *matter-psyche*

The twin process in the ego:

The conscious transformation of the Logos ego into the introverted Eros ego and the spontaneous observation of the vegetative image:

2a: Transformation of the Logos ego into the Eros ego, which accepts its identity with the Eros Self, the *unus mundus*, the psychophysical reality

And

2b: *Spontaneous* **but conscious observation of the appearance of the vegetative image, the** *psychophysical* **symbol = the discharge of the acausal condenser in the vegetative body**

In colloquial language we can write the process of SST as follows:

The twin process in the physical body/vegetative body:

The symptom of the disease and the constellation of the potential transformation into the vegetative symbol:

1a: Constellation of the vegetative symbol as an effect of the symptom of the disease

And

1b: *Spontaneous* **transformation of the symptom into the inner vegetative image, into the** *psychophysical* **symbol**

The twin process in the ego:

The conscious transformation of the Logos ego into the introverted Eros ego and the spontaneous observation of the vegetative image:

2a: Conscious transformation of the Logos ego into the Eros ego, which accepts its identity with the Eros Self, the *unus mundus,* **the psychophysical reality**

And

2b: Conscious introverted Eros ego *spontaneously* **observes the appearance of the vegetative image, the** *psychophysical* **symbol**

If we translate the process described in neutral language into colloquial language we receive the result that *the matter-psyche with higher order corresponds to the realized vegetative image, the psychophysical symbol.* Since, in contrast to the UFO phenomenon the vegetative image is consciously observed, this *leads to a third process, the sustained incarnation of increased order in physical matter of the body*:

The healing process:

3: {*Matter-psyche* with realized higher quality → outer spirit-psyche with realized higher quality}

Or expressed in colloquial language:

3: {Observed vegetative image = observed psychophysical symbol → corporeal matter/energy with realized increased order}

The latter process we can also describe as the observation of the acausal healing activity in one's own body realized by the patient. It is thus exactly the third process, which corresponds to the healing or recovery effect in the gross body, the creation of increased order in it.

If we compare now the process happening in SST with the Odeon Pauli effect, we realize the following differences[202]: Since Pauli is completely unconscious of the possibility of an observation with the help of the Eros ego, and since matter-psyche behaves psychophysically nonlocal, the produced matter-psyche with altered order is 'projected' into the outside, there transformed into physical energy with altered order, and in a destructive manner lets the car catch fire. In the case of SST, however, *since the Eros ego is consciously realized and the vegetative image is observed, a constructive third process becomes possible, an autonomous transformation of the realized psychophysical matter-psyche with increased order, the vegetative image, into physical energy with higher order—the life essence.*

The third process of SST characterizes also the difference of it to UFO encounter and abduction. As we have seen, in the latter no stable product is created, and the process looks somehow unfinished. *In SST, however, the consciousness of being in the Eros ego leads to a transmutation in the unus mundus itself (and not only in 'our world') which leads to a third process, in which a sustainable effect in corporeal matter/energy, an increase of order in the body is created, which is observable as the recovering and healing of the physical disease.*

We are now able to realize a further difference between the Pauli effect and SST: When such an effect happened, the Nobel laureate always sensed a release in his belly. In SST the easing is also experienced, however not together with a destructive event in the outside, but together with the realization of the vegetative image, the psychophysical symbol. Since one accepts the transformation of the Logos ego into the Eros ego, one is also able to change the destructive into a constructive process with the result that bodily energy has increased order, and the healing essence is created.

---

[202] *The first process of SST corresponds to the second of the Pauli effect, and vice versa.*

/ / /

At this place we realize also the difference between my definition of the symbol term and Jung's: Expressed in the neutral language his symbol term consists in inner spirit-psyche, objective psychic energy; my symbol term however relates to (psychophysical) matter-psyche. The difference is created by the fact that the Eros ego does not observe with the help of the extraverted or introverted sensation of the CNS, with Jung's sensation function, but with the deeply introverted vegetative sensation of the VNS. In this way also the difference between Active Imagination and SST/BCI becomes much clearer.

In section 6.11 I used a term which is new to the reader: Negentropy. It is very interesting that quantum physics dealt with this problem. It was Erwin Schrödinger who postulated the possibility of negative entropy, of negentropy. It means that higher order—thus increased negentropy—could be created. In the year 1943 he held a lecture at Trinity College in Dublin, which he published in 1944 in a little booklet with the title: *What is Life?*[203] In this little booklet we find an endnote about negentropy[204]:

> The remarks on negative energy have met with doubt and opposition from physicist colleagues. Let me say first, that if I had been catering for them alone I should have let the discussion turn on free energy instead. It is the more familiar notion in this context. But this highly technical term seemed linguistically too near to *energy* for making the average reader alive to the contrast between the two things. He is likely to take *free* as more or less an epipheton ornans [a dispensable term] without much relevance, while actually the concept is a rather intricate one, whose relation to Boltzmann's order-disorder principle is less easy to trace than for entropy and 'entropy taken with a negative sign' [i.e., negentropy; RFR], which by the way is not my invention. It happens to be precisely the thing on which Boltzmann's original argument turned.

I have to comment on this very important little remark a little further: Physics believes that in all energetic processes the so-called entropy (disorder) of a state is always increased, i.e., the system becomes more chaotic. This shows for example when one breaks a glass. Only in the movie (and in science fiction) can we 'realize' the negentropic process, i.e., let the glass again become whole, when we let the film move backwards. This necessity of the decrease of entropy is the

---

[203] Schrödinger, E.: What is Life, The Physical Aspect of the Living Cell, *Cambridge University Press*, 5th ed., 1955
[204] Schrödinger, p. 89

so-called second law of thermodynamics of Boltzmann. Thus, today everyone believes that all physical/materialistic processes follow this law.

Originally Boltzmann talked however of disorder *and* order. This means that he accepted first the concept of negentropy besides entropy. The creation of higher order (increased negentropy) was thus not excluded. Physics of today however excludes this possibility.

Live processes are negentropic, which means that in them, in contrast to physics, the creation of higher order is possible. However, biology believes that for this task it is necessary that the living organism must be supplied with energy from the outside. (Light for plants; food for animals and humans, etc.). In the following it will become clear that for SST this is not the case. There *the higher order, increased negentropy, is created by the deeply introverted acausal twin process observed by the Eros ego.*

We see further that Schrödinger equates the terms negative energy, free energy and negentropy. This is important since there are today many fantasies of pseudo-inventors of making use of exactly this free energy (zero-point energy, Tesla energy, vacuum energy, and so on) physically and *by will* to create a *perpetuum mobile*.

I postulate now that with the help of SST it is possible to *observe* the spontaneous increase of order without supplying physical energy to the 'system,' the body. This increase of order happens itself, spontaneously, i.e., acausally in the *unus mundus*. As we realized, such a spontaneous increase of order corresponds to the Hermetic alchemical process of the *coniunctio*, which I describe in a modern language as the acausal twin process.

If we observe as demonstrated above, singular acausal quantum leaps happen; the image coming out of the belly heals. The process corresponds to what medicine (mostly in a pejorative way) calls a spontaneous healing process. These 'singular acausal quantum leaps' lead to the creation of higher order. In the case of SST this means the recovery and healing of the disease.

The difference to the above mentioned pseudoscientific attempts of using zero-point energy is the acceptance of the impossibility of forcing such singular acausal processes with the help of the will. On the contrary, we have to abandon the will and thinking and enter the Eros ego. In such states we just observe and do not wish to influence the process happening spontaneously in the *unus mundus*. Thus the difference is also that all these pseudo-inventors are will-possessed and believe that in this way *they can make the thing*[205], *whereas in SST we give up the will and trust the world soul, the 'ruler' over the matter-psyche and the potentially increased order that she does the job.* In this way, the world soul becomes some sort of a psychophysical *perpetuum mobile*: she creates higher order, recovery and healing.

---

[205] *It seems that this attitude of will-based making has now also entered Jungian psychology. The title of Victor Mansfield's book on synchronicity is* Synchronicity, Science and Soul-Making *(Open Court, 1995)*

6.14 Body-Centered Imagination—conscious 'UFO abduction' for the healing of the world's disease

6.14.1 The theory of Body-Centered Imagination

If corporeal matter is psychophysically nonlocally connected to the vegetative image, to matter-psyche or subtle body matter, we can also hypothesize that a similar relationship is true for *inorganic* matter and the world soul, since, as we have seen, because of the abolishment of physical space and time in a nonlocal world the world soul is secretly identical with the subtle body. Of course we enter here the realm of Hermetic speculation. Thus, we have to look for empirical proofs for such an assumption. If we remember the hypothesis of the preconscious knowledge of the unconscious empirically observable in synchronicities leading to new knowledge on the Logos level, we could ask ourselves if the content of certain BCIs could not talk about similar phenomena on the Eros level. We could pose the question whether there could exist creation and even incarnation phenomena on the level of inorganic matter, which should be observed by the Eros ego and like this become real.

Actually one of the most important reasons for beginning my research about the psychophysical reality was the fact that at the end of the year 1995 and the first months of 1996 I was myself overwhelmed by visions which some years later I began to understand of being spontaneous Body-Centered Imaginations. I will demonstrate the reader the most important aspect of them below.

Before we can deal with the contents of the BCI we have to realize its formulation with the help of the neutral language and to compare it with the other paranormal phenomena. The general description looks as follows:

The twin process in the universe:

The symptom of the disease of the *unus mundus* and the transformation into the psychophysical symbol described in the neutral language:

1a: {X = unobservable matter/psyche/spirit → 'collective' matter-psyche with potentially increased order}

And

1b: {'Collective' matter-psyche with potentially increased order → 'collective' *matter-psyche* **with realized increased order}**

The twin process in the ego:

The conscious transformation of the Logos ego into the *introverted* **Eros ego and the observation of incarnation phenomena in the** *unus mundus* **described on a psychophysical level:**

2a: {X = unobservable matter/psyche/spirit (Logos ego) → conscious *'individual'* **matter-psyche with potentially increased order (Eros ego)}**

And

2b: {Conscious 'individual' matter-psyche with potentially increased order (Eros ego) → consciously observed *'collective' matter-psyche* **with realized increased order (Observed image corresponding to the increased order in the psychophysical background of the universe}**

In the physical-symbolic language we can write:

The twin process in the universe:

The symptom of the disease and the transformation into the vegetative symbol:

1a: Charge of the acausal condenser in the *unus mundus* **and potential creation of disorder (the world's disease) as an effect of the artificial fission of the atom**

And

1b: *Spontaneous* **discharge of the acausal condenser in the** *psychophysical* **world, in the** *unus mundus,* **in the world of the** *matter-psyche*

The twin process in the ego:

The conscious transformation of the Logos ego into the introverted Eros ego and the spontaneous observation of the vegetative symbol:

2a: Transformation of the Logos ego into the Eros ego, which accepts its identity with the Eros Self, the *unus mundus*, the psychophysical reality

And

2b: *Spontaneous* but conscious observation of the appearance of the vegetative image, the *psychophysical* symbol = result of the discharge of the 'collective' acausal condenser in the *unus mundus*

Or in colloquial language:

The twin process in the universe:

1a: Creation of matter-psyche with destructive influence as an effect of artificial fission

And

1b: Transformation of the destructive into constructive matter-psyche in the *unus mundus*

The twin process in the ego:

2a: Conscious transformation of the Logos ego into the Eros ego

And

2b: Observation of the spontaneous healing processes in the universe with the help of the symbolic images of BCI

Since, however, only the observation leads into incarnation, process 1b happens only in the moment of the observation of the vegetative image by the Eros ego (process 2b). Otherwise, it remains potential.

In the case of the conscious observation of the vegetative image in BCI, in analogy to SST we can postulate a third process, the incarnation of energy/matter with increased order in 'our world,' based on the increased order or quality created in the *unus mundus*:

3: {*Matter-psyche* with realized increased order in the *unus mundus* → 'outer' and/or 'inner' spirit-psyche with realized increased order}

Or expressed in colloquial language:

3: The observed vegetative image = observed psychophysical symbol in one's inside transforms into physical matter/ energy with realized increased order and/or objective psychic energy (C.G. Jung) with realized increased order

If we translate the process described in neutral language into colloquial language we receive thus the result that because of the artificial fission potential disorder in the *unus mundus* is created (Process 1a). As we have seen, *in the moment of the forced observation in UFO abduction, the disorder is realized—the rape of and/or the cruel experiments with the victims. In the case of BCI, however, because of the conscious observation of the transmutation processes in the unus mundus, not matter-psyche with destructive quality is produced, but the inner vegetative image, series of images or the vegetative sensation, which lead to a constructive process of transmutation and the creation of increased order in the psychophysical reality, in the Beyond. Since the latter is nonlocally connected to our world, also in the outer, the inorganic and organic world as well as in the inner, the psychic world increased order is created.*

As we have seen in the case of SST such a process is observable as the patient's sensation and feelings of their recovery. In the case of BCI we abandon however the empirically observable world and enter mere speculation since it seems that such effects are only observable *ex post*. As I mentioned above, the only chance is to have a look at the contents of certain BCIs and ask ourselves if their symbolism talks of such phenomena as the creation of increased order, the healing of the world and of the universe. This is just what we will do.

Here I would like to return to Hermetic alchemy and compare BCI with its *opus*. As we remember, Gerardus Dorneus embedded the *coniunctio* into a multistage process: The Neoplatonic *unio mentalis*, the liberation of the psyche out of matter and its union with the spirit in the Heavens, was followed by the *unio corporalis*, symbolically equivalent to the *coniunctio* or Hierosgamos. Then, however, he added a third step: The reunion of the ego with the *unus mundus*. What I described above as BCI is nothing less than this third process.

I would like to present now the content of a personal BCI, which completely autonomously invaded my consciousness in 1995/96. As we remember, such BCIs are the only proof for possible incarnation phenomena on the collective level, on the level of physical spacetime, since no immediate change in the world after a successful imagination is observable. Thus, we have to trust the preconscious knowledge of the unconscious or of the psychophysical reality observable in such BCIs, in which analogous to the meaning of synchronicities, i.e., to incarnation phenomena in the world of the mind, possible incarnation events in inorganic matter could be described.

Before I begin with the description of the BCI, I have perhaps to give the uninformed reader the following explanation: On the basis of his experience as a psychiatrist C.G. Jung was convinced that having visions is not at all per se an indicator of a psychosis. It depends of the state of the ego what really happens. If the ego is strong enough—and here I mean especially the Eros egoéit is not swallowed by the archetypal images, and thus does not become psychotic. On the contrary: As I showed above, such processes can help to heal.

6.14.2 Body-Centered Imagination with the turtle and the UFO, who lead me to Anubis in the beyond resulting in a rotation as a dance with the UFO:

Body-Centered Imagination

1. At the end of 1995 'it' began spontaneously to do BCI in me: I see before me a tortoise or turtle which develops slowly into the pregnant belly of a huge woman. On it I realize an also huge Seal of Solomon. I sense that in it something lives. I feel that this huge belly is *The hub of the world*.

Comments and Interpretations

The reader can believe me that this experience was a real shock, especially since I felt all this so incredibly corporeally. It was as if this woman lied before me in all her physical presence.

In Taoism the tortoise/turtle is a symbol of the *coniunctio*, since above it is round and below a square, the union of the masculine and the feminine principle. It is pregnant, which means that a creation and incarnation process is constellated.

We assume that the turtle is a being of the intermediate world, since as we will realize it creates a UFO which is a means of a relationship between the two worlds (a 'wormhole,' as I called it above). Thus it symbolizes animated matter possessing a psychophysical aspect, as defined above.

Using the physical-symbolic language we can also say that the tortoise/turtle represents the acausal condenser charged because of the artificial fission since 1945.

The Seal of Solomon is the symbol for the bipolarity of the energy term. Containing matter-psyche, the Seal is a hint that the turtle in fact possesses a psychophysical aspect.

Thus, in contrast to Genesis, the hub of the world has its seat in the intermediate world. The described process is further not a *creatio ex nihilo*, but a *creatio continua*. Thus it can acausally begin in any moment at any place (as actually it did in me).

2. The woman lies in some sort of a swamp, which gives me the feeling and sensation of the 'primal hill' coming out of the 'primal waters,' which is a symbol of Atum, the primal god of old Egypt.

This image shows again that a creation myth is constellated. My spontaneous association shows that the constellated myth has not to do with a 'heavenly' but with an 'earthy' creation, since the ancient Egyptian culture was very earthy. Further, obviously a creation is meant which leads to a change in the Beyond, since the Egyptian culture dealt especially with the afterlife.

Atum, who created the world out of himself by masturbation, is a parallel motif to the self-fertilizing world soul and thus in a modern terminology a symbol of the singular acausal quantum leap, extraverted visible in UFOs/'aliens,' and introverted in BCI. Thus, the BCI talks of itself.

3. Then, an incredible synchronicity happened: In the evening of the same day my brother-in-law drives us to the house of his uncle, a physician, where we are invited to stay (we were in Italy for the holidays). In the car his wife plays a CD, always the same piece, which completely fascinated us both (no one knew anything about my BCI; it was so crazy that I decided not to talk about it, especially since my wife and other relatives there were physicians). In this piece always one term is repeated:

Ombellico del mondo, ombellico del mondo, ombellico del mondo
(Hub of the world)

A second time I was really shocked. Obviously the preconscious knowledge of the unconscious liked to tell me that I have to deal with this creation myth, and to realize what it could mean. Today I know that it is a confirmation of the above insight that in certain humans of today compensatory to the destruction of the world creation myths are constellated.

4. Two to three weeks later, on Jan 16th, 1996 I had a dream in which I played my beloved *Schwyzerörgeli*. I am composing (as I did in reality) a 'dream melody,' which is incredibly beautiful and moving. It reminds me of the sphere music belonging to the Holy Wedding, the *coniunctio* (as Wolfgang Pauli describes it in his Kepler/Fludd essay). I am also reminded of the dreams with sphere music I had during this time. I have further the sublime memory that this sphere music belongs to Mercury, who played the sphere music on an instrument built out of a shell of a tortoise.

Figure 6.14:
The Schwyzerörgeli
[Source: Remo F. Roth]

The *Schwyzerörgeli* is a very specific harmonica. It is diatonic, which means that the tones one produces in pushing and pulling are different. Further, the arrangement of the innermost of the three rows of buttons at the right side is completely 'weird.' The buttons were added accidentally when in the course of time the instrument was extended to further keys (Originally one was only able to play in three keys).

Composing music on the *Schwyzerörgeli* was for me an act of chance. Since nothing is logical, my fingers created new melodies 'by chance.' Thus, together with my association the 'dream melody' means the 'sphere music' of the Pythagoreans, which belongs to the *coniunctio*. However—and this is the decisive detail—the sphere music is composed by accident, and becomes like this a symbol of the above described twin process happening spontaneously, i.e., acausally. Further, it is a human being and not the universe, who creates the sphere music.

5. Since I am reminded of Mercury's tortoise's instrument, immediately after the dream I begin a BCI with the tortoise: I sense with my hands the shell of the tortoise. Once again it immediately changes into the pregnant woman's belly. I have the feeling and the sensation that it is the earth itself, which became pregnant. I am also reminded of the hills near the place where I then lived (Hirzel above Horgen, Zurich, Switzerland), which look like pregnant women's bellies.

Figure 6.15:
The hills of Hirzel, Switzerland
[Source: Remo F. Roth]

The spontaneous association with the hill's landscape shows that in addition to the above incarnation process in animated matter demonstrated is now a creation process beginning in so-called inanimate matter, which thus possesses a potential psychophysical aspect.

6. I am standing over the belly and look down on it. Its diameter is perhaps one meter. I realize that an aperture is built and out of it a small tortoise is born. Everything happens very spontaneously, what today to me is the proof that an *acausal* quantum leap happens, in which in the psychophysical reality something new is born.

7. Then, something further and very surprising happens: Out of the belly, but not through the aperture but through the closed surface a UFO is born. It has the typical shape of the saucer.

It seems that the UFO dematerialized in the belly and rematerialized outside of it. The UFO then hovers perhaps one meter over the belly.

I was very surprised and astonished that the UFO came out of the 'earth' and did not appear in the sky. Thus it must have something to do with the liberation or even the release of the *anima mundi* out of matter. The imagination showed me that UFOs and the liberation of the world soul belong together. I was reminded of a development of the motif in my dreams: First the UFOs came down from the sky, then, however, they began to come out of the earth.

Figure 6.16:
UFO
[Source: Wikimedia Commons]

Today I know that 'dematerialization' means the first of the twin process, 'rematerialization' the second.

The birth of the UFO symbolizes the constellation of a deeply introverted 'wormhole' between the Eros ego and the Eros Self, which allows the former to observe twin processes with their acausal quantum leaps. This is why, as we will see, the UFO can lead us to Anubis/Osiris in the Beyond.

Further, my experience is not a concrete UFO encounter, but the result of a BCI, a deeply introverted event. Thus, we can guess that an incarnation in the psycho physical reality as well as the above *third process*, the incarnation into 'our world' will later happen. Since I am conscious about living in the Eros ego, the incarnation will be sustainable.

8. In February 1996 I get sick with a mysterious disease, some sort of a flu but somehow different.

As compensation my then eight-year-old son dreams that we have discovered Atlantis, the immersed continent.

On February 27, 1996 I decide to return to the tortoise: It seems to be very pleased by this and licks my face with its tongue. It does this more and more intensely, and I begin to feel a little uncanny. I feel however that in this way it would like to tell me something in its language, but I don't understand what. Thus, I lie on its back, which gives me a feeling of calmness.

Today I know that the disease was the effect of not continuing with the BCI though I was inundated by visions and deeply archetypal dreams out of the collective unconscious respectively the psychophysical reality.

As C.G. Jung realized, children often dream the dreams of their parents in the case that they suppress such messages out of the unconscious. In my case I failed to continue with the BCI; thus my son dreamed its result: Atlantis is the immersed continent, which we have to discover anew, which means a 'renewed earthy principle.' It is exactly what is represented later in the dance at the end of the BCI, namely the creation of the vegetative body/world soul.

The continuation of the BCI was insofar the solution as I very soon recovered from this mysterious disease.

Lying on the back of the tortoise, the symbol of the *coniunctio*, symbolizes the complete handing over to the Eros Self. Before my Logos ego renounced this. This is why I got sick. However with the help of the disease my ego was defeated.

Here we realize also the difference between SST/BCI and Active Imagination: The tortoise is not able to speak in a human language. Thus, I have to feel and sense what I have to do. It is the nonverbal communication on the level of the Eros.

9. All the time the UFO is hovering over us. It has changed its shape and has now the form of a cylinder with a cone above and a cone below. At the upper end there is also a sphere. Like this it looks a little odd, like a fool. It reminds me of an early dream, in which the pope orders that in all churches the cross has to be replaced by a sphere. Further I remember the many dreams I had about fools.

As we realized, the UFO is the 'wormhole' between the Eros ego and the Eros Self, the world soul. Thus, as soon as I give in to the Eros ego, the wormhole opens.

The UFO looks a little foolish. Later I was reminded that I many times fell ill at the carnival, and realized that I always got sick or had an accident when I lived the fool, the Eros ego unconsciously and too extraverted.

Of course this foolishness of the UFO, of the 'wormhole,' is related to the Eros Self, which seems to be as foolish as the Eros ego. This means especially that in it there is no causality, but acausality. Further, this means that not an incarnation by cognition (synchronicity), but a magic incarnation by (mere) observation is constellated.

10. I discover that I can let the UFO rotate. I do this clockwise. Surprisingly I feel that this makes the UFO happy!

    I am reminded of an earlier dream in which it was stated that the rotation developing out of oscillation is the only important aspect of the UFO.

As we will see below, rotation means incarnation into our world. The motif thus means that it is the Eros ego which can co-create with the world soul.

The mentioned dream is quoted below.

11. Now the tortoise shows me with a waggling motion of the shell, that it too is happy, obviously because I confide in it. With me on its back it goes into the water, into the sea. Thus it seems to be a turtle. In this way we swim to an isle. On it there are mountains like the *Zuckerhut* (sugar's hat) of Rio de Janeiro. Perhaps these are also trees in this form.

My spontaneous association was the Carnival of Rio—the foolish party.

Today I realize that this foolishness is a symbol for the Eros ego/Eros Self connection. As long as I lived it extraverted, I was in danger of disease or accident.

Water is the element of the second chakra svadhisthana, in which, as much as I know today, one enters in BCI.

12. We now enter a castle. I realize first that the entrance room has a ceiling, which reminds me of the Sistine Chapel in the Vatican.

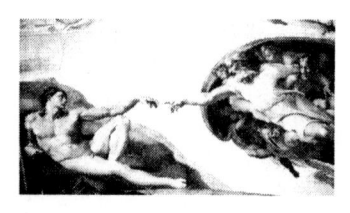

Figure 6.17:
God creating Adam
[Source: Wikimedia Commons]

Figure 6.18:
The iconic image of the Hand of God giving life to Adam
[Source: Wikimedia Commons]

The ceiling of the Sistine Chapel contains nine scenes from the Book of Genesis. Wikipedia writes:

Along the central section of the ceiling, Michelangelo depicted nine scenes from the Book of Genesis, the first book of the Bible. The pictures fall into three groups of three.

The first group shows God creating the Heavens and the Earth. The second group shows God creating the first man and woman, Adam and Eve, and their disobedience of God and consequent expulsion from the Garden of Eden, where they have lived and where they walked with God. The third group of three pictures shows the plight of Humanity, and in particular the family of Noah.

The most famous image is the one in which God with the help of his hand gives life to Adam.

The preconscious knowledge of the unconscious shows us that it is in fact an incarnation myth that is constellated. Since by leaving the mainland and landing on the isle we three entered the Beyond (or Atlantis of my son's dream). We are now sure that the incarnation myth begins in the *unus mundus*. In my modern terminology we can say that an increase of order in the psychophysical reality is constellated. Since to this incarnation the creation of a human being is connected, we have also to expect the creation of 'new life' in our world.

13. I hesitate a long time with entering, since I am afraid I will not come out. The turtle and the UFO wait patiently beside me up until I have decided to enter.

14. Then we enter the Vatican. We three are a really peculiar trio. I am on the left (from behind), to my right the turtle and over it the UFO.

Since number three symbolically seen represents energy, the energetic aspect of BCI/SST is stressed here.

15. We cross the Sistine Chapel. Then another room comes which looks like a Germanic 'Langhaus.'

Figure 6.19: Germanic Langhaus [Source: Wikimedia Commons]

What a difference to the Sistine Chapel!

For a long time I did not understand this motif. Then I realized that in my BCI a creation myth is demonstrated, and thus that I had to amplify with the Germanic world's creation myth. In contrast to the Jewish/Christian myth described in the motifs at the ceiling of the Sistine Chapel above, the Germanic myth is completely vegetative. Everything in this world is created out of the world's ash tree Yggradsil combining the sky, our world and the underworld. The vegetative aspect of the myth is stressed by the self-sacrifice of Odin, originally the god of aggression and war. In contrast to Jesus Christ he hangs himself into the ash tree killing himself with the lance's thrust. In this way Odin on the one hand obtains the secret knowledge, however, since Yggrasil is also the source of the life essence, he also becomes immortal. In a modern terminology the Germanic creation myth symbolizes thus my above presented results: On the one hand the goal of interpreted synchronicities, the creation of inner spirit-psyche with realized increased order (meaning), on the other the creation of outer spirit-psyche, physical energy with higher order as a result of BCI/SST (as just demonstrated in the next sequence).

16. Then we approach a throne. First I believe that on it sits the Black Madonna in Einsiedeln, Switzerland:

The Black Madonna in Einsiedeln, Switzerland possesses magic healing power. Thus, the motif of healing comes up. As we know, I distinguish between two ways of healing: The healing of personal disease with the help of SST, and the healing of the disease of the world with BCI. As we will see, here the latter is stressed.

Figure 6.20: Black Maria in Einsiedeln, Switzerland[206]

I realize then that the figure of the head is not the one of the Black Madonna. Further the figure is veiled (covered up), and one sees only the black head.

---

[206] *Source: Foto P. Damian Rutishauser, Klosterarchiv Einsiedeln, Switzerland*

17. I try a long time to recognize this figure, but the important aspect is this veiling. I am reminded that Jung or Marie-Louise von Franz talk somewhere of the veiled figure and realize that this is an attribute of Osiris. Then, for a short moment I see the figure and spontaneously the term 'Anubis' comes to my mind. Consciously I do not at all remember who this god is, but I remember that he has the head of a jackal.

*Figure 6.21:
Anubis
[Source: Wikimedia Commons]*

Here the crucial highlight of the BCI comes in, since by mere observation of the Eros ego the archetypal Egyptian recreation myth develops:

Osiris is the god of the underworld or of the Beyond. In a modern language we would say that it is the energetic principle of the psychophysical reality, of the *unus mundus*. Thus he is a symbolical equivalent to the *anima mundi,* the world soul.

In Egyptian mythology Osiris was murdered by Seth. He cut him in pieces and scattered them all over the world. Then, together with Isis, Osiris' wife/sister, the god Anubis collected the parts of Osiris' body, put them together and revitalized him.

Interpreted in a psychological/psychophysical way the reassembling motif means on the one hand an *increase of order* in the Beyond, and second *the bringing back of the life essence* to Osiris. Thus, an increased quality is reached, which is the main goal of the singular acausal quantum leap happening in the twin process.

Thus, it is not too astonishing anymore that Anubis was also the protector of the dead against evil forces and later the servant of Osiris! Obviously the turtle (the symbol of the *coniunctio* as well as of the pregnant world soul) and the UFO (symbolizing the 'wormhole' between the Eros ego and the Eros Self) liked to bring me to Anubis with the purpose that by mere observation of the events happening in the Eros Self I become a co-creator of incarnation events in the *unus mundus*. We remember that exactly this is the main goal of C.G. Jung's point A creation and of Isaak Luria's *tikkun*.

18. I implore Anubis/Osiris to protect me and my family against evil forces.

Figure 6.22:
Osiris in Bandages with Tutanchamun, his Ka and Isis

19. All this happens in the following formation of us: The turtle is below, on the floor; I knee behind it and prop my elbows on the shell; the UFO hovers over us.

20. I thank Anubis/Osiris and we go back. It is all open, and we can leave unhindered.

21. Finally we come back to the shore of the island, which reminds me of the landing stage in Jung's Bollingen Turm (tower).

C.G. Jung was convinced that the Bollingen tower was a symbol of the Self, in my terminology of the Logos Self. Thus, when we three above entered the castle, we must have been in a realm behind or even beyond the Logos Self. My hypothesis of the Eros Self is confirmed. In it the incarnation phenomena in the *unus mundus* and because of psychophysical nonlocality also into the physical aspect of our world happen. The BCI shows further that for a successful incarnation the observation of a human being, of its Eros ego, is necessary.

22. Then the turtle leads us back to the mainland.

The castle, as well as C.G. Jung's Bollingen tower, was thus situated on an island. This is why my son anticipated in his dream that we had discovered Atlantis. The latter, the Eros Self as well as the Logos Self, are in fact 'immersed continents,' since today not too many people are conscious about them, the deeply introverted God-images, the Hermetic alchemical queen and king.

23. When we are there something really crazy happens: The UFO seems to be so happy that it extends a so-called 'solid light.' This light is really solid. It has the form of a bowed arm.

Since we are back in 'our world,' this motif means that a creation of increased order in it as an effect of the increased order in the Beyond has taken place. The increased order has to do with 'solid lights' on the one hand and rotation on the other (see below).

'Solid lights' are very peculiar attributes of UFOs. In contrast to normal light they are finite, and are extended and retracted by the UFOs like telescopes. Further, they seem to have their root in an anti-gravitational force. Thus, with the help of the UFOs these solid lights have the ability to lift objects and humans up. This reminds us of course of the UFO abduction symbolism.

24. The UFO's arm then takes my arm, and thus I sense the real solidity. To do so it comes from the front to the right of me and with its bowed solid light (its right arm) goes around my right arm. We are now on the shell of the turtle. The UFO begins a clockwise dance with me. The UFO/Remo dance!

As I mentioned above, in an earlier dream I was told that *rotation developing out of oscillation is the only important aspect of UFOs*. On the basis of some of Wolfgang Pauli's dreams and visions, in which an oscillation transforms into a rotation, and of some of my similar dreams, I concluded further that the process {oscillation → rotation} symbolizes the incarnation of subtle matter out of the *unus mundus* into our world.

6.15 A case example of Symptom-Symbol Transformation: The Cure of Multiple Sclerosis

A scientific theory has to be confirmed by empirical results. I will fulfil this task in the next sections first with an example of my professional work as a healer, and second with the interpretation of some of Wolfgang Pauli's most decisive dreams.

Physical, psychophysical and psychic events happening during the treatment	My comments and interpretations
1. I begin the case example with the description of a very impressive synchronicity, which I only realized some months after the beginning of the treatment: What the patient did not tell me during the first months was the fact that she was so desperate that she decided to commit suicide. In Switzerland, there are some organizations which help hopelessly sick people to commit suicide. My patient already had the poison in her flat and had only to phone one of the 'helpers' to come and assist her for this last task of her life. Some months later she showed me a little brochure of the organization with the name EXIT. On its front page the *Radbild*, the Wheel Image of the Swiss Saint Nicholas von Flue is shown!	Four years before the beginning of my first treatment with SST in January 1987, Sara, as I will call my patient, after many tests was officially diagnosed with Multiple Sclerosis. When I first visited her, she was not able to walk anymore, could only crawl, and this with great effort. She was convinced that the only way out is committing suicide. However—as she told me later—she decided to give me as the collaborator of a famous pastor which she admired, a last chance. Sara's CNS was in a very lamentable state. She was no longer able to write; could barely sense her fingers and toes; her eyesight was failing and she could no longer walk. Some years after the treatment Sara had recovered completely. Today, many years after its end, she is still fully recovered and has never had a relapse.

Figure 6.23: Brochure of EXIT

Most people, including my patient, did not have any knowledge of this symbol. In my interpretation it is a symbolic equivalent to the Seal of Solomon. As the reader immediately realizes, it possesses the two times three structure and is thus a symbol of the bipolar energy term and of the twin process, as well as of its singular inner quantum leap. It even shows the process more clearly since there are three lance points directed to the center—Nicholas interpreted it as his heart—the other three are pointed to the outer two circles interpreted by me as the body/subtle body relationship.

'EXIT' in the interpretation of the above organization means of course leaving this world by committing suicide. However the synchronicity shows that what is meant is *the 'exit' to the 'realm' of the world soul during this life*, to the *unus mundus*, which lead, as we will see, to a complete cure of the disease after some years.

I and all the other people who were able to follow the development, believed in a miracle. Of course physicians, as always when they do not understand a cure with their limited world view, in a depreciative manner called it a 'spontaneous cure.'

It was exactly the incomprehension of the official medical world, which was the incentive to my research, and this book is one of the most important results of my attempt to understand the development in a scientific way—the latter term understood in a more extended manner. In a synchronistic way the treatment fell together with my autodidactic studies of quantum physics, and in my book I can now present the theory as well as practical applications of the method. It was exactly the incomprehension of the official medical world, which was the incentive to my research, and this book is one of the most important results of my attempt to understand the development in a scientific way—the latter term understood in a more extended manner. In a synchronistic way the treatment fell together with my autodidactic studies of quantum physics, and in my book I can now present the theory as well as practical applications of the method.

2. When I enter my patient's residence I experience an almost unbelievable sensation, which reminded me of C.G. Jung's situation in 1916, when he was forced to write *Septem Sermones ad Mortuos*: 'The atmosphere was thick... The whole house was...crammed full of spirits.'[207]

I sit on Sara's bed and accidentally looking at her feet I experience a spontaneous vision:

I see one of her feet having a hollow in the instep. I look closer and realize standing in it is the Black Madonna in Einsiedeln, Switzerland (see figure 6.19 above).

I spontaneously associate the fact that she is a 'wonder healer,' who cures physical disease. I tell my patient this vision and ask her, if she sometimes also sees inner images. In this moment she experiences a spontaneous vision:

She tells me that she sees a frame with embroidery containing a flower. I ask her which one. The answer: 'A lily.'

I experienced the synchronous apparition of the two visions as a real miracle: The lily is one of the most well known symbols of the Holy Mary! Thus the magic (acausal) healing force, which I will later be able to describe as the twin process and its singular inner quantum leap, is constellated.

Now, more than 20 years after this event I am still very moved, since I realize that with my spontaneous application of SST I had also found the way out of all these paranormal phenomena: The use of SST and BCI can help one to listen to the spirits, be it in the personal or in the collective situation. The *prima materia* for this process seems to be personal disease and/or the disease of the earth and of the universe.

As the reader perhaps knows, Marie-Louise von Franz had a dream about the Black Madonna[208]:

'She is working in the laundry at the cloister in Einsiedeln. She is given to understand that Jung would come down from heaven to the wedding of the Black Madonna. Marie-Louise is among the one hundred elect who are permitted to take part in the wedding.

---

[207] *MDR, p. 216*
[208] See for example http://psychophysical.free.fr/viewtopic.php?t=76

Marie-Louise von Franz was thus convinced that what we need and what is constellated is the *coniunctio*, not in the Heaven, as in C.G. Jung's interpretation of the Assumption, but in the Hermetic intermediary world between Heaven and earth, in the *unus mundus*.

However, to reach the Holy Wedding we have to work, sometimes very hard. This is why in Sara's vision the lily is an embroidery—woman's work!

Figure 6.24: The lily [Source: Wikimedia Commons]

3. In the second session I propose that we just be silent and wait to 'see' what may happen. Perhaps we will see further images out of the belly.

Sara suddenly experiences the second vision:

She sees the shore of a lake with reeds.

Amplification:

In *The Golden Ass of Apuleius: The Liberation of the Feminine in Man*, 1980, p. 94, Marie-Louise von Franz writes about the reed:

'In many fairy tales the reed betrays, as it does here, a secret knowledge. One finds in folklore many stories in which, for example, someone is murdered and buried in a swamp. A shepherd comes along, cuts a reed and makes himself a flute, and the flute sings and betrays the secret of the murder, and the murderer is discovered and punished. So the reed can also betray or convey divine wisdom to man by the wind which whistles through it. There is an ultimate instinct of truth in the human psyche which, in the long run, cannot be suppressed. We can pretend not to hear it, but it remains in the unconscious. And Psyche in this story has a kind of secret inspiration about the coping strategy. The whistling reed has a role analogous to that of the ants; they represent tiny little hints of truth which we get from the unconscious.

Figure 6.25: Reed [Source: Wikimedia Commons]

Dr. Jung always said that truth did not speak with a loud voice; its tiny little voice is manifested by a malaise, or a bad conscience, or some subliminal intuition of this nature. Great quiet is needed to attend to these small, truthful intuitions.

When the unconscious begins to talk loudly, and to work upon the ego with car accidents and such things, then the situation is really bad. But normally it has been whispering for years before producing the thunderclap of catastrophes. In analysis, we try to hear what the reed says before these happen.'

Thus, the vision tells us first that in Sara a rebirth myth is constellated. It is the rebirth of the vegetative body, of the subtle body. Further, the amplification with the reed tells us that she is connected to the preconscious knowledge of the unconscious.

4. In the same session a further, the fourth vision:

   Sara sees a Christmas tree on which I light the candles.

   The Christmas tree is originally heathen and means the solstice tree: After the darkness of winter spring and summer are in sight. It is the new light and the new life after death. Nature begins to awake and to flower anew. A very good omen for our work.

5. The fifth vision, one week later:

   With her inner eyes Sara sees the crater of a volcano. In it she realizes the fiery magma, which comes out of the dark opening. It is not too much, and thus the crater does not overflow. The red/yellow mass begins to rotate.

   The fire lily is also of red and yellow color. Thus we have what I call a symbolic equivalence. Both symbols mean the twin process.

   The vision of the volcano tells us however something more: First, there is not too much magma coming out of the volcano, thus not too much energy is leaving the *unus mundus*; the ego is not overflowed by the magma; there is no danger.

Second, a rotating motion begins. As we will see in the interpretation of Wolfgang Pauli's dreams and visions (see section 6.16), the rotation symbolizes the new life created as an effect of the singular inner quantum leap. The vision thus speaks of the process constellated in my patient, and it confirms that it is the right thing to just passively observe what is happening in the inside of Sara.

6. The sixth vision, three weeks after the beginning of the treatment is a very decisive one:

   An apple tree, the left half (seen from her standpoint) is dried up, the fruits are riddled with worms and rotten. The right half, however, lives and carries green leaves and healthy fruits.

The tree is a symbol of the vegetative life which Sara was forced to live because of the MS. For the apple tree itself the left side is its right side et vice versa. Thus, the right side, the side of the consciousness, the side of the CNS is deadly sick. However the left side, the side of the 'unconscious,' in my interpretation the side of the Eros ego, the Eros Self and of the VNS is healthy.

The apple I associate to the paradise scene: Eve receives the apple from the snake. The snake is the devil, i.e., acausality (see section 6.3 for the explanation of this motif). Thus: The acausal processes in the Eros Self, in the psychophysical reality (W. Pauli) or in the *unus mundus* (Dorneus/Jung) is healthy and thus itself able to heal and to cure.

7. The seventh vision four weeks after the beginning of the treatment:

   Sara sees a cashbox. It is full of money, but up until now no one opened it. I have a key to this cashbox and open it. All the money comes out.

SST seems to open the treasury in the Eros Self, when Sara concentrates on it with the help of the Eros ego.

Symbolically seen money is energy. Thus it seems that my unconsciously applied method liberates Sara's inner energies.

8. Eighth vision, six weeks after the beginning:

    Sara is placed in the center of a ring of anthropoids.

The anthropoid is a symbol of the archaic body, thus of the vegetative body and its contents, the images out of the belly.

The mandala tells us therefore that Sara is protected by the vegetative body and by its contents, the images.

9. Ninth vision, seven weeks after the beginning:

    Sara sees a source. Water comes out and 'jumps' around the stones and looks for its way down into the valley. There the water calms and ends in a meadow with beautiful kingcups (or marsh marigold; *Caltha palustris*.

Figure 6.26:
Kingcups
[Source: Wikimedia Commons]

In her vision all the kingcups—remember the king and the queen of the *coniunctio*—are still closed, like golden spheres. Later she experiences the same symbol as a golden sphere which she senses and feels in her upper belly (solar plexus, 3rd chakra manipura). She tells me that it contains an energy which is completely different than any energy she ever sensed in her body. It is the matter-psyche, which transforms into outer spirit-psyche, physical energy with increased order.

When I looked up these visions and the symbols contained in them again for the formulation of the example of SST in this book, I realized that then, in 1988, I approached for the first time the empirical existence of matter-psyche, later theoretically postulated by me.

Water always follows 'the path of least resistance.' The interpretation is that Sara has to give up all resistance of the Logos ego against experiencing these visions. She should completely *give up her will* and begin to trust the transformation and transmutation processes out of the *unus mundus*.

The water is also the 'life's water,' the life essence, which begins to flow anew.

10. Sara tells me that she is very happy that I take seriously what she 'sich ein*bilde*' [imagines].

'Einbilden' [imagining in English] means on the one hand being conceited about something and is a pejorative term in German. However, literally it means 'realizing images.' Thus, the pejorative term has changed its meaning: 'Einbildung' becomes positive.

11. Two months after the beginning of the treatment with SST:

    Sometimes my patient senses her body in a very strange manner. It is as if there would be an intense tension in it. I propose to transform this symptom into a symbol. Sara enters an SST and experiences the following, the tenth vision:

    The red and white blood corpuscles play a children's game: *Päärlifangis*. This Swiss German term means catching each other, however in pairs, which means a girl must catch a boy and vice versa.

The perfect symbol of the *coniunctio*! Red and white are the alchemical colors of the opposites, e.g. the *servus rubeus* and the *femina candida*, the red slave and the white woman, a very wide-spread motif.

The opposites of femininity and masculinity 'catch each other,' i.e., they try to consummate the sexual union.

The vision happens in the blood, which is the essence of life.

The culmination point of the series of vision has arrived. The Holy Marriage has taken place. The absolutely decisive circumstance is that all this happens out of an extreme tension in the gross body. The Hermetic alchemists say: *In stercore invenitur*—in the dirt we find the gold. Out of the sick body the vegetative body is created, which finally leads into the complete cure of the disease.

12. Nine months after the beginning of the treatment the recovery begins. Sara can walk three steps without help. The nervous system that controls the fine muscle motor skills begins to recover in a really astonishing manner. The sensations in the hands and feet come back. She does not need a ruler for writing anymore. The vision improves. The sensation that her body is split into two parts disappears. She begins to walk anew, first some steps, then 50, and at the end she is completely cured.

    My experience has shown that the recovery process always begins some months after the *coniunctio* symbol has manifested. Also in Sara's case we had to wait more than half a year. Perhaps another hint of the preconscious knowledge of the unconscious that we have anew to learn to be patient, to give up our will-possession and to trust in the inner nature.

13. Many further synchronicities happen the most impressive of them I would like to tell the reader:

    One and a half years after the beginning of the treatment:

    Sara possesses a flower, an *Asclepias asperula*. She was never able to let it bloom, though she cared a lot for the flower. Now, however, on a morning she realizes that it had begun to flower.

    The flower is named after the primordial Greek physician Asclepios. Thus, the synchronicity means that she has become her own physician, and—she begins to let the milk from the milkweed, the VNS, flow its healing 'juices' which heal her.

Figure 6.27:
Asclepias asperula
[Source: Wikimedia Commons]

Figure 6.28:
Asclepios
[Source: Wikimedia Commons]

14. To end the description of the treatment, I would like to present the psychological progress of Sara. At the beginning she was an extreme perfectionist, was very hard with her body and overburdened it completely. Today I am sure that the MS was the physical compensation to this auto-aggressive behaviour: MS is a so-called auto immune disease, which means that the immune system destroys itself—auto-aggression. Thus, Sara once told me: 'Some of my organs began to rebel since I demanded too much of them.'

    On the other hand she was much too weak in her extraverted life and was not able to establish borders. During the treatment she learned to be much weaker with her body, to let it flow, to give up her will-possession.

    This fact was impressively demonstrated by the circumstance that suddenly an inner archetypal figure emerged, a fairy. She was the personification of the Eros Self. Sara began to ask her what to do, and the fairy told her exactly what her body was allowed to bear. Up until today the fairy, who she experiences even corporeally, is her guide. She began a dialogue with her—the connection of the Eros ego with the Eros Self.

    She further realized that her soul and her body had become split, but now began to re-unify. Thus she also consciously realized the *coniunctio* between her soul and her body. Today, more than 15 years after the ending of the treatment she remains symptom free, though during our work she began to reduce the Cortisone medication dramatically.

    For me this was the first and an incredibly impressive example of the powerfulness of Symptom-Symbol Transformation.

6.16 Interpretation of some of Pauli's most decisive dreams, visions and auditions as an empirical confirmation of the psychophysical theory

6.16.1 'People who know what rotation is'

One of the most important goals of this book is the understanding of some of Wolfgang Pauli's very informative dreams and visions. According to C.G. Jung we can interpret a series of archetypal dreams without any associations, just by comparing the common motifs and their chronological development[209]. I will apply this method to the interpretation of some of the Nobel laureate's most decisive dreams.

I would like to begin with the earliest dream, which I mentioned several times, the dream of the objectification of rotation[210]:

THE DREAM OF THE OBJECTIFICATION OF ROTATION:

The 'Blond' is standing next to me. In an ancient book I am reading about the Inquisition trials against the disciples of the teachings of Copernicus (Galileo, Giordano Bruno) as well as about Kepler's image of the Trinity.

Then the Blond says: *'The men whose wives have objectified rotation are being tried.'* These words upset me greatly. The Blond disappears, and to my consternation the book also becomes a dream image: I find myself in a courtroom with the other accused men. I want to send my wife a message, and I write a note: 'Come at once, I am on trial.' It is getting dark, and for a long time I cannot find anyone to give the note to. But finally

---

[209] CW 12, §§ 48-50.
[210] AaA, p. 30-32; PJB, p. 34-36; not yet published in WB. My title of the dream. Since the dream dates of Oct 28, 1946, it cannot be an enclosure of letter [32P] of Oct 25, as Meier believes. Enz supposes that it was sent together with letter [35] of Nov 7, 1948 [Enz, No Time to be Brief, p. 455].

a *Negro* comes along and says in a friendly way that he will deliver the note to my wife.

Soon after the Negro has left with the note, my wife turns up in fact and says to me: 'You forgot to say good night to me.' Now it starts to get lighter, and the situation is as it was at the beginning (except that my wife is now present, too): The 'Blond' is standing next to me once more, and I am reading the ancient book again. Then the Blond says to me sadly (apparently referring to the book): 'The judges do not know what rotation or revolution is, and that is why they cannot understand the men.' With the insistent voice of a teacher he goes on to say: '*But* you *know what rotation is!*' 'Of course' is my immediate reply, 'The cycle [German: der Kreislauf] and the circulation of light[211] — all that is part of the basic rudiments.' (This seemed to be a reference to psychology, but the word is never mentioned.) Whereupon the Blond says: 'Now you understand the men whose wives have objectified their rotation for them.' Then I kiss my wife and say to her: 'good night! It is terrible what these poor people who have been charged are going through!' I grow very sad and start crying. But the Blond says with a smile: 'Now you've got the first key in your hand.'

We realized that this dream of the year 1946 initialized Pauli's intensification of his research on the conflict between Johannes Kepler and Robert Fludd, the empirical scientist and the alchemist at the beginning of modern science during the 17th century. We have further seen that the Nobel laureate half consciously anticipated a conflict in his soul, and that he expressed this presentiment in a letter with the remark that he carries Kepler as well as Fludd in himself. However, exactly this conflict did not play any role when he wrote *Background Physics*, the theoretical paper dealing with a possible world behind the split into physics and depth psychology, in which he definitely repressed the yin/yang bipolarity of the energy term. However, in contradiction to this he compared the physical radioactive nucleus with the psychophysically defined *infans solaris*, symbolically equivalent to the quintessence and the red tincture, the last goal of the Hermetic alchemical *opus*. Though he compared physical radioactivity with its radiation with the red tincture[212], the 'psychophysical radioactive core,' which at the end of the *opus* also sends out a radiation, he was however not able to realize that the radioactive decay could be a process happening on a deeper, on the psychophysical level of reality. He was however already conscious of the fact that the background of Fludd's *opus* was the *coniunctio* archetype. Since in the latter the energy term

---

[211] *This sentence is differing from Roscoe's translation. The term 'of the blood' does not exist in Pauli's original handwritten letter.*
[212] See section 5.4.6 in Part 1

is defined in a bipolar way, a big conflict arose in the Nobel laureate, the deepest background of which he was however not able to become conscious of.

Thus, we have to understand what the dream of the objectification of rotation means. A very interesting detail concerning my research is the fact that in the context of this dream Pauli mentions for the first time the idea of the creation of a neutral language for the description of processes happening in the unified psychophysical reality, the *unus mundus,* a task I tried to fulfil with the definition of the twin process using exactly such a neutral language.

The beginning of the dream talks about the Nobel laureate's deepest problem: He is reading in an ancient book about the Inquisition trials against the disciples of Copernicus, i.e., about Galilei, Giordano Bruno, as well as about Kepler's image of the Trinity. Then, however, the scene changes and Pauli is now himself the accused in the courtroom.

It is obvious that the dream talks about the physicist's half conscious conflict between the worldview of Hermetic alchemy and modern science beginning with Galilei and Kepler. He is accused of remaining on the side of science! What a heavy reproach for 'the conscience of physics,' as Pauli was called by his colleagues. However, as we will see[213], the magician is also an 'antiscientist.' Thus the Inquisitor is an aspect of the Eros Self in Pauli, which does not agree with his strictly scientific attitude.

The Inquisitor being an aspect of the magician is the reason why at the beginning of the dream he—here he is called the Blond—is present. He formulates the reproach in a different way: 'The men whose wives have objectified rotation are being tried.' Later, in a letter of 1953 to Marie-Louise von Franz, Pauli interprets the white woman as his inner *femme inspiratrice*[214] fertilizing him with creative physical ideas. Thus we can interpret the wives in the dream as his Anima, which is also present as the (one-dimensional) 'light, fruitful Anima' in both Seals[215] which Pauli drew the day before the visual-auditive experience of the dancing Chinese, the quintessence and the square in November 1953[216]. As he mentions as a comment to the second Seal[217], at the beginning of the fifties this light physical Anima became more and more negative; the dark however, the Chinese, which I interpret as a symbol of the *anima mundi* became more and more positive. Thus, we realize that the opposition between the physically creative Anima and the psychophysical *anima mundi,* exactly the two archetypes C.G.

---

[213] See section 6.16.4
[214] For the following see WB 4/II, p. 354; letter [1672] of Nov 10/11, 1953 which contains also the vision/audition with the Chinese anima mundi.
[215] WB 4/II, p. 345-346; die 'lichte Anima' mit ihrer 'Fruchtbarkeit'
[216] See section 4.3.3 in Part 1
[217] WB 4/II, p. 346; 'lichte Anima wird negativ bewertet und erscheint...böse'

Jung as well as Wolfgang Pauli were not able to distinguish from each other[218], produces the conflict in the Nobel laureate.

Later, in the year 1956, Pauli confesses the same conflict to C.G. Jung. In an interpretation of one of his dreams of the new houses (see below) he writes[219]:

> The 'light anima' has entered into a secret relationship with the shadow (Devil, *princeps huius mundi*), and this is precisely why this light female figure has become so suspect for me.

And he continues with his solution of the problem[220]:

> In my view, only a *chthonic*, instinctive wisdom can save mankind from the dangers of the atom bomb, which is precisely why the material-chthonic, ostracized by Christianity as unspiritual, acquires a positive value sign. This manifests itself particularly in the fact that the dark-chthonic anima [*anima mundi*; RFR] now seems to me superior, and its connection with the light (spiritual) side of the 'Master' is a source of hope. So for me, light and dark no longer coincide with good and evil. Down in the dark depths of the earth an *assumptio* of the woman is required, and not far away from humans in the Heaven.[221]

Here Pauli again attacks C.G. Jung's quaternities kept up in the heaven at a great distance from people, and with it of course also the depth psychologist's (one-dimensional) Anima concept. As we have seen[222], the Nobel laureate's solution was the definition of the chthonic principle as the 'trinity to below.' Since he is however not yet able to really differentiate between C.G. Jung's Anima, symbolic thinking, and the *anima mundi*, the magic principle of Hermetic alchemy that I call the matter-psyche aspect of energy, he cannot return to Robert Fludd, as his Fludd/flood synchronicity had demanded. In this way he is neither able to abandon the strictly scientific attitude. This is the real reason why in the dream of the objectification of rotation he is accused by the Inquisitor/stranger and magician.

The next passage talks of Pauli's personal feeling problems, of course a result of the identification with the physically creative Anima. The problem is solved by a black man, an Eros aspect, who becomes a messenger of his note to his wife, in which he tells her that he was withheld at the court.

Then, the scene at the very beginning of the dream repeats: The magician/stranger comes back and Pauli reads once again the ancient book. Now the former

---

[218] See section 5.2.1.6 in Part 1
[219] AaA, p. 140; PJB, p. 140; WB 4/III, p. 718
[220] AaA, p. 140-141; PJB, p. 140; WB 4/II, p. 718
[221] The last sentence translation mine, since Roscoe's translation is not correct.
[222] See section 5.1 in Part 1

says with a sad voice: 'The judges do not know what rotation or revolution is, and that is why they cannot understand the men,' and he continues: 'But you know what rotation is!'

This is a very enigmatic passage. Pauli is accused by the Inquisitor/magician because of his scientific standpoint; however, the magician is an antiscientist and does not understand anything of science. The antiscientific aspect of the magician, the Inquisitor, knows however that Pauli is able to anticipate the answer: The principle of rotation seems to be the decisive answer to the problem. Of course, since the Nobel laureate more than 20 years previous had invented the spin, some sort of an internal rotation, we first assume that the spin is meant. However Pauli answers with thorough conviction that the solution is 'the cycle and the circulation of light.'

Before I can interpret this part of the dream, I have to tell the reader an important aspect of depth psychological dream interpretation: Experience has shown us that sometimes in dreams the real ego is not present, and thus the 'dream ego' behaves in a completely different manner than the former. This is also the case in Pauli's dream: Actually it talks of what I defined above as the Eros ego.

The clarification of this motif in the dream helps in the interpretation of the setting of the sun in the Taoist text above. It means the transformation of the Logos ego into the Eros ego and the possibility of its relationship with the Eros Self, whereas the chaos we can translate with the disease of the individual as the starting point of Symptom-Symbol Transformation and the chaos in the *unus mundus* as the collective destruction created as an effect of the artificial fission, which, as we realized, has to be overcome by Body-Centered Imagination.

It is thus the complementary Eros ego—not known by most people but connected to the deepest roots—that knows more than the Logos ego. This is why the physicist's alter ego can give the above answer: 'Of course, the cycle and the circulation of light—all that is part of the basic rudiments.'

With this remark out of the preconscious knowledge of the collective unconscious (C.G. Jung) we approach the essence of the dream. The circulation of light is an exercise of the Taoist contemplation process with its goal, the creation of the Golden Flower described in the *T'ai I Chin Hua Tsung Chih* (The Secret of the Golden Flower)[223], which Richard Wilhelm translated into German and published in 1929 together with a comment of C.G. Jung. In this Chinese alchemical

---

[223] See Jung, C.G., Wilhelm, R., Das Geheimnis der Goldenen Blüte, Ein chinesisches Lebensbuch, Dornverlag, München, 1929; I use here the 10th edition of 1973; English translation: Wilhelm, R., Jung, C.G., The Secret of the Golden Flower, A Chinese Book of Life, Routledge & Kegan Paul Ltd., London, 8th ed., 1950. Since the 5th edition of 1957 the German original contains also a second tractatus with the name Liu Hua Yang. Hui Ming Ging, *which is not contained in the English translation of 1950.* See also CW 13, § 27 and footnote 1.

treatise, which Pauli knew when he had the above dream[224], a contemplation method is described, in which one let circulate the 'light' in one's own body.

Since the old Chinese master's goal consisted in creating the Logos ego, they suggest a circulation which begins in the coccyx and there rises up in the back to the parting. Then one lets the light flow back in the front of the body[225]. We in the West should however be conscious of the fact that we have already developed the Logos and have to come down into the belly. Thus, as an introduction to Body-Centered Imagination I turn around the flow: One lets the light or the water or any other substance chosen by the creative human itself flow down the back to the coccyx. Then one turns it around into one of the lower three chakras. In this way the shape of a 6 is reached. Then, one goes back to the parting and begins anew. This exercise—I call it also the reverse circulation of the light—helps to enter the Eros ego, i.e., the concentration onto one of the three lower chakras.

One of the most important preconditions of the Taoist/alchemical contemplative method is the opinion that this specific light belongs on the one hand to one's own body, on the other, however, also to the whole universe. To show the reader the revolutionary transformation that is described as the goal of *The Secret of the Golden Flower* and similar texts, I cite the decisive part literally[226]:

> It is said: The seed-blossom of the human body must be concentrated upward in the empty space...Immortality is contained in this sentence and also the overcoming of the world is contained in it. That is the common goal of all religions.
>
> The Light is not in the body alone, neither is it only outside the body. Mountains and rivers and the great Earth are lit by sun and moon; all that is this Light; therefore it is not only within the body. Understanding and clarity, knowing and enlightenment, and all motion (of the spirit), are likewise this Light; therefore it is not just something outside the body. The Light-flower of Heaven and Earth fills all thousand spaces. But also the Light-flower of one body passes through Heaven and covers the Earth. *Therefore, just as the Light is circulating, so Heaven and Earth, mountains and rivers, are all rotating with it at the same time.* To concentrate the seed-flower of the human body above in the eyes, that is the great key of the human body. Children, take heed! If for a day you do not practise meditation, this Light streams out, who knows wither?[227] If you only meditate for a quarter of an hour, you can set ten thousand aeons

---

[224] See AaA, p. 29, letter [31P] of June 3, 1940
[225] Geheimnis, p. 120; not published in the English translation.
[226] For the following see Secret, p. 36; Geheimnis, p. 87
[227] On the background of this insight we can perhaps understand why Pauli produced the Pauli effect.

and a thousand births at rest. All methods take their source in quietness. This marvellous magic cannot be fathomed. [Emphasis mine]

In my terminology we could express the goal of *The Secret of the Golden Flower*—corresponding to C.G. Jung's identity of point A with the whole collective unconscious and Isaak Luria's *tikkun*—in the way that during the exercise of the rotation of light as described above psychophysical nonlocality is reached. On the background of the results of my research we know that in the moment, in which the state of the Eros ego is created it is simultaneously connected to the Eros Self and is able to observe the singular inner quantum leap in it—the twin process happens, and the new content, mostly an inner image and/or a vegetative sensation out of the belly, is realized.

In the text psychophysical nonlocality is described as the identity of the inner rotation with the rotation of the whole universe. This state of affairs is verified by a late dream of Pauli. On September 28, 1952 he dreamed the following dream[228]:

DREAM OF THE CHINESE WOMAN WHO TRANSFORMS THE OSCILLATION INTO ROTATION AND LIKE THIS DISSOLVES SPACE:

The Chinese woman walks on ahead and beckons me to follow. She opens a trapdoor and walks down some steps, leaving the door open. Her movements are oddly dancelike; she does not speak but only expressed herself in mime, almost as in ballet. I follow her and see that the steps lead into an *auditorium,* in which 'the strangers' are waiting for me. The Chinese woman indicates that I should get up onto the rostrum and address the people, apparently to deliver a lecture. As I am waiting, she 'dances' rhythmically back up the steps, through the open door into the open air, and then back down again. As she does so, she keeps the index finger of her left hand and her left arm pointing upward, her right arm and the index finger of her right hand pointing downward. The repetition of this rhythmic movement now has a powerful effect, in that gradually it becomes a rotation movement (circulation of light). The difference between the two floors seems to diminish 'magically.' As I am actually mounting the rostrum of the auditorium, I wake up.

We realize first the motif of the oscillation, a topic which appeared very often in Pauli's dreams[229].The dance reminds us of the dancing Chinese in the

---

[228] AaA, p. 88-89; PJB, p. 90; WB 4/II p. 50; *my dream's title*
[229] *See for example his remarks in* Background Physics, *AaA, p. 187; PJB, p. 183-184; here Pauli also mentions that this motif lead to a 'fear of death.'*

visual-auditive experience of her and the Seal of Solomon, the quintessence and the square, but also of the dancer Käthe Deppner, whom the physicist divorced and immediately after invented the neutrino. I interpreted the Seal as the bipolarity of the energy term on a psychophysical level. In *Background Physics* of 1948 Pauli mentions[230] 'the ancient idea of polar opposites, such as the Chinese Yang and Yin,' which he however again reduces to complementarity.

We can therefore be sure that the oscillation of the Chinese woman means the bipolarity of the energy term as well as the potentiality of the constellated twin process, especially since the *anima mundi* is here presented as a Chinese, and thus as a symbol of the yin principle, of the matter-psyche, or of the Eros Self.

This interpretation is backed by the fact that during the oscillation the Chinese 'keeps the index finger of her left hand and her left arm pointing upward, her right arm and the index finger of her right hand pointing downward.' Symbolically seen, 'left' and 'downwards' are synonymous, as well as 'right' and 'upwards.' Here, however, 'left' is combined with 'upwards,' and 'right' with 'downwards.' It is obvious that the 'preconscious knowledge of the unconscious' (C.G. Jung) would like to stress that with the help of the oscillating movement an exchange of attributes takes place. Or as Taoism expresses the process: In the moment of the Tao yang becomes yin, and in the same moment yin becomes yang, and an incarnation has taken place. The latter process, as well as the exchange of attributes in Hermetic alchemy corresponds exactly to what I call the singular quantum leap happening during the twin process, or in a physical-symbolic language the discharge of the acausal condenser in the *unus mundus* that leads to incarnation.

The next step in the above dream of 1952 consists in *a magic change of space*. By dancing the oscillations or the up and down rhythm the Chinese *anima mundi* causes first a rotation of space. Exactly this transformation is also presented in the *Golden Flower*: 'Just as the Light is circulating, so Heaven and Earth, mountains and rivers, are all rotating with it at the same time.' In contrast to Pauli's dream such a *collective* rotation of the universe is connected to the *individual* exercise of the circulation of light. It is thus the psychophysical nonlocality between the microcosm and the macrocosm, of which the Nobel laureate is not conscious of, since he cannot see the necessity of the transformation of the Logos into the Eros ego for the realization of spatial nonlocality.

We can further conclude that in the dream as well as in the exercise of the *Golden Flower, a transformation of oscillation into rotation* is described. Obviously the development into a rotation is connected to the exchange of attributes, which we can characterize as a spontaneous singular quantum leap happening during the above described twin process in the Eros Self observed by the Eros ego.

But this is not yet the end of the magic process described in the dream: Next, obviously caused by the rotation and thus as an effect of the singular quantum

---

[230] *AaA, p. 185; PJB, p. 182*

leap space is contracted. This means nothing less than the abolishment of the idea of physical space: 'Point-space' and 'all-space' become identical. Thus, described is exactly the same situation as in the *Golden Flower*: The identity of the microcosmic human body with the macrocosmic universe, corresponding to C.G. Jung's Point A hypothesis and to the *tikkun* of Isaak Luria. As we have realized, in a modern terminology we can say that psychophysical nonlocality of space is reached. Since physical time is only possible with its definition in space—we measure time with the help of motion in space—also this concept is overcome. Further, as we will just see, the idea of physical matter is replaced by the concept of the subtle or vegetative body.

The Nobel laureate must have had a hunch of such processes, since shortly after the remark of the yin/yang polarity in *Background Physics* he compares the oscillating motion, which appeared always together with the 'Anima' [the *anima mundi*; RFR], with the *multiplicatio*, the last goal of Hermetic alchemy. He writes[231]:

> What is meant by *multiplicatio* is the tendency of a psychic situation to be repeated or become more widespread...[a] phenomenon [which] is mentioned frequently in Western alchemy. I first came across it in the text of the *goldenen Blüte* [Golden Flower] translated by Wilhelm...: 'The Book of Successful Contemplation (*Ying Kuan Ching*) says: The sun sinks in the Great Water and *magical pictures of trees in rows arise*. The setting of the sun means that in Chaos...a foundation is laid: That is the condition free of polar opposites'.

Then he compares the situation of the oscillation also with the one described in hexagram #51, Chên, The Arousing (Shock, Thunder) of the *I Ching* and tells us that it is exactly 'the *multiplicatio*, [which] is circumscribed in the Commentary: "The upheaval alarms everyone for one hundred miles around".'

In a modern terminology we can interpret the *multiplicatio* as the effect of psychophysical nonlocality, the spreading out of an incarnation event into the surrounding. According to my hypothesis, such events happen during the singular quantum leap, in the moment of the discharge of the 'acausal condenser.' As we know, this situation is symbolically represented as the rotation principle, so that we can describe the general process as a transformation of oscillation into rotation—exactly the motif that pursued Wolfgang Pauli in many dreams and visions[232].

---

[231] AaA, p. 187, note 3; PJB, p. 183-184, note 3

[232] For example in the dream of the Chinese woman, the dance, the quintessence and the square, in which the motif of 'rhythms and rotations' is mentioned. See section 4.3.3 in Part 1 and 6.16.8.

Since, however, Pauli neither knows the Eros ego nor its ability to observe the singular quantum leap happening in the Eros Self—in a symbolic language: the oscillative ego, the Eros ego is able to observe the spontaneous transformation of oscillation into rotation in the Eros Self—he is not able to realize that exactly by this transformation 'the condition free of polar opposites' is created, which is equivalent to the overcoming of the objectification of rotation, of the mathematical definition of the spin. Therefore he cannot realize that in such moments, as shown in the above examples of BCI and SST, in the Eros ego 'magical pictures arise,' which correspond to the symbolic term 'rotation,' and mean acausal incarnation.

As we know, the *multiplicatio* belongs to the second goal of Hermetic alchemy, the 'radiation' of the gold, the extraction of the red tincture or of the quintessence, and to the birth of the *infans solaris*, which is reached after the first goal, the creation of the intermediary realm symbolized by the Seal of Solomon, the philosophical gold or the *lapis*. In a modern terminology I interpreted the *multiplicatio*, the essential attribute of the last goal, as one of the most important effects of the observed twin process, the singular (acausal) quantum leap. Now we can concretize this final goal, the Hermetic alchemical *multiplicatio*, a little further: The result of the twin process corresponds to the individual creation of the 'magical pictures,' which, as a result of psychophysical nonlocality, seems also to influence the surrounding or perhaps even the whole universe. My hypothesis concerning the result of Body-Centered Imagination is verified: The creation of the vegetative or subtle body in oneself leads to a higher quality of the *anima mundi*, of the world soul.

How close to the solution of the psychophysical problem the Nobel laureate came, shows the following passage, also formulated in *Background Physics*. After interpreting the bipolarity of the oscillation process as a separation into two components and comparing it with the physical doublet splitting of the spectral lines and with the birth of a child he writes about the 'psychic birth' as a result of yogin meditation[233]:

> The 'child' is a pictorial representation of the…'spirit body' or 'adamantine body' or the *'corpus subtile'* [the subtle body; or vegetative body in my terminology; RFR]—a concept that has been very familiar in the West since late antiquity (especially to the Gnostics). This is linked to the idea of a 'superior personality part,' which is more constant than the ego, can outlive it, and is said to express itself by appearing as a specter

---

We know that in the early fifties Pauli because of this repeating oscillation symbolism was afraid that he approaches a psychosis. In Pauli's opinion the danger of a pychosis is banned as soon as the oscillations transform into rotation. See letter [1625], in WB 4/II, p. 252; see also WB 4/II, p. 303, note 2

[233] *AaA, p. 186; PJB, 183*

or ghost...This *corpus subtile,* as its name suggests, would have not only a psychic existence assigned to it but also a physical one (the latter, it seems to me, in a way that would be very unclear to us).

Thus it is the Nobel laureate of physics who combines the *coniunctio* with the idea of the subtle body, the microcosmic aspect of the macrocosmic world soul created during this life for the afterlife. The 'conscience of physics' becomes like this some sort of a modern mystic. As we have seen, he proposed to reach this goal with the help of a combination of modern physics with parapsychology.

After the interpretation of the contemplation process and its revolutionary effects with the help of a modern terminology including quantum physical as well as depth psychological insights we can now return to Pauli's dream of the objectification of rotation. After his alter ego's realization of the replacement of the physical rotation, the spin, by the contemplation method of the *Golden Flower,* the magician says: 'Now you understand the men whose wives have objectified the rotation for them,' and 'Now you have got the first key in your hand.' By understanding that the rotation means an inner process, the circulation of light, Pauli's alter ego has overcome the spin, the invention of his creative physical Anima. Simultaneously physical space, time and mass is abolished and replaced by the subtle body hypothesis.

Since, however, the Nobel laureate is not yet able to accept the bipolarity of the energy term and thus cannot realize the corresponding bipolarity of the Logos ego and the Eros ego consciously, he is not able to concretize the process of the creation of the vegetative body more clearly. Thus, the empirical way of the creation of this 'physical/psychic body' remains very unclear to him. Today, however, we can neither remain in the modern scientific worldview nor unconsciously regress into the worldview before Copernicus, Galilei, Bruno and Kepler, i.e., the esoteric worldview of today, which is not able to include modern quantum physical and depth psychological insights. On the contrary we have to create a psychophysical theory which includes both. This is exactly what I have tried in the course of my book.

/ / /

Summarizing, we can postulate that Pauli's dream of the objectification of rotation symbolizes the following process: On a psychophysical level the spin hypothesis, the objectified rotation has to be replaced by the Taoist exercise of the (reversed) circulation of light. Following this process helps to abandon the Logos ego and enter the Eros ego. The latter, the wave-like ego, the 'conscious oscillation,' is then able to observe singular acausal processes in the Eros Self, in the oscillative *unus mundus.* The observation of such singular processes in oneself—mostly the viewing of inner images and/or vegetative sensations out of one's own belly—is symbolized by a rotation process happening in the moment of the *kairos*, in which the spontaneous singular quantum leap happens and physical and/or objective psychic energy transmutates to an increased quality. This process leads into psychophysical nonlocality, in which C.G. Jung's point A situation or the *tikkun* of Isaak Luria is reached: What happens in one human, in the extreme case has happened in the whole universe. The result of this process is a higher quality of the subtle or vegetative body on the individual level as well as of the world soul on the collective. Like this a healing of individual as well as of the disease of the world becomes possible.

6.16.2 The radioactive experiment of the revenant and the death of the neutrino

Two years after the dream of the objectification of rotation, at the inauguration ceremony of the C.G. Jung Institute in 1948 in Zurich the Pauli effect with the overturned Chinese vase happened. As we remember, Pauli was convinced that the effect named after him was caused by revenants which come back now since in the 17th century science went too far into a one-sided direction. The next dream of August 16, 1953 confirms Pauli's supposition. Further I show that this dream on the one hand horrible and on the other hopeful, backs one of the most important aspects of my theory, the idea of Body-Centered Imagination being the Alexipharmakum, the counter-poison against the artificial fission poisoning the *unus mundus*.

Since the dream has never been translated into English, I give the whole text in my translation here[234]:

THE DREAM OF THE RADIOACTIVE EXPERIMENT OF THE REVENANT AND THE DEATH OF THE NEUTRINO:

> With the help of chemical retorts out of radioactive uranium a man produces another yellow substance, which looks like bromine. Then the man disappears. The two women present (one of them of the motherly

---

[234] German original in WB 4/II, p. 251; letter to Marie-Louise von Franz of August 16, 1953. Pauli had the dream in the morning of this day. My title of the dream.

type) begin to scream out of fright. They say that the man had died a long time ago, and his ghost has returned. The younger adds that she is so afraid, since it is he who produces the stripes.

I contradict the two and say that he was not at all dead, and that I do not see any stripes. The women calm a little.

Now a man resembling Einstein enters and says that radioactivity is always a provisional state, the end substance however is stable; this is why the experiment of the man is a great success.

Then a man resembling C.A. Meier enters, having red rims around the eyes and an imbecilic face. He says: 'I have read in the newspaper that Kertino (or a similar Italian sounding fantasy name) has died.'

It seemed to me that he liked to imply that it was that man, who did the chemical experiment. Therefore I only say: 'Do not read the newspaper so much.'

Now I try to consult Professor Jung, however only come across the two women, who tell me that he is not achievable.

It is obvious that the topic of the dream is transmutation, the essential ambition of alchemy. The experimenter is a deceased that comes back from the Beyond into our world, a revenant. In a general language we can say that a content of the *unus mundus* which consists of living matter comes back into our world— exactly the result of the above defined twin process caused by artificial fission. Of course we are also reminded of the psychokinetic Pauli effect, which he looked at as being a revenge of the repressed world soul.

Revenants live in the Beyond and in our world as well. Thus we can conclude that the deceased man's radioactive experiment is based on psychophysical radioactivity, is thus psychophysically nonlocal, and therefore influences both worlds, the Beyond as well as our world. This means concretely that not only our material and psychic world, the here and now, but also the *unus mundus* or the Beyond is contaminated. The term 'the radioactive experiment of the revenant' presents thus a confirmation of my above hypothesis that the 'radioactive experiment of mankind,' the nuclear bomb and the nuclear power plants influence our world as well as the *unus mundus* and thus the Beyond. As we will see this influence is destructive as long as we do not become conscious of the fact that radioactivity is a process happening on the psychophysical level of reality.

The two women scream of dread; collectively seen we can say that femininity per se, the Eros principle that is conscious of psychophysical nonlocality knows that we should realize the deep but completely repressed angst in the world because of the absolutely dreadful invention of the artificial fission of the atom.

One of the women knows the reason why we should become conscious of the collective angst: The experiment of the revenant, of the active principle behind psychophysical nonlocality, produces 'the stripes.' Surely the Nobel laureate was aware of the fact that these stripes were a parallel motif to the oscillation and to the black and white stripes he mentions in 1948 in *Background Physics* in the section 'Frequency symbolism and level of consciousness.'[235] It is exactly this symbolism which belongs to his life long wasp phobia, since wasps have a striped body. Thus, the interpretation of this motif would on the one hand show us Pauli's deepest unconscious problem and on the other the collective problem which is constellated because of the invention of fission.

For Pauli the oscillation's symbolism was not only equivalent to the motif of the black and white stripes as well as to the frequency motif, but also to the above mentioned doublet splitting of the light spectrum's emission, which, as we have seen, he brings together with the birth of the 'child' in the contemplative process described in *The Secret of the Golden Flower*, the subtle body. For our concern it is now extremely important that it was exactly a specific form of this splitting, the so-called anomalous Zeeman effect[236], which forced Pauli to invent the spin as the fourth quantum number. As we further remember, the spin splits the world into 'masculine' forces and 'feminine' matter. Thus we obtain the following association chain: Oscillation—black and white stripes—doublet splitting—subtle body—spin—active masculine/passive feminine split of the material world. We will deal with these connections below.

Here we remember first that I have shown above that the oscillation's and the stripes' motif leads us to the idea of the bipolarity of the energy term and thus to the twin process on the background of the Eros Self, with its result, the singular acausal quantum leap observable, however, only by the Eros ego, the wave-like consciousness. We can therefore conclude that it was exactly this idea which was constellated in Pauli and shown in the dream of the radioactive experiment. In slightly different words we can say that it is the radioactive experiment of the revenant, a figure belonging to the Beyond as well as to our world, which symbolizes the twin process on the psychophysical level of reality. Thus, the dream of the radioactive experiment confirms my hypothesis of the twin process happening between the physical world and the *unus mundus*.

---

[235] AaA, p. 187; PJB, p. 183-184
[236] *For a detailed description of Pauli's struggling with this topic see Miller, Arthur, I., Deciphering The Cosmic Number, The Strange Relationship of Wolfgang Pauli and C.G. Jung, 2009, Chapters 3 & 4*

In contrast to the first dream above, in this one it is not the Nobel laureate's potential Eros ego, which acts, but the Logos ego. This is why he cannot accept the hypothesis of the two women of the revenant coming back into our world and producing the stripes, the potential quantum leap on the psychophysical level. Of course this is also the reason why he has no dread. This shows that in this moment a destructive regressive development in the physicist begins, which is, as we will later see, the reason for his early death. Since, however, the psychophysical reality is involved, the dream possesses the meaning of a collective danger, as we will realize.

We know that it was Pauli's Logos ego that invented the spin for the explanation of the peculiar 'stripes' of the anomalous Zeeman effect. On a psychophysical level the terms 'black and white stripes,' 'oscillation' and 'frequency' symbolize the bipolarity of the energy term, thus the necessary precondition for the twin process and its singular acausal quantum leap, which leads to an increase of order in matter, to the creation of the subtle or vegetative body. Thus, we realize that Pauli on the one hand anticipated the connection of the spin and the subtle body, on the other, however, was not able to replace the former by the latter, since his Logos ego did not accept the psychophysical aspect of the oscillation symbolism.

Let us return to the dream: Now the great opponent of Pauli, Albert Einstein enters the scene. As we know, the latter never accepted statistical causality of quantum physics and postulated that behind it there must exist a further dimension of the physical world which is again causal. Pauli was convinced that this was a regressive tendency in Einstein[237]. To understand the Einstein figure in the dream we have to consult another of the quantum physicist's dreams, the dream of Einstein Pauli dreamed about in the year 1935, exactly in the moment when the physical-symbolic terminology began. Pauli tells the dream to C.G. Jung in a letter of May 27, 1953 after discussing the above 'regression' (W. Pauli) of Einstein. He writes[238]:

> I remarked to Bohr…that Einstein was regarding as an imperfection of wave mechanics [quantum physics; RFR] within physics what in fact was an imperfection of physics within life.

Then he tells the dream:

> A man resembling Einstein is drawing the following figure on a board:

---

[237] AaA, p. 121; PJB, p. 121; WB 4/p. 164
[238] For the following see AaA, p. 121-122; PJB, p. 121-122; WB 4/II, p. 164

```
(hachured
surface
crossed
by graph)
```

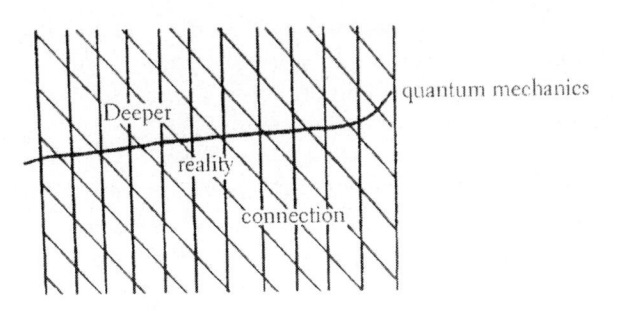

The reality beyond quantum physics

This was apparently connected with the controversy described and seemed to contain a sort of response to it from the unconscious. It showed me quantum mechanics and so-called official physics in general as a one-dimensional section of a two-dimensional, more meaningful world, the second dimension of which could be only the unconscious and the archetypes.

In the figure the line symbolizes quantum mechanics which is however only a section of the whole, the deeper reality connection. Since 'Einstein' in the dream talks of a reality beyond physics, he does not correspond to the real scientist. As Pauli mentions[239] he corresponds to an inner aspect that confirms that the great colleague is wrong. Instead of looking for a further physical reality behind quantum physics, we have to look for a union of physics and depth psychology on a deeper, on the psychophysical level.

In my interpretation this deeper level, the *unus mundus*, does not only include physical and depth psychological concepts, but paranormal as well, as also Pauli some months after the above dream realized. In a letter to Marie-Louise von Franz of October 30, 1953 he concludes[240]:

> In fact a less far-reaching assumption [than the integration of depth psychology into physics; RFR] is sufficient for the explanation of the physical symbolism in my dreams, namely: *The tendency of my dreams*

---

[239] *AaA, p. 122; PJB, p. 122; WB 4/II, p. 164*
[240] ‚*Es genügt in der Tat schon eine weniger weitgehende Annahme [als die Integration der Tiefenpsychologie in die Physik; RFR], um die physikalische Symbolik meiner Träume zu erklären, nämlich:* die Tendenz meiner Träume ist eine Assimilation alles dessen an die Physik, was... '"sychoider Archetypus" genannt wird. Mit anderen Worten: Parapsychologie und Biologie sollen in eine erweiterte Physik aufgenommen werden.' *(WB 4/II, p. 327; letter [1667] to Marie-Louise von Franz)*

consists in the assimilation of all of what...is called the 'psychoid archetype'. In other words: Parapsychology and biology should be integrated into physics. [Translation mine]

Thus we can conclude that 'Einstein' in the dream of the radioactive experiment symbolizes the idea of a psychophysical theory describing the permissible processes in and out of the *unus mundus* as developed above. With the help of my comments about the double twin process we can interpret radioactivity being only a provisional state as follows: In the *unus mundus* there exists an 'acausal condenser' containing a 'psychophysical radioactive core,' which is charged by the 'radioactive experiment' of the artificial fission. The stable state that 'Einstein' mentions would then correspond to the state after the acausal discharge of the condenser—exactly my hypothesis above.

The stable state consists of bromine, a highly toxic substance. Since it is a revenant, living in the Beyond as well as in our world, who undertakes the experiment, we can conclude that the poisoning leaks out of the *unus mundus* into our world. Its basis is a radioactive substance. Thus, also my hypothesis is confirmed that fission has a destructive effect not only in our world but also in the *unus mundus*.

Today, the great majority of mankind knows that radioactivity is a very destructive radiation. However, they only know of its concrete toxicity. That the artificial fission of the atom could 'poison' the *unus mundus* and with it the Beyond is not an idea which too many humans of today would accept. However, if we base our experience on the preconscious knowledge of the unconscious, we have to face this truth: Not only our planet, but also the whole universe and the *unus mundus* are poisoned by some sort of an unconscious and thus destructive subtle body energy created as an effect of the artificial fission[241].

However, the great hope for mankind lies in the statement of 'Einstein'—the symbol for a content of the psychophysical reality; in this case for its preconscious knowledge—that with the radioactive experiment great progress is made. As we just will see, this progress we can interpret as Body-Centered Imagination, the Alexipharmakum, counter-poison to artificial radioactivity, which 'cleans' the *unus mundus*.

C.A. Meier, Pauli's friend and editor of *Atom and Archetype*, is described as going gaga. We know that the physicist did not think highly of Meier's intelligence. For example he refused to back him in the intention of becoming a professor of depth psychology at the ETH, the Federal Institute of Technology in Zurich, Switzerland[242]. Thus, we can interpret Meier as the Eros ego, which during the process of Body-Centered Imagination represses thinking.

---

[241] *I know also of dreams and visions of friends and patients, in which the preconscious knowledge talks like this.*
[242] See *WB 4/III*, p. 434; see also *WB 4/II*, p. 77-78 and p. 496

Meier knows that 'Kertino' died. The latter is equated with the revenant at the beginning of the dream. It is an Italian fantasy name, which reminds us of Pauli's neutrino[243]—originally 'baptized' not by Pauli but by the *Italian* physicist Enrico Fermi. Thus, 'Meier' would state that on a psychophysical level the postulate of the neutrino/antineutrino, Pauli's 'foolish child of [his] life's crisis,' has to be abolished. This is exactly the case in Body-Centered Imagination in the Eros state, in which the introverted observation of the matter-psyche replaces the neutrino hypothesis.

The death of 'Kertino' corresponding to the 'radioactive experimenter' we can also interpret as the return of the revenant into the Beyond. Thus, as a deceased he does not live in our world anymore, as he did before as a spirit, i.e., as paranormal events, and the 'radioactive experiment' in the *unus mundus* does not influence our world anymore. The 'acausal condenser' is emptied; the destructive effect caused by artificial fission stops, the stable state is reached, and the poisoning of our world as well as of the *unus mundus* ends. Such a death of the neutrino can only happen when the above replacement of the neutrino hypothesis by the matter-psyche postulate is realized and when the latter is consciously observed in the deeply introverted process of BCI. Only then the poison changes into the counter-poison, the Alexipharmakum, the *medicina catholica*, the all-healing substance for the universe as well as for the individual human as was sought by the medieval alchemists.

Here the reader is perhaps reminded of my above BCI with the turtle and the UFO with the help of which I can enter the Beyond. There, at the hub of the world, we find Anubis, the Egyptian god, who recollects the parts of Osiris' dead body, puts them together again and puts new life into it. As much as I can see, this motif corresponds to the positive aspect of the 'radioactive experiment' mentioned by Pauli's Einstein figure, the one, who realizes the psychophysical reality behind or beyond the split into the outer and the inner world. Since Osiris is the god of the underworld and thus of the *unus mundus*, this motif means that in the latter a negentropic process had happened, the creation of higher order in the world of the vegetative body/world soul.

The end of the dream shows Pauli's tragedy. He tries to talk to C.G. Jung but does not find him anymore. This means that Jung cannot help him, since his theory does not embrace the psychophysical reality: It cannot explain paranormal events like the Pauli effect, UFO encounter and abduction, since in it the transmutation of matter into subtle matter as a result of the twin process in Body-Centered Imagination is not included.

The Nobel laureate could only be helped by the two women. As we realized they symbolize the dread rooted in the invention of the nuclear bomb, which we should become conscious of. However, too many humans still repress this dread,

---

[243] *In German, especially in the Austrian German spoken by Pauli, the two terms sound much more similar than in English*

thus cannot face it and remain in will- and power-possession, instead of sacrificing themselves to the modern Hermetic *opus*.

As a last aspect of the dream we can eventually deal with the spin. As we realized, Pauli's invention of the spin must somehow be connected with the idea of the subtle body, or vegetative body as I call it here. In the above I wrote that in the description of the psychophysical reality not only the idea of the neutrino but also of the spin must be abolished. With the help of the above association chain we realize now that Pauli was haunted by the oscillation symbolism in his dreams and visions since in him *the idea of the subtle body was constellated. Instead of realizing that the oscillation phenomenology represents the potential vegetative body, which in an introverted process should be transformed into rotation, the realized vegetative body, the physicist objectified rotation, and invented the spin.* As the dream of the 'oscillating Chinese' above shows, the oscillation is transformed into a rotation which causes the annihilation of physical space. If physical space is wiped out, also physical time and mass do not exist anymore. We enter a space-, time- and massless world, the *unus mundus* with its content, the subtle body and the world soul. As we realized above, because of the dimensionlessness of the *unus mundus* and the subtle body the Hermetic alchemical idea 'As above, so below, as without, so within,' the identity of the microcosm and the macrocosm in the moment of the singular quantum leap, i.e. psychophysical nonlocality, is reached. Thus, also this hypothesis is backed by Pauli's dream and his reflections about the contemplative process of the *Golden Flower*.

We realized above that the spin splits the world into the active masculine principle of force and the passive feminine of matter. If there is no spin anymore, this split is also annulled. For the healing of a split between enemies it is however first necessary to accept each other as of equal worth. This means concretely that we also accept that the feminine principle per se, matter, possesses its own force—the matter-psyche. The abolition of the spin leads thus to the bipolarity of the energy term, and in this way to an acceptance of the parapsychological complement to physical as well as to objective psychic energy, matter-psyche. Pauli's demand of the integration of parapsychology into an 'extended physics' is fulfilled. The world soul/vegetative body is accepted as the principle behind the transformation into matter-psyche and the creation of increased order in the observation of the singular acausal quantum leap, the twin process, which leads to the reunion and its 'child,' the incarnation process.

Contemplation and imagination methods similar to the one described in the *Golden Flower*, especially Body-Centered Imagination, seem to be the means for the observation of the creation of the vegetative body, the subtle body. This process leads on the one hand into Paracelsus' *vita longa* mentioned above, which with the help of an introverted transmutation process serves the healing of individual physical disease and the creation of the subtle body as a necessary vehicle for the afterlife; on the other to the Alexipharmakum, the counter-poison to the poisoning of our world as well as of the Beyond and the *unus mundus* by the realization of the fission of the atom.

/ / /

If we summarize the interpretation of the above dream, we can state its meaning as follows: The artificial, will-possessed fission of the atom has triggered a destructive process on the level of the psychophysical reality or *unus mundus*. As an effect of this development the latter as well as the here and now are 'poisoned.' This is the reason why the oscillation symbolism is constellated, representing the charge of the acausal condenser in the psychophysical reality of the Eros Self. If this constellation remains unconscious, the discharge of the acausal condenser, symbolized as rotation, also appears in a negative way. One effect of this destructive development could be the UFOs characterized exactly by oscillation and rotation phenomena.

This development is the direct effect of the definition of the spin as the fourth quantum number. On a psychophysical layer, it must therefore be replaced by the fourth principle on the basis of the Axiom of Maria Prophetissa, the Seal of Solomon and the bipolar energy term. Only with the help of this replacement we become able to realize the 'inner spin,' the (inverse) circulation of light and its result, the spontaneous production of inner images and/or vegetative sensations out of the belly, happening not on the physical but on the psychophysical level of the universe. In this way, the destructive consequences of artificial fission in the nuclear bomb and in nuclear power plants, the 'poisoning' of the *unus mundus* as well as of the here and now—the physical as well as the psychic—can be overcome.

The abolishment of the spin and its replacement by the bipolar energy term on the psychophysical layer would further lead to the abolition of the split between matter and force, between the principle of femininity and masculinity in the *coniunctio* of Body-Centered Imagination. In it the *multiplicatio* happens, in which psychophysical nonlocality is reached since in the moment of the *kairos*, in which the introvertedly observed singular quantum leap happens, the microcosm and the macrocosm become for a short moment identical. As a result of such a 'psychophysical inflation'[244] the positive effects in the psyche and the body of the imaginating human become at the same time positive effects in its surrounding and in the extreme case in the whole universe—C.G. Jung's point A situation or the situation of the *tikkun* of the Cabbalist Isaak Luria.

---

[244] *The term is consciously chosen on the basis of Alan H. Guth's and Andrei Linde's inflation theory of the universe.*

6.16.3 The secret laboratory, the radioactive isotope unknown to Pauli, and the sun eclipse

Chronologically seen the next message of the unconscious is the visual-auditive experience of the dancing Chinese, the Seal of Solomon, the quintessence and the square, which I already presented to the reader in Chapter 4 in Part I of the book. Since this message shows in some way a summary of all the others, I will interpret it at the end. Thus we continue now with the next but one, again a dream about radioactivity, which Pauli dreamed on July 15, 1954[245]:

DREAM OF THE SECRET LABORATORY AND THE RADIOACTIVE ISOTOPE:

I am in Sweden, where Gustafson (professor of theoretical physics in Lund) is present. He says to me: 'This is a *secret* laboratory in which a radioactive isotope has been isolated. Did you know anything about it?' I reply that I knew nothing about it.

Pauli must have been very impressed by this dream, since he wrote it to all people he thought of being able to deal with it in a meaningful way: To Marie-Louise von Franz[246], to Aniela Jaffé[247], and also to C.G. Jung[248]. As the physicist mentions in the letter to Jung as well as to von Franz, the dream happened only a short time after his visit in Lund, Sweden. The reason for this visit was the observation of the total sun eclipse there on June 30, 1954, and it is the Nobel laureate himself, who associates the sun eclipse with the radioactive core of the dream. The sun eclipse we can of course interpret as the 'darkening' of the 'individual sun,' the Logos ego[249], which leads into the Eros ego and its ability to observe the singular quantum leap in the Eros Self, the *unus mundus*. The secret radioac-

---

[245] Originally published in German, PJB, p. 134; also published in WB 4/III, 2001, p. 712; English translation in AaA, p. 134

[246] WB 4/II, letter [1847], p. 714

[247] WB 4/II, letter [1865], p. 747; here in the context to his feelings of quantum physics being a 'black measuring mass.'

[248] WB 4/III, letter [2367], p. 712 respectively PJB, 1992, letter [69], p. 134 and AaA, p. 134

[249] Pauli anticipated the 'darkening' of the Logos. In his letter [69P], p. 134, note 1 (PJB, p. 134; WB 4/III, p. 729, note *), to Jung he quotes the latter's remark in GW 14ii, par. 322 (CW 14, par. 657), that the eclipse of the sun is a symbol for the 'darkened' moment, in which the synthesis happens. See also WB 4/III, p. 729, note *. In my interpretation the

tive isotope *unknown* to Pauli becomes the potential twin process, the charged acausal condenser (replacing the spin and the neutrino hypothesis), of which he is unconscious exactly since he does not know the Eros ego and its ability to observe the spontaneous creation and incarnation—the decay of the psychophysical radioactive core. However, he should isolate the radioactive core, which means that he should become conscious of the psychophysical process described in this book. As we know, his tragedy was that he was not able to do so, since C.G. Jung's depth psychological theory does not comprehend the psychophysical processes described above.

In Hermetic alchemy the sun eclipse is a symbol of the *coniunctio* of the king and the queen, as described in extenso in this book. In Holy Wedding[250] I show that this motif is equivalent to the so-called *sol niger*, the black sun. It is also represented as Osiris, the *vegetative* god of the underworld. In the alchemist Gerardus Dorneus' *opus* the sun eclipse is described as the *unio corporalis*, which corresponds to the *coniunctio*. In it the king must be decapitated, which means of course on a personal level the renunciation of the Logos ego and its replacement by the Eros ego, which solely is able to observe the acausal processes in the Eros Self, in the *unus mundus*. The decapitation activates the instinctive Eros, sexuality. This is why the king, Osiris and also Mercury/Hermes, the god of Hermetic alchemy are imagined ithyphallically[251]. In Christian texts they are therefore identified with the devil. This motif leads us back to Pauli's remark of acausality being regarded as evil[252]. Everything that the Western Logos cannot control is looked at as being devilish. However, in Body-Centered Imagination one hands over to the willessness of the Eros ego and becomes able to observe the singular acausal quantum leap, the (white!) magic creation processes replacing the Christian devil.

In contrast, C.G. Jung interprets the decapitation as 'an emancipation of the "cogitation" [cognition] which is situated in the head'[253], which in modern terms is obviously the conscious development of the thinking function. For the depth psychologist the decapitation becomes in this way 'significant symbolically as the separation of the 'understanding' from the "great suffering and grief"'. Therefore, it seems that conscious suffering is substituted by thinking, a procedure which is 'a freeing of the soul from the "trammels of nature"'! This 'sublimation' of the suffering into thinking is then, according to Jung, the *'unio mentalis* "in the overcoming of the body"' ['in superatione corporis' in the German original]. This overcoming of the body according to the depth psychologist happens especially in

---

synthesis is the coniunctio, or in a neutral language the singular quantum leap in the moment of the twin process.
[250] Digital publication, http://paulijungunusmundus.eu/hknw/holy_wedding_alchemy_modern_man_contents.htm
[251] For the following see CW 14, § 726
[252] See section 3.3.9 in Part 1
[253] For the following see CW 14, § 730

Active Imagination, the Neoplatonic creation by cognition. As the reader knows, I, however, propose Body-Centered Imagination, the letting go of the will and the Logos, which is based on the Hermetic creation by observation. It seems however that the acceptance of such a procedure is mostly only possible when the human concerned is forced to suffer, for example in a severe disease.

Osiris leads us back again to my above BCI, in which the turtle, the UFO and I eventually meet Anubis in the Beyond. As we realized, Anubis is the one who puts together the pieces of Osiris' body and revitalizes him. He is so to speak the one who reincarnates the god of the Beyond. In psychophysical language I expressed this fact in the way that in the *unus mundus* living matter with increased order is created, which corresponds to the vegetative body and the world soul.

The place where Pauli's dream happens, Sweden, leads us back to his physical-symbolic dreams beginning around the end of his psychoanalysis with C.G. Jung in the year 1934. In the letters to Jung as well as to von Franz he mentions the fact that during his analysis the 'child in Sweden' was a very important motif[254]. He writes that already at the beginning of psychoanalysis he dreamed of this symbol and that it appeared frequently at the end—'wurde [aber] niemals aufgeklärt'[255] (was [however] never cleared up). 'This is why,' he also says, '[he] still today thinks of this motif often.'[256] At the end of the introduction of the letter to Jung—it is the one named as *Statements by the Psyche*—he then remarks that the best context to the above dream is a series of dreams which then follow. They contain the new houses' motif, with which we will deal in the next section.

When we remember the child above, the product of the separation into two which Pauli associates with the oscillation's and stripe's symbolism and then with the subtle body as the result of the contemplation method of the *Golden Flower*, we realize that the child in Sweden is exactly the *infans solaris*, the red tincture or the quintessence, the last result of the *coniunctio* of the Hermetic *opus*, which I interpreted as the result of the twin process, of the observed singular quantum leap—the creation and incarnation process happening out of and even in the *unus mundus*. As we have also seen, in UFO encounter this process creates matter/energy with altered quality in our world, in abduction some sort of subtle matter in the psychophysical reality, happens completely unconscious and thus does not create something sustainable. In SST, however, by mere observation the symptom of the disease is consciously transformed into the symbol, and thus as a result creates stable bodily matter/energy with higher order—the healing process. In BCI the conscious process leads to an increased order in the *unus mundus*, and

---

[254] WB 4/III, p. 713, PJB, p. 134, respectively AaA, p. 135; letter to von Franz from July 18, 1954, WB 4/II, p. 714. There he also mentions that this motif was represented as 'besonders entwicklungsfähig,' especially *capable of development [Pauli's italics]*.

[255] WB 4/II, p. 714 and WB 4/III, p. 713; PJB, p. 134; AaA, p. 135; See also the remark of v. Meyenn in WB 4/I, p. 114

[256] For the following see WB 4/III, p. 713; PJB, p. 134; AaA, p. 135

thus heals it of the destructive effects caused by the nuclear bomb and the nuclear power plants.

As a scientist I agree with critics who will answer the last sentence with the remark that such a statement is a mere hypothesis. I know that only future history can prove it. However it is my great hope that my conclusion is true and that in a deeply introverted manner some individuals can influence the course of world's history. This idea is backed by the preconscious knowledge of the collective unconscious shown in Pauli's unpublished dreams of 1934 and 1935, which I mentioned shortly in connection with the interpretation of my dream about the synchronous synchronicities[257] and earlier in the demonstration of Pauli's loneliness. These 'extremely surprising and unexpected' dreams[258] show, as we have seen, a magic connection between the Eros principle on the one hand, and political or historical events on the other, triggered by the Chinese *anima mundi*. As the Nobel laureate further writes, these dreams also showed 'close links with...parapsychological areas that are not easily accessible.' Body-Centered Imagination is a method based on (white!) magical effects. Thus, my above hypothesis could be proven as correct in the future.

The letter to von Franz contains two further very important thoughts of the Nobel laureate. At the beginning he writes that the dream belongs to the ones 'which mentally isolate me from the environment for circa 18 years'—thus since 1936. He is forced to speak two different languages; with his colleagues the language of physics, with the depth psychologists their language. Though both speak of the same content—the reader is reminded of Pauli's and Jung's hypothesis of complementarity between physics and depth psychology—none of them is good enough and they are not sufficient. This is why the unconscious expresses itself in a third language—obviously the physical-symbolic language. As we know, Pauli also tried to find a forth, the neutral language[259], which has to serve the description of these physical-symbolic images in a consistent rational language which can be understood by the Logos ego. I try exactly this in my book.

The second aspect, which Pauli stresses in the letter to von Franz[260] deals with the above mentioned dream[261] of her, which says that she has to find 'the psychological equivalent to the atomic bomb.'[262] He thinks that the motif of the radioactive nucleus in the above dream is intimately connected to this symbolic term in her dream, and interprets both as the task of creating an 'extended physics,' which includes parapsychology. With the idea of the singular quantum

---

[257] See section 6.12.3.2
[258] For the following see AaA, letters [9P], p. 9, [16P], p. 16, and [18P], p. 17.
[259] For example in Background Physics, AaA, p. 182-183; concerning radioactivity also in letter [47P] in AaA, p. 66-67)/[PJB, p. 179-180 and p. 69]
[260] WB 4/II, p. 713-716; letter [1847] of July 18th, 1954
[261] See section 5.1 in Part 1
[262] WB 4/II, p. 352; p. 713

leap, observable in one's own inside—one of the most important contents of my theory—we have however found this 'psychological equivalent,' or better: the psychophysical correspondence.

/ / /

The letter to Aniela Jaffé[263] does not mention the dream, however the motif of the radioactive laboratories, and that for military reasons they are in fact secret, since in them nuclear bombs are produced. Then Pauli adds his idea of the detached observer in quantum physics: The physicist observes first but then shirks taking the responsibility. He does not sacrifice himself, but a part of the outer world. Then, the Nobel laureate of physics writes something incredible: He confesses that his feelings tell him that quantum physics is a 'black mass' and he begins to feel remorse, obviously for the invention of the spin and the neutrino, which helped to complete quantum physics, and only then was applicable for the construction of the bomb. Pauli's statement shows that the 'cold and cynical devil'[264] four years before his death changes into a human, who begins to doubt the meaning of quantum physics. However, he fails to advance to the conscious insight that the renewed observer, which in fact is a participant, in the deeply introverted state of Eros is able to observe the twin process and as a consequence reaches the possibility together with the world soul to co-create compensations to the 'black mass' of quantum physics.

In a very decisive letter to his colleague Markus Fierz also written on August 10, 1954 he goes as far as possible that an epistemologist can go. He attacks now the quantum physical mode of observation[265] and postulates that[266]

> we (regarded in the sense of life) do not treat matter 'in the right way,' if we observe it in the way quantum physics does, namely completely desist from the inner condition of the 'observer. [Translation mine]

Then he goes one crucial step further[267]:

---

[263] WB 4/II, letter [1865], p. 747
[264] Pauli about himself; AaA, p. 27; letter [30P] of May 24, 1934; PJB, p. 31.
[265] For the following quotations see WB 4/II, p. 744-745; letter [1864] of August 10, 1954
[266] 'wir die Materie, z.B. im Sinne des Lebens betrachtet, nicht "richtig" behandeln, wenn wir sie so beobachten, wie wir es in der Quantenphysik tun, nämlich vom inneren Zustand des B "eobachters' dabei ganz absehend."'
[267] 'Es kommt mir so vor, wie wenn die nicht beobachteten "Nacheffekte" der Beobachtung dann doch eintreten würden (als Atombomben, allgemeine Angst, "Fall Oppenheimer z.B". etc.), aber in einer unerwünschten Form.'

> It seems to me as if the non-observed 'side effects' of the observation then take place anyway (as nuclear bombs, general dread, 'case Oppenheimer,' etc.), however in an undesirable form. [Translation mine]

And he continues[268]:

> The famous 'incompleteness' of quantum mechanics (Einstein) actually is somehow/somewhere existing; it is of course not at all removable by the return to classical field physics (this is only a 'neurotic misunderstanding' of Einstein). It has rather to do with holistic relationships between 'inside' and 'outside,' which today's natural science does not contain (which, however, alchemy has anticipated, and which can also be proved in my dream's symbolism, of which I think that it characterizes exactly a modern physicist's situation.) [Translation mine]

Afterward the co-creator of quantum physics realizes that with these thoughts he reached the border of today's epistemology, and that he even approached magic. Then he writes about his fear concerning quantum physics being black magic also to his colleague[269]:

> [The quantum physical act of observation appears like] a 'black mass' ... after which 'tortured' matter by indirect revenge shows its counter-effect against the observer' as a shot that has backfired. [Translation mine]

Including philosophical concepts of Schopenhauer these deepest thoughts of Pauli culminate in the remark that[270]

> Beside the 'nexus physicus' ... there exists a further connection between the phenomena of our world; a connection which as 'somehow

---

[268] *'Die berühmte "Unvollständigkeit" der Quantenmechanik (Einstein) ist doch irgendwie - irgendwo tatsächlich vorhanden, sie ist natürlich gar nicht behebbar durch Rückkehr zur klassischen Feldphysik (das ist nur ein 'neurotisches Missverständnis' Einsteins), hat vielmehr zu tun mit ganzheitlichen Beziehungen zwischen "Innen"und "Aussen," welche die heutige Naturwissenschaft nicht enthält (die aber die Alchemie vorausgeahnt hat und die sich auch in meiner Traumsymbolik nachweisen lässt, von der ich meine, dass sie gerade die eines heutigen Physikers charakterisiert).'"*

[269] *'[Der quantenphysikalische Akt der Beobachtung erscheine einem wie eine] "schwarze Messe"...nach welcher die "misshandelte" Materie, indirekt "sich rächend", ihre Gegenwirkung gegen den "Beobachter" als "hinten hinausgehender Schuss" manifestiert. '*

[270] *"[es] ausser dem 'nexus physicus' ... noch eine andere Verbindung zwischen den Erscheinungen dieser Welt [gibt], eine 'durch das Wesen an sich aller Dinge gehende', 'gleichsam eine unterirdische Verbindung', den 'nexus metaphysicus'".*

subterranean' is stamped by the fact that it penetrates the essence of all things, the 'nexus metaphysicus'. [Translation mine]

This subterranean connection[271] would then be[272]

> A direct effect of the essence of the things per se, thus of the inside onto nature,' whilst 'the causal law would only be the outer ligament of the phenomena'. [Translation mine]

Then[273] Pauli translates Schopenhauer's terms into the language of C.G. Jung's depth psychology. 'The essence of the things per se' would thus become Jung's collective unconscious, Schopenhauer's Will 'the stream of the archetypes following their energetic decline,' and 'metaphysicus' becomes 'psychologicus,' depth psychological.

If we insert the depth psychological terms into the above context, we obtain the following hypothesis: The subterranean connection takes place in the collective unconscious, which Pauli at this time surely understood psychophysically. Thus, he very closely approached the singular acausal twin processes in and out of the *unus mundus*. Since, however, he did not realize the bipolar energy term and thus neither the Eros ego as well as the Eros Self he was not able to differentiate between the collective unconscious, the Logos Self, with its content, the spirit-psyche, and psychophysical reality, the Eros Self with its matter-psyche. Without the bipolarity of the energy term he was neither able to realize the singular acausal twin process. Of course as a consequence he was also blocked to realize Body-Centered Imagination, though so many of his dreams talked about the development of such an introverted method based on the Eros ego.

However, the Nobel laureate was on the right track, and his brilliant thoughts paved the way for my discoveries. Somehow he realized that—though not with the help of the ;nexus psychologicus' but with the 'nexus psychophysicus'—it could perhaps be possible to influence outer nature with the help of a deeply rooted inner process, without using any outer influencing, as it is necessary in physics. This would however only be possible, if the ego follows Schopenhauer's Will, i.e., the natural energetic decline of the archetypes, which in contrast to Pauli and Jung I regard as being an acausal process. Concretely this means that we have to give up the idea that we can observe the totality of the processes in

---

[271] *The reader perhaps realizes that Pauli talks of this essence in a similar way as of how today's physicists talk about the neutrino/antineutrino. Further we are spontaneously reminded of Marie-Louise von Franz' hypothesis of the one-continuum. I would say that this 'essence' consists in what I call the matter-psyche.*

[272] *"ein unmittelbares Wirken vom Wesen der Dinge an sich, also vom Inneren auf die Natur', während 'das Kausalgesetz bloss das Band der Erscheinungen' sei.'*

[273] *For the following see WB 4/II, p. 746*

the universe with the help of the experiment designed by the conscious will and accept that our observation must become acausal, as described above. This would further mean that we should very carefully examine UFO encounter and abduction, in which, though unconsciously, exactly this mode of observation happens. This would further mean that as many humans as possible should begin to do Body-Centered Imagination, in which exactly the accidental observation mode is applied.

In the letter [1864] to Fierz the Nobel laureate mentions C.G. Jung's and his postulate of psychic relativity of space and time. He states that Schopenhauer's Will, the energetic stream in the collective unconscious (I would say, as well as in the psychophysical reality) following its own decline can[274] break through space and time. In a further letter to his colleague two days later[275] he stresses that in contrast to the opinion of the natural scientific 'classicism' [causal Newtonian/Einsteinian physics; RFR] space and time are connected to human consciousness. Thus, he almost realizes the ability of an altered consciousness being able to let dilate the measure of space and of time[276]. Since he is however not conscious of the possibility of the altered Eros state, he is unable to realize that it is exactly the moment of the *kairos*, in which the Eros ego observes the quantum leap in the Eros Self, in the *unus mundus*, in which space and time of physics are broken through and an incarnation event in the world of the world soul/subtle body is reached.

In the same letter Pauli mentions[277] that he—for a last time—met C.G. Jung in his Tower in Bollingen, Switzerland. He writes that Jung pointed to the fact that Albertus Magnus (circa 1200 to 1280 A.C.), the church father and alchemist, was stamped by magic ideas, especially the one of an 'überschwere Form von Materie,' an overly-heavy form of matter. Of course we are immediately reminded of uranium and the transuranian elements, which all are radioactive. Further we remember the higher-energetic quarks and leptons as well as the efforts of physicists to empirically prove the existence of the so-called Higgs boson—it is also called the God particle!—also an overly-heavy form of matter, which should help to unify the four elementary forces. Could this effort perhaps be a first, however unconscious and thus incomplete (and destructive) attempt to approach Hermetic magic, which was constellated in Wolfgang Pauli? Could it also be that by these physical imaginations my hypothesis is backed that these endeavors of the conscious will and power of the Logos ego will lead to destructive effects, as it is the case with artificial fission? Only the future can answer this question. Perhaps it will soon be answered on the day when the first Higgs particle is produced in CERN in Geneva, Switzerland[278].

---

[274] WB 4/II, p. 745
[275] WB 4/II, p. 748-750; letter [1867] of August 12, 1954; especially p. 748-749
[276] See section 6.12.2.4
[277] For the following see WB 4/II, p. 749
[278] See http://en.wikipedia.org/wiki/Large_Hadron_Collider

We know that the idea of a possible replacement of the quantum physical black mass by a more conscious form of magic did not let go of Pauli. When he died four years later in the Rotkreuz Hospital on the other side of the street of his ETH office, one found as his last reading matter before his early death the book *Der Magier, Das Leben des Albertus Magnus* (The Magician, the life of Albertus Magnus) by Rudolf Baumgardt[279].

/ / /

Here I would like to present the reader the essence of the above dream. It shows that radioactivity—artificial as well as natural—is a phenomenon that happens not only on the physical but also on the background of the psychophysical reality. The motif of the sun eclipse shows however, that the psychophysical aspect of it is only observable with the help of the 'dimmed consciousness,' the Eros ego. On the psychophysical layer the motif means of course the *coniunctio* of the divine feminine with the divine masculine principle, the result of which is first the creation of the intermediary layer (W. Pauli), the Seal of Solomon, the philosophical gold or the *lapis*. Its second goal consists in the creation of the red tincture, the 'psychophysical radioactivity' symbolically equivalent to the quintessence and to the *infans solaris*. In connection with the place where the dream happens, the latter motif comes back in my association/amplification with Pauli's 'child in Sweden,' which is nothing less than exactly the above second goal of the *coniunctio* or *unio corporalis*. Translated into a modern language, the creation of the *infans solaris*—symbolically equivalent to the extraction of the red tincture or of the quintessence—means the observation of increased order in one's own body on the one hand—the creation of the vegetative or subtle body—on the other the observation of increased order in the *unus mundus*, in the vegetative or subtle body of the universe, the world soul.

We have further seen that in the year 1934 Pauli began to have dreams, which connected such a work on the basis of the Eros principle with magic influences on the development of the world, which he interpreted as a parapsychological phenomenon. The Nobel laureate already realized that the solution of this problem lies in an 'extended physics,' which includes parapsychology and in this way integrates the enigmatic statement of Marie-Louise von Franz's dream that she has to integrate 'the psychological equivalent to the atomic bomb,'[280] which in fact is the psychophysical equivalent. We can thus conclude that a method like BCI/SST could be this solution for in some way it helps create the 'anti-nuclear bomb'[281].

---

[279] *WB 4/II, p. 750; note 4 of the editor K. v. Meyenn*
[280] *WB 4/II, p. 352; p. 713*
[281] *I thank Gregory J. Sova for the definition of this term*

Such a task, the real challenge of the 21st century, is only possible, if the physicist transforms into a 'psychophysicist.' This way the detached observer (W. Pauli) of the supposed inanimated outer nature becomes a real participator and counteracts what the Nobel laureate called the 'black mass' of quantum physics. He half consciously realizes that this black mass is a result of his inventions, especially of the spin and of the neutrino, and even feels remorse and repentance for his inventions.

As an enthusiast of Schopenhauer, Pauli looks for the solving of this problem with the help of some of his concepts. He realizes that besides the causal and statistically causal laws of physics, 'the outer ligament of the phenomena,' there could exist 'a direct effect…of the inside onto nature' that he anticipated as a third type of law of nature. I translate this idea of Schopenhauer/Pauli into the concept of the *nexus psychophysicus*, the possibility of parapsychological/psychokinetic and magic action with the help of Body-Centered Imagination and Symptom-Symbol Transformation. In it, in the moment of the *kairos*, the completely willless moment of the singular quantum leap, a new creation and incarnation happens, in which by mere introverted participation the quality of the subtle body/world soul, the background of the here and now of the physical body as well as of the universe, is spontaneously increased. Since in this moment the physical/metric spacetime is broken through, the incarnation happens not only in one part of the body and in one human, but in the whole body and in the whole universe. In this way the destructive effects of the artificial fission of the atom as a result of the deification of man—who in 1945 with the help of the first fission physicists began to ape the world soul—can be annulled and a positive and constructive development of the individual as well as of the collective situation can be reached. Since Wolfgang Pauli's last reading was a book about magic, it seems that he half-consciously anticipated this crucial task of the beginning 21st century.

6.16.4 The new house dreams: the vegetative body, the Seal of Solomon and the singular quantum leap

As we remember, Pauli stated that the series of dreams following the one about the radioactive core and the eclipse of the sun provide the best context to this dream. Most of these dreams contain the house motif, which then began to occupy the Nobel laureate very intensely. Further, we realized that in my 'synchronous synchronicity' dream I parallelized the house in the bridge's pier with an old image showing the house as a symbol of the gross body/vegetative body. My occupation as a healer, which I began in 1987, showed me many times that this is in fact the case: Houses in dreams often speak of the gross body/ vegetative body relation, of the perception of the body with the CNS on the one hand, with the VNS on the other. I will therefore include this empirical fact to show that Pauli's dreams speak of the transformation of the physical body into the vegetative body, the process only observable with the help of the Eros ego.

Pauli's new house dreams are of great importance insofar as they connect Hermetic alchemy with the deepest problem constellated in him. This we see explicitly in a statement of C.G. Jung's about the round house in Rypley's *Cantilena*[282]:

> The 'house of the sphere' is the *vas rotundum*, whose roundness represents the cosmos and, at the same time, the world-soul, which in Plato surrounds the physical universe from outside. The secret content of the Hermetic vessel is the original chaos from which the world was created. As the filius Macrocosmi and the first man the king is destined for 'rotundity,' i.e., wholeness...

Thus, though C.G. Jung talks in a Neoplatonic way of psychic wholeness and not of a new creation on the physical level, he equates the (round) house with the world soul as well as with the savior of the universe, and since they are secretly identical with the vegetative body, also with the latter.

To make the development of the gross body into the vegetative body for the reader more understandable, I must first flash back to a development in my life of the year 1982. In this year, without knowing of the reproaches of Wolfgang Pauli discussed above, for scientific and ethical reasons I renounced the diploma of the Zurich C.G. Jung Institute. I had to professionally orient myself anew. I began to learn that instead of desperately running around and looking for a job, I had just to wait and have a look what my dreams could tell me about my professional future. Then on March 27, 1983 I had a crucial dream about Albert Einstein:

DREAM OF EINSTEIN'S SILVERY PLAQUETTE ON HIS BELLY:

> I am together with my father and my brother. Einstein visits us and to my great surprise he tells me that he is my grandfather. He wears a very old-fashioned suit, similar to the ones of Sigmund Freud or of the orthodox Jews. The inventor of Special and General Relativity Theory shows me a big silvery plaquette, which he always wears on his upper belly, in the

---

[282] CW 14, § 373

region of the solar plexus. He tells us—and I become even more astonished—that it protects him against injuries.

In more or less two hours Einstein will be honoured. Strangely enough this will happen in a church by a divine service. All three of us would like to take part in this service. We all must first take a bath, first my father, then my brother and I as the third and last.

The end I do not remember very clearly. I know however that it has to do with dimming my consciousness.

As usual in Jung's depth psychological methodology one first associates to the motifs of the dream. I give here these associations together with some further ideas I had later:

My father: He would have liked to become a physician. Since he was one of 16 children, because of financial reasons this was impossible. Thus he became a businessman, however he was not happy with his profession. He sometimes tried to be a healer, however he did not really do goal-directed work for becoming one. Thus he died without having lived his life.

Einstein: SRT and GRT. Later I realized that 'Einstein' is an aspect in me which is very similar to Pauli's magician, stranger and master, and that he has to do with the Eros Self.

Sigmund Freud: The couch. I did not like this association, since for me C.G. Jung's change to sitting face by face during psychoanalysis seemed to me a better setting. Today, however, in my healing profession in some way I returned insofar to Freud's couch as during doing SST/BCI my patients lie.

Silver: In my mandala presented above the innermost circle of triangles is silvery, protecting in this way the hole in the middle.

Plaquette: The Einstein plaquette, which is some sort of a Nobel award for mathematicians.

Solar plexus: In the course of time I realized that the plaquette protects the solar plexus, the place where Paracelsus' Archaeus was situated. The latter symbolizes what I call today the matter-psyche or yin energy. I further associated the fact that Siberian shamans believe that disease enters through a hole in the belly. Further during this time I suffered psychosomatic symptoms, especially cramps in the upper belly, together with cramps in the neck, and many times I had a heavy headache.

Divine service: It seems that all this has to do with a religious attitude.

Bathing: I had read of the alchemical *albedo*, the whitening, which Jung interprets as the dealing with the shadow. Today I would say that the *albedo* corresponds to the passive Eros state of Body-Centered Imagination. Of course I was also reminded of the white aspect of my red/white mandala. Later I had dreams, which showed me that 'white' meant 'the white lady,' a synonym of the *anima mundi*, of the world soul.

Dimming the consciousness: As a means against my psychosomatic symptoms I began during that time to do exercises, which brought my energy from the head down into the belly. It was the spontaneous, completely unconscious beginning of Body Centered Imagination respectively Symptom-Symbol Transformation, which always begin with some exercises like this.

With these associations and later insights we can interpret the dream: My father means my healer aspect which I neither lived—my 'inner Paracelsus.' After this dream I had to develop the healer myself, i.e., to concentrate on the great Renaissance physician's *Archaeus*, which according to him has its seat in the upper belly. Further I had to give up depth psychological analysis except dream interpretation, which I combine today with SST. 'Einstein' of the dream is the 'guru,' the magician. This is a funny detail, since in reality he was of course a very intellectual scientist. Here however he becomes the magician. The Einstein plaquette, the 'Nobel award' for mathematicians is related to the belly, to the solar plexus and thus to the Eros ego. Thus, this motif means that the Logos ego and the Eros ego have to come together, exactly what happens in BCI and SST.

Much later I better understood why 'Einstein' played such a decisive role in my dreams (I dreamed many dreams of him): The symbol Einstein means Special Relativity Theory applied to the psychological and psychophysical level. Like this 'Einstein' has in fact some heritage for me, the idea of SRT (and also of GRT), which I applied to the psychophysical level. The reader remembers that in my theory and empirical experience in the state of the Eros ego the measures of space and of time are dilated and in the extreme case even abolished and overcome—my psychophysical relativity theory. The divine service for Einstein means a religious attitude, the behavior of modern mystics beyond any religious confession, who are related to the deceased in the Beyond on the one hand, and on the other to their vegetative body. To do so it is however absolutely necessary to dim the Logos ego: The realization of the transformation of the Logos ego into the Eros ego centered on the belly, the solar plexus.

After this dream of March 1983 I began to test Symptom-Symbol Transformation on myself, and after four years fate decided that I have to work with a famous Swiss pastor who dealt with the poor and sick people. In 1987 I met by chance the above mentioned woman who suffered a severe Multiple Sclerosis[283]. Half unconsciously I applied SST to her disease and to my great surprise she recovered completely. Today she no longer has any symptoms of MS.

At the beginning of school, age 7, the woman concerned began to draw many images with a house—her parents' home—with what she called the mole's tunnels (see image 6.28):

Figure 6.29:
The house with the mole's tunnels
[Source: Image collection of Remo F. Roth]

Of course we are immediately reminded of Pauli's above subterranean connections, which in my interpretation symbolize the world of the vegetative body as a counterpart of the gross body. Entering primary school is critical, since the original Eros ego of children has to change into the Logos ego. Thus, we can be sure that these images were like compensations to the 'rape' by the intellectualism of our education system. Future historical research could perhaps establish that Pauli suffered the same situation.

---

[283] *See section 6.15*

These images presented to me in the year 1987 were the first hint for my supposition that the symbol of the house in dreams and other products out of the unconscious shows mostly the gross body/vegetative body relationship. This remark leads us back to Pauli's house dreams. Before we can deal with them I must tell the reader of a further crucial dream, since it contains a parallel motif to one in Pauli's house dreams that I will present. I had the dream much earlier than the above, on February 14, 1975, on Valentine's Day, the day of Eros, a circumstance which I later interpreted as being synchronistic.

In the evening of February 13, 1975 I listened to a lecture of Marie-Louise von Franz. There she told us first that C.G. Jung was once asked if there could exist something else behind the Self. He answered that this is possible. However, it is meaningless to talk about it, since people do not even understand what he means by the Self. In the lecture she backed Jung's statement with an age-old alchemic text: *Komarios to Cleopatra*. She showed that in this text between the four original steps of the *opus*, the *nigredo,* the *albedo,* the *citrinitas* and the *rubedo* there are four further steps as shown below (see figure 6.31).

The fourth of these in-between steps is called 'The treatment with the vessel with breasts.' It is an alchemical vessel and similar to the one known as the pelican. The latter looks like this (see figure 6.30):

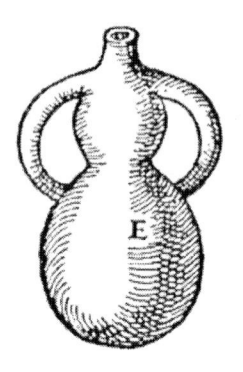

Figure 6.30:
The pelican
[Source: Jung, CW 13, plate B7 after § 190]

It is the retort with the help of which the so-called circular distillation is realized: After pouring the liquid into it, one corks the top. Then one heats the bottom, and in this way the liquid vaporizes. This is the distillation. Since the vessel is closed and possesses the two tubes, the 'breasts,' lead back to the bottom, the vapour condenses again and a circulatory process begins. The alchemists believed that as a consequence the liquid becomes more and more refined. This refined liquid was the goal of the *opus*, corresponding to the philosophical gold or the *lapis*, the alchemical stone, the first goal of the *coniunctio*, but also to the red tincture and the quintessence, the second goal.

In modern language we can postulate that with the circular distillation the Hermetic alchemists anticipated the twin process and its quantum leap: The vaporizing corresponds to the first process, the creation of the matter-psyche with potentially altered quality, the condensing to the 're-materialization,' to the creation of the spirit-psyche with realized altered quality as a result of the singular quantum leap. As we realized, this was a complete projection, since in such processes nothing new was created. The physicist would say that an energy transformation had taken place. However, applied to one's own body in SST, the procedure is in fact acausal and leads into the singular quantum leap with its healing effect.

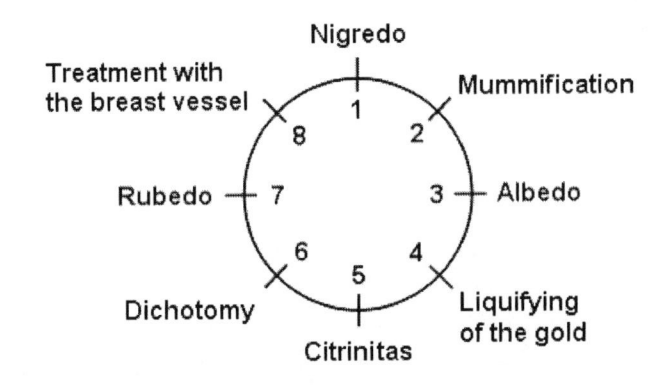

Figure 6.31:
The eightfold alchemical opus
[Source: Remo F. Roth according to Marie-Louise von Franz]

But let us now return to the *opus* of Komarius. Figure 6.31 shows how the four further steps are integrated into the original *opus*. They are called the mummification, the liquifying of the gold, the dichotomy and, as I mentioned above, the treatment with the breast vessel, the pelican. For Marie-Louise von Franz the breast vessel, in which the last step of the extended *opus* of Komarius happens, was a symbol for the archetype behind Jung's (Logos) Self. Thus she yet half consciously anticipated the Eros Self[284].

---

[284] As I was able to observe, because of her severe disease Marie-Louise von Franz began to deal with SST and thus with a relation of the Eros ego with the Eros Self. However, she was not yet able to integrate SST into C.G. Jung's theory (which had required an extension of the latter). Thus, she found the empirical solution of the problem, Wolfgang Pauli however the theoretical. As we have seen in section 6.16.1, he was not able to step further to the

I was very impressed by the content of this lecture, but of course did not understand anything. I went to bed and in the morning dreamed the following dream[285]:

THE DREAM OF THE WOODEN SCULPTURES IN THE ADJACENT ROOM OF C.G. JUNG'S AND MARIE-LOUISE VON FRANZ' HOUSE

> I am in a villa, and around it there is a big and very beautiful park with large trees. It is the house where C.G. Jung and Marie-Louise von Franz live together. There are also other people there, and we sit at a very long rectangular table.
>
> C.G. Jung begins to speak and says: 'I'd like now to speak about the one that comes behind the Self...' He explains then what it is, but I forgot what it was.
>
> After this reunion I walk into a 'Nebenraum' (the *adjoining room*), a hall. Its entry is from outside (like the garages). Here at the walls there are *wooden sculptures*, which I palm. (Association of today: As a sculpturer I always palm sculptures. Only in this way I can really feel their soul—the soul of matter, matter-psyche.)

I did not understand this dream then. I wrote under it: 'I'm struggling with the Anima integration, and the unconscious comes with such a dream...' I did not yet know that it was a dream about the *anima mundi* and that the latter, as we realized above[286], is something completely other than C.G. Jung's Anima.

The dream is more or less self-explaining. It is obvious that it talks about what I call today the Eros Self symbolized in the ancient alchemical text *Komarios to Kleopatra* as the vessel with breasts, which is of course also a symbol of Eros. The villa (a big house) means the extension of Jung's and von Franz's theory by including the gross body/vegetative body relationship. The park with the beautiful vegetation means the *vegetativum*, the vegetative nervous system.

---

empirical way. On the other hand Marie-Louise von Franz was unable to find the theoretical solution. In my opinion this fact is a symbolical complement to the complete breaking, with which they ended their relationship. Since then this split between depth psychology and physics was never really overcome.

[285] *It is a funny and even synchronistic detail that I had this dream on February 14, 1975; on Valentines Day.*

[286] *See section 5.2.1.6 of Part I*

But now the very interesting and crucial detail comes: I abandon the house and enter from outside the *adjacent* room, a real hall. In the course of time I learned with the help of my own dreams and those of my patients that the adjacent room means the vegetative body. It is the 'vegetative space,'[287] the place where vegetative life happens. Thus, the adjacent room is a symbol of the belly brain or gut brain.

In the adjacent room there are wooden sculptures. 'Wood' means 'vegetative;' thus again the stressing of the VNS. Sculptures are 'formed matter,' thus both symbols together mean the vegetative body to be created. Further, sculptures mirror reality and are in this way an *image* of reality—as is the image out of the belly in BCI/SST.

The end of the dream consists in the palming of the wooden sculptures. Later I realized that I had to integrate my hands into Symptom-Symbol Transformation: The patients lie on the couch—Sigmund Freud in his old-fashioned frock coat comes back—and with the help of my hands I assist them to come down from the head and enter the belly brain. Then everything else happens itself, spontaneously, acausally.

/ / /

I will discuss three new house dreams of Pauli. He wrote about them to von Franz in 1954[288], in which the new house is however a laboratory, further to Fierz in 1955[289], and to Jung in 1956[290]. I chose these dreams since they contain motifs which are also very important in my theory.

The first dream is of February 17, 1954, and Pauli dreamed it in Princeton where he for some months studied biology. As we remember, four years before exactly in Princeton the physicist experienced the Pauli effect with the cyclotron catching fire. We will realize that there is in fact a close connection between the dream and the Princeton Pauli effect. Let us first have a look at the dream[291]:

---

[287] *In German the terms for room and space are identical: Der Raum.*
[288] *WB 4/II, p. 575, letter [1772]; see also WB 4/II, p. 729-730, letter [1856] where Pauli interprets the new house as a stable end product of the 'radioactive' processes*
[289] *WB 4/III, p. 434, letter [2209]*
[290] *WB 4/III, p. 713-715, letter [2367]*
[291] *WB 4/II, p. 575; translation mine*

DREAM OF THE JAGGED SQUARE IN THE ADJACENT ROOM[292]:

> I am in a laboratory in which strange experiments are done. The Master calls me with the words '*Professor* Pauli.' Then he leads me into an adjacent room and points to an image and says: '*This* seems to interest you much.' The image looked like this:

2, 4, 8, 16, 64, …
(also die Potenzen von zwei)⁴

Hier *fremde* Worte –
wie „Gir" „Mati" etc.,
die ich *nicht* verstehe

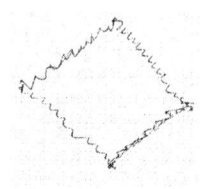

(Die Seiten des auf der Spitze stehenden Quadrates waren in eigentümlicher Weise *zackig* – wie Drähte.)

The adjacent room with the jagged square

[English translation of the German remarks:
Above left: 'Thus the powers of two.'
Below left: 'Here unfamiliar words as "Gir," "Mati," that I do *not* understand.'
Below right: 'The sides of the square standing on its point were *jagged* in a peculiar way—like wires.']

As the editor of the *Wissenschaftliche Briefwechsel* remarks[293], the laboratory is of course again one in which there are radioactive substances. The strange experiments concern thus exactly the above psychophysical radioactive cores of which Pauli does not know anything, i.e., is not conscious of. The laboratory seems to have an adjacent room, obviously a motif related to the new house, and the very important event happens there: The magician/master shows Pauli there the jagged square. We must therefore discover what it symbolizes.

As we have just realized, the adjacent room means the 'vegetative space,' i.e., the place where the vegetative process happens, the belly brain or gut brain. Thus the jagged square belongs to or is created in the belly brain. As we have further seen, this is only possible with the help of the Eros ego, for example in Body-Centered Imagination.

---

[292] My dream's title
[293] WB 4/II, p. 577, note 3

To find out what the square could symbolize we must first deal with the powers of #2 noted left above. In a letter to C.A. Meier of August 1st, 1950 Pauli writes[294] that #2 and its powers are insofar attributes of the continuum as we divide it with the help of these numbers. Obviously he talks of the infinite division of the angle, which is in fact only possible with the powers of #2. The continuum is insofar connected to causal Newtonian and Einsteinian physics as their equations have always to be continuous. This means especially that no discontinuity is allowed. Thus #2 and its powers symbolize the continuum of causal physics.

In a footnote[295] in the same letter [1145] to Meier of August 1st, 1950, Pauli states that the three rhythms of his World-clock vision are not continuously related, but *discontinuously*. #3 would so become a symbol of discontinuity and thus of acausality. A day later in letter [1146] he writes to Aniela Jaffé a similar hypothesis[296]: In the symbolism of the mandala of the World-clock the three represents discontinuity; the four continuity. We will just see that the interpretation of #3 and #2 (respectively #4) in this way connects the World-clock vision to the above dream.

The understanding of a further aspect of the dream needs some knowledge in quantum physics. The reader remembers the wave function. It is a linear combination of some terms each of which describes a potential incarnation, similar to the *potential being* of the matter-psyche with potentially altered quality of the above defined twin process. Every term of the wave function is imaginary, which means that all are multiplied with i, the root of -1.

In the image below I show the so called unity circle in the plane, defined by the imaginary numbers i and -i and the real numbers 1 and -1.

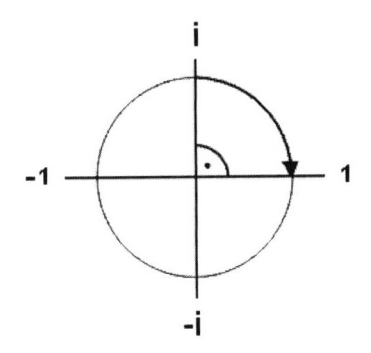

Figure 6.32:
The unity circle in the complex plane

---

[294] WB 4/I, p. 145-146
[295] WB 4/I, p. 147, note **
[296] WB 4/I, p. 147

As long as the situation is potential, i.e., the wave function has not yet collapsed, as long as 'the acausal condenser' remains charged, all terms of the wave function are defined on the straight line i/-i and its prolongation. In the moment of the quantum leap, of the collapse of the wave function, all terms except one become zero (we do not know which one; this is why the process is acausal). The one acausally chosen, however, becomes real, which means that it lays on the horizontal line 1/-1. Thus, geometrically seen, the quantum leap means a rotation through a right angle or of 90 degrees on the circle. This is what is demonstrated in the image.

If we now take a further look at the square in Pauli's dream we realize that it is created by jags. As we just realized, the '90 degree jags' symbolize quantum leaps or collapses of the wave function. Thus on a psychophysical level we reach the following result: *The square is created by singular quantum leaps*. Or in a slightly different terminology: *The square is created by the union of continuity with discontinuity* (which the quantum leap in fact is). In alchemical terms: the square is created by the *coniunctio* of the queen and the king. In fact, Pauli stresses in his letter to Fierz[297] as well as in the one to Jung[298] that the main motif of the dreams of this time, especially of the dream of the new houses, is the union of the opposites, the *coniunctio*.

The above is a very important result, since it combines the visual-auditive experience of the dancing Chinese with the World-clock vision that I will interpret at the end of the book[299]. The result of all the activities in this dream are four squares which are arranged in the spiral order, with which in *Aion* C.G. Jung demonstrates the development of the Self during the Christian aeon[300].

We can now interpret the whole of the dream: In the belly brain [= the adjacent room] a union of continuity [= #2 and its powers] and discontinuity [= the jags; #3], i.e., singular quantum leaps [= union of continuity and discontinuity] happen, which create the square. The latter term is still symbolic, and I can only interpret it in the discussion of the dream of the dancing Chinese, the *anima mundi*. Thus, I mention here without any proof that the square is a symbol of what I call a 'renewed spacetime.'

As we know, the 'adjacent room' and its contents are only observable with the help of the Eros ego. This is what Pauli because of his identification with the Logos is not conscious about, and this is exactly what annoys the magician extremely. In a letter to C.G. Jung's wife Emma Jung[301] from 1950 the physicist

---

[297] WB 4/III, p. 434-438, letter [2209] of December 10th, 1955
[298] AaA, p. 134-152, letter [69P] of October 23rd, 1956; WB 4/III, p. 712-731; PJB, p. 131-151, letter [69]; Pauli titles the letter with 'Statements of the Psyche'
[299] See section 6.16.8
[300] CW 9/II, §§ 390-391
[301] AaA, p. 49-53; letter [44P] of November 16, 1950; the following on p. 50-51; PJB, p. 53-54; WB 4/I, p. 185

writes that the magician/stranger resembles Mercury and Merlin, and that he unifies 'a spiritual-light figure with superior knowledge' with 'a chthonic natural spirit'[302]. Then the most important aspect of the magician is mentioned: He is 'the one who prepares the way for the quaternity, which is always pursuing him.' This statement corresponds completely to the content of the above dream. What we should have in mind here is the fact that the magician is not a symbol of C.G. Jung's quaternity. As Mercury he is symbolized as the Seal of Solomon. Thus, somehow the Seal prepares for the quaternity. We will come across this process again in Pauli's visual-auditive experience of the Chinese woman.

Women and children, who are in dreams a frequent symbol for the Eros principle, like the magician[303], much more than men, who represent the Logos principle. We can understand this refusal, since the magician regards scientists as well as the Nobel laureate as 'completely ignorant and uneducated compared with himself.' He likes magic but thinks that the ancient books about it are only 'a popular preliminary stage for people with no education,' the latter especially being meant for Pauli. The magician/stranger is not an 'Antichrist,' but an 'Antiscientist.' He hates the scientific approach taught in universities today, and he sees them as a place of oppression. He criticizes Jung, insofar as he replaces the term 'synchronicity' by 'radioactivity.'

The physicist summarizes then as follows[304]:

> The stranger's attitude toward science is very similar to that of Ahasuerus toward Christianity: This stranger is something that did not accept the scientific world picture about 300 years ago [during the 17th century when modern science was born; RFR] and is now running around autonomously in the collective unconscious like a loose cannon; in doing so, it is becoming more and more loaded with 'mana'.

In a modern terminology we would say that Pauli's magician is loaded with matter-psyche. He is symbolically identical with the acausal condenser, and thus charged. We can also say that he corresponds to the principle of the potential twin process. The Nobel laureate, however, is not conscious of the existence of matter-psyche, of the Eros ego and thus neither of the twin process. Thus the magician causes his 'moods of depression or incomprehensible affects'[305] £and of course also the Pauli effects.

---

[302] *In my terminology: The Logos philosophicus combined with the Logos Spermatikos, the combination of causality and acausality in the twin process.*
[303] For the following see AaA, p. 51, PJB, p. 54; WB 4/1, p. 185
[304] AaA, p. 51; PJB, p. 54; WB 4/1, p. 185
[305] AaA, p. 51; PJB, p. 54; WB 4/1, p. 185

Let us now have a brief look at two dreams of the new house, which happened after the above, on July 20, 1954 and on May 20, 1955. Both have further to do with three popes. I quote here a shortened version of the first dream in the English translation[306]:

DREAM OF THE THREE POPES, WHO GIVE PAULI A NEW HOUSE AS A PRESENT[307]:

I am in Copenhagen, at the home of Niels Bohr and his wife, Margarethe. He makes an announcement to me, a very official one: 'Three *popes* have given you a house.'...He then presents me with a sort of document of the gift, and I *sign* it. ...

I regret very much that my wife is not present, for what can I do in a new house without her?

(Here I wake up briefly but soon go back to sleep. The dream continues.)

A late uncle of mine form Austria, a Catholic, appears to me in the dream, and I say to him: 'The new house is for you and your family. I hope you will enjoy it.'

With Bohr Pauli associates complementarity. However, it was exactly Bohr who was ready to accept the violation of the energy conservation law in the case of the beta decay. This is also the reason why his interests gravitated more and more toward the question of the connection of physics and life. The acceptance of the violation would have opened the way for the inclusion of the paranormal twin process. In fact, to the deceased Catholic the Nobel laureate also associates magic and parapsychology. He states that behind the Catholic mass—remember quantum physics as a 'black mass' above—a magic thinking is hidden, since in contrast to quantum physics, the transformation of the 'experimenter' is included—a topic Pauli in connection with the 'detached observer' of physics dealt with intensely. Further, it is a deceased who is invited to live in the house. Thus, including the above interpretation of the house as the gross body as well as the vegetative body and the place of the transformation, we can conclude that besides dealing with the vegetative body on the one hand, on the other some sort of a relationship with the Beyond is presented in the dream. This is exactly the topic of Symptom-Symbol Transformation and Body-Centered Imagination.

---

[306] *AaA, p. 135-137; PJB, p. 135-136; WB 4/III, p. 713-714*
[307] *My dream's title*

The dream helps us to realize that the creation of the vegetative body, which corresponds to Dorneus' second phase of his *opus*, to the *unio corporalis*, is in fact followed by a third phase. Dorneus called this third and last phase the reunion with the *unus mundus*. In a modern terminology I call the second phase Symptom-Symbol Transformation with the goal of the transformation of the gross body into the vegetative body. On the other hand the third phase corresponds to Body-Centered Imagination, dealing with the observation of the creation of increased order in the world of the world soul, in the psychophysical reality or *unus mundus*. My experience as a healer shows however that the two phases cannot be distinguished too exactly, since one never knows when SST suddenly develops further into BCI.

There are three popes who give Pauli the house as a present. After all that we have seen above, three means of course 'energy.' This interpretation will be backed by the other dream I will interpret here, in which there are three 'anti-Popes,' with whom he spontaneously associates the above dream. The symbol 'pope' we can interpret as a belief, a hypothesis. Together with the 'anti-Popes' this symbol means thus the bipolar energy term, which is in fact a hypothesis which has to be proven by observable events.

Then the Nobel laureate laments the absence of his wife. Of course we can interpret this motif on the one hand as the absence of the Eros ego the main function of which is the feeling (= wife). Pauli gives us another hint. He says that his wife is a sensation type—exactly the contrary to him, who was intuitive. He mentions that the main function of his wife as well as his inferior function, both being sensation, is missing in his new house.

If we remember once again that the symbol house means the vegetative body and further that the latter can only be experienced and observed with the help of the Eros ego and the *vegetative* sensation, we realize that the dream talks of the task of observing the creation of the subtle body with the help of the Eros ego and its introverted vegetative sensation—thus, Body-Centered Imagination and/or Symptom-Symbol Transformation.

/ / /

The third dream, of May 20, 1955, does not really deal with a new house which is given as a present to Pauli. However, as I mentioned above, it is connected to the second dream by the motif of the 'lower mirror image of the three Popes.' This is why the dream becomes very important to him. Its (shortened) translation into English is as follows[308]:

---

[308] *AaA, p. 148-149, PJB, p. 147-148*

DREAM OF THE LOWER MIRROR IMAGE OF THE THREE POPES[309]:

Once again I am in a laboratory, and this time Einstein is conducting the experiments. All they consist of is intercepting rays on the screen. Above the screen is the 'unknown woman' (this time resembling a certain Miss M.). On the screen, there now appears an optical diffraction pattern, consisting of one central and two subsidiary maxima. This is how I describe the image as a physicist; it looks somehow like this:

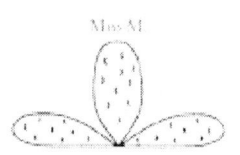

The threefold optical diffraction pattern

The picture resembles a leaf. Marks now appear on the 'leaves' then the woman fades away and finally disappears. But now *children* appear on both sides of the picture; the woman has gone and is forgotten—only the children and the pictures are important.

Context: I regard Einstein as a manifestation of the 'master' [thus also of the magician; RFR]. I cannot see what is behind the screen. It is the unconscious, which is visible only when it comes up against a material object (screen). And yet it has its own autonomous energy, such as rays, against which the screen is also a protection.

I regard the image as a lower, *chthonic triad*…and it now looks to me like the *lower reflection of the three popes* from the earlier dream (20 July 1954). The appearance of the 3-leaf image and the disappearance of the 'anima' are parallel actions…

The labor we can again identify with the one in which radioactive experiments are conducted. This interpretation is backed by the physicist's remark in a letter to Marie-Louise von Franz of July 29, 1954[310], in which he interprets the house of a further new house dream as the '*stable* end product of the 'radioac-

---

[309] My dream's title
[310] See WB 4/II, p. 730, letter [1856]

tive' processes.' Pauli's 'Einstein' has now transformed into the magician. If we combine him with 'my Einstein,' we can conclude that he corresponds to an effect which allows the dilation of space and time, and as a consequence constellates the space-, time- and massless *unus mundus*. The second motif in the dream consists in the rays, which are directed to the screen, which leads to the effect that the three-fold 'leaf' is created.

In the same letter, in the associations to the dream before the above, Pauli mentions experiments with 'two neutrinos' and adds that neutrinos are an especially penetrating radiation. Thus, if we combine the two dreams we obtain the result that it is the neutrino/antineutrino, which creates the three-fold 'leaf.' The vegetative character and the three-foldness make us think of the matter-psyche, which I defined as the compensating aspect to the spirit-psyche, both together based on the bipolar energy term. *The dream would therefore like to convince Pauli that on a psychophysical level instead of the neutrino/antineutrino we should define the matter-psyche aspect of energy*. Further, it stresses the fact that artificial fission and in this way the creation of neutrinos/antineutrinos constellate the matter-psyche aspect of the universe, or expressed in a physical-symbolic language: Artificial fission charges the acausal psychophysical condenser. As a consequence also the twin processes and their spontaneous quantum leaps, the discharges, are constellated, which happen on the background of the double-triadic Seal of Solomon. Since the Seal as well as the bipolar energy term are constellated in the Nobel laureate's unconscious, he consistently associates with the three-fold leaf 'the lower mirror image of the three Popes.' Then he quotes the fact of the disappearing of the woman in the dream in the moment when the three-fold leaf is created, and adds that the disappearance of the Anima and the becoming visible of the leaf are parallel processes. There is only one possible interpretation of this scene: C.G. Jung's (one-dimensional) Anima disappears in the moment when the three-fold *anima mundi* appears. This motif reminds us immediately of the creation of the philosophical gold, the Seal of Solomon and the *lapis* as the first goal of the Hermetic *coniunctio*. The second goal, symbolized by the children of the dream is the creation of the *infans solaris*, synonymous to the red tincture and the quintessence.

/ / /

The summary of the above interpretation and conclusions gives the following result: Pauli was convinced that the dreams of the radioactive core belonged together with the new house dreams. As we realized, the house and especially the room/adjacent room is a symbol of the connection between the body perceived with the CNS and the subtle body observed with the help of the VNS. My dream of the Einstein plaquette shows further that such a transformation happens in the belly brain. The latter is symbolized by the alchemical breast vessel or the pelican.

The circular distillation in the vessel we can interpret as a series of twin processes and their result, the singular acausal quantum leaps. Since in my other dream in the adjacent room of Jung's and von Franz' house I find the sculpture, an image of reality, we realize that the sought after result of the *opus*, the red tincture or quintessence, corresponds to such images out of the gut brain.

With this information we can interpret the Nobel laureate's new house dreams. The first shows that it is in fact the adjacent room, the 'vegetative space' of the gut brain, in which the 'radioactive experiment,' the singular quantum leap of the twin process takes place. This process we can also interpret as the *coniunctio* of causality and acausality, symbolically seen as the union of number 2 and 3. Physically seen such processes are symbolized by the jag of 90 degrees. The square of Pauli's first new house dream is created by exactly such jags. Thus we can interpret that the singular quantum leaps create a new quaternity, a 'renewed spacetime.' We can further conclude that the master of this process, the 'producer,' is the magician, who chased Pauli in so many dreams.

A further of Pauli's new house dreams shows that the acausal transformation process does not only lead to the development of the vegetative body and thus to new health, but also to a relationship with the Beyond and the deceased. Further, the dream tells us that such phenomena are observed with the help of the *vegetative* sensation the relation with which requires the development of the Eros ego. This is a very important result, since most psychiatrists of today would interpret the above phenomenology as the symptoms of a psychosis, of schizophrenia. As already in the year 1981 Lee Sannella has shown[311], we must however very carefully distinguish these processes from the psychic disease[312].

The third of Pauli's new house dreams eventually leads us back to the double-triadic structure, the bipolar spirit-psyche/matter-psyche energy term symbolically represented by the Seal. It shows that it is in fact the neutrino radiation, the result of the artificial fission that leads to the creation of matter-psyche energy in the *unus mundus* and as a consequence to the charging of the acausal condenser. Since the psychophysical reality is space-, time- and mass-less and psychophysically nonlocal its constellation leads to phenomena, which contradict the physical laws of nature, the causal Newtonian/Einsteinian as well as the statistically causal of quantum physics. The phenomena connected with the matter-psyche aspect of energy are thus ruled by a 'third type of law of nature,'[313] unsuccessfully sought after by the Nobel laureate. As we realized above, the effects are UFO encounter and abduction

---

[311] See Sannella, Lee, Kundalini, Psychosis or Transcendence?, H.S. Dakin, San Francisco, 1981

[312] *We know that in the early fifties Pauli was afraid that he approached a psychosis. See letter [1625], in WB 4/II, p. 252. In Pauli's opinion the danger of a pychosis has very much to do with the oscillation symbolism, and it is banned as soon as the oscillations transform into rotation. Thus Pauli was not conscious about the difference between schizophrenia and the creation of the vegetative body described in my text. See also WB 4/II, p. 303, note 2.*

[313] WB 4/II, p. 310-311, 335-336 and 387-389

as well as other 'physically impossible' phenomena. Further, the dream tells us that in Pauli's case the Anima problem in Jung's meaning is a pseudoproblem, and that the real problem is the integration of the *anima mundi* and of the vegetative body.

6.16.5 Brass tones engraved in a metal plate and eggs as a confirmation of the psychophysical theory

The above conclusions are confirmed by two dreams Pauli had already in March 1948[314], shortly before he and the audience of the C.G. Jung Institute's foundation ceremony experienced the Fludd/flood synchronicity with the Chinese vase. The physicist quotes them in *Background Physics*[315], and one feels that he is deeply touched by them.

DREAM OF THE BRASS TONES ENGRAVED IN A METAL PLATE:

> My first physics teacher appears and says: 'The change in the splitting of the ground state of the H-atom is a fundamental one. Brass tones are engraved on a metal plate.' Then I go to Göttingen.

Since Pauli became a physicist because of his first impressions about the subject mediated by his first physics' teacher, we can interpret the motif of the doublet fine structures of spectral emission as the most important aspect of physics for him. As we realized, the splitting means the bipolar aspect of the energy term also expressed in so many dreams of Pauli by dark and bright stripes—remember his wasp phobia—and oscillations.

To the metal plate and the tones engraved in it the Nobel laureate gives the following remarks[316]:

> The metal plate...represents the material physical world (physis) in a relatively stable form. ...The tones...serve very well as symbols; with

---

[314] Date quoted according to *Enz*, p. 423
[315] For the following see *AaA*, p. 192-196; *PJB*, p. 188-192
[316] *AaA*, p. 194; *PJB*, p. 190-191

their connection to music, they represent feeling—the very thing that physics cannot express. With their connection to the music of the spheres (I was very involved with Kepler at the time), they have a cosmic character. As an acoustic phenomenon, they also belong to physis, so they are a symbol uniting physis and psyche.

We remember the stable substance in the dreams[317] above. It is the end product of the Hermetic *opus*, the result of creating the red tincture or the quintessence. The reader is further reminded that in my interpretation it symbolizes the incarnated product of the *coniunctio*, of the union of the continuous and the discontinuous world, of the twin process' singular quantum leap. It also symbolizes the destructive aspect of the *incarnatio* in the unconscious case, the Pauli effect, UFO encounter and abduction.

The end of the dream mostly shows the solution of the constellated problem. There the physicist has to go to Göttingen. In Göttingen a very famous Pauli effect happened[318]: Pauli's colleague Otto Stern prepared a large-scale experiment at the University of Göttingen, when one of the measuring instruments exploded. Since one did not find the reason, one began to believe in a Pauli effect in his absence. Pauli was thus asked what he did in the moment of the explosion. Exactly when the misfortune happened, he waited on the railway station of Göttingen, since coming from Zürich he had to change trains to visit Niels Bohr in Copenhagen. Once again, his presence close to the experiment caused a Pauli effect.

Symbolically seen, 'Göttingen' means therefore that Pauli should have become conscious of the background of the paranormal effect named after him. As we realized, this would have meant to give up the objectification of rotation, the spin, on the psychophysical level and its replacement by the concept of the subtle body/world soul located in the space-, time- and massless psychophysical reality with its nonlocal quality.

The tones, 'uniting physics and psyche,' engraved in the 'relatively stable' brass plate, i.e., in inorganic matter, tell us why the twin process with the singular (acausal) quantum leap can happen: *Matter/energy itself possesses a psychophysical aspect*[319]. *It is not just inanimate matter without any soul as materialistic science would like to make us believe. This is the naked truth science will have to accept against its materialistic worldview. The dream gives in this way a confirmation of the fact that UFO phenomena are real*[320]. *It is only the prejudice of the one-sided Logos, which prevents us from the observation of the psychophysical*

---

[317] See sections 6.12.2 and 6.12.3
[318] Quoted according to Fischer, E. P., An den Grenzen des Denkens, Wolfgang Pauli, Ein Nobelpreisträger über die Nachtseiten der Wissenschaft, Herder, Freiburg, Basel, Wien, 2000, p. 135-136.
[319] It can however only indirectly be observed, by the spontaneous quantum leap.
[320] And not a projection of the Self into the sky, as Jung believed.

aspect of the universe. However, this onesided view will more and more be compensated by phenomena like the above, and since most people are unconscious about the psychophysical reality they will be destructive.

The Nobel laureate then mentions that the tones as the creators of music have to do with the feeling function. Further, since during the time when he had this dream he was deeply involved in the Kepler/Fludd studies, he also associates with the cosmic character of this music, the music of the spheres both of the two antagonists were deeply impressed by.

Let us first have a look at the feeling aspect, which, as Pauli mentions, is absent in physics. As we remember, the introverted feeling belongs to the Eros ego defined above. Thus, the dream tells us that a necessary condition for the creation of the 'tones engraved in the metal plate' is the development of the Eros ego. The physicist further spontaneously associates the cosmic character of this specific music. Without knowing the process that I propose, Body-Centered Imagination, he thus anticipates half consciously that with the help of the Eros ego one can observe the sphere's music.

As he knows of his Kepler/Fludd studies, the sphere's music, an originally Pythagorean concept, belonged to the Hermetic *coniunctio*, creating as we realized in Chapter 4 as its last result the[321] '*infans solaris* [symbolically identical with the red tincture and the quintessence; RFR], which is at the same time the liberated world-soul.' This procedure leads into the harmony of the world and of the universe. It is exactly this harmony, which I hypothesized to be the result of BCI. Thus Pauli's very impressive dream confirms my hypothesis: By a completely introverted procedure it seems to be possible to create the red tincture or the quintessence—the latter comes back in the last dream I will interpret. In this way, it seems, the disease of the world and of the universe caused by the artificial fission can be healed. However, this is only possible, if mankind becomes conscious of the necessity of the development of the Eros ego, since only the latter can observe the 'subterranean connection' (W. Pauli), the psychophysical nonlocality, between the microcosm, the imagining human, and the macrocosm, the *unus mundus* with its energetic principle, the world soul or Eros Self. As we further know, only in this way the potential singular quantum leaps become actual and can enter the reality of our world.

/ / /

The second dream, which is in fact a visual-auditive experience, is a perfect illustration of the background of my theory, the bipolar energy term, derived from the modern interpretation of the Axiom of Maria Prophetissa.

---

[321] For the following see Pauli, W., Writings on Physics and Philosophy, *Springer, Berlin,* 1994, p. 247-250, and section 4.3.1 in Part I

THE VISUAL-AUDITIVE EXPERIENCE WITH THE EGGS[322]:

It consists in seven pictures in a row. No words are spoken until right at the end and Pauli is the one speaking:

Picture 1: A woman comes with a bird, which lays a large egg:

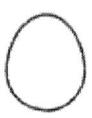

Picture 2: The egg divides itself into two:

Picture 3: Pauli goes closer and notices that he has in his hand another egg with a blue shell:

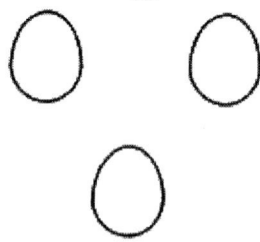

Picture 4: Pauli divides the *third* egg into two[323]. Miraculously, they remain whole, and he now has two eggs with blue shells.

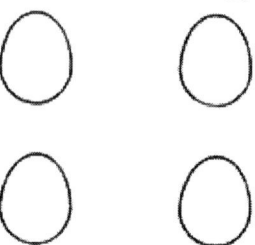

---

[322] AaA, p. 192-193; PJB, p. 189-190; *my title*
[323] *My italics*

Picture 5: The four eggs change into the following mathematical expressions:

$$\cos \partial/2 \quad \sin \partial/2$$
$$\cos \partial/2 \quad \sin \partial/2$$

Picture 6: This gives the formula:

$$\frac{\cos \partial/2 + i \sin \partial/2}{\cos \partial/2 - i \sin \partial/2} = e^{i\partial}$$

Picture 7: Pauli says: 'The whole thing gives $e^{i\partial}$, and that is the circle.' The formula vanishes, and a circle appears.

The egg is a symbol of potential life. Thus we can interpret it as the potential incarnation process in the *unus mundus*. The first three images of the vision/audition correspond exactly to the Axiom of Maria Prophetissa: One becomes two, two becomes three.

Then, however, the dream tells us that the third and thus the energy term is bipolar. The blue color of the third and doubled egg reminds us of Pauli's amplification of it in connection with his World-clock vision contradicting Jung's[324]. Thus, we can conclude that the fact is stressed that the energy term consists of the Logos philosophicus, causality, spirit-psyche, as well as of the Logos Spermatikos, acausality, matter-psyche[325]. The third and thus the energy term must consist of a quantitative-qualitative bipolarity. Only by accepting the bipolarity the unconscious split in the energy term can be overcome, the repression of the qualitative aspect of energy is withdrawn and the fourth is created as the re-union of the opposites, 'the One as the fourth,' as the Axiom states. And it continues[326]: 'In this way the two [aspects of the energy term; RFR] become one,' in the circle—and not in the square, thus not in C.G. Jung's quaternity! This is why, as compensation to Pauli's and Jung's view, the fourth of the square—the Neoplatonic prejudice—is replaced by the fourth as the circle. As we have seen above, with the help of the circle it is a very easy task to create the Seal of Solomon, the symbol of the bipolar energy term as the background of the twin process.

---

[324] See sections 3.3.9 and 6.5 in Part 1

[325] As I mentioned before, this other aspect of the bipolar energy term Hermetic alchemy of the Renaissance also called the Pneuma (of the Stoa). It is a form of energy that is not lead by the first cause, by God, but is the autochthonous energy form of the feminine principle. See Stadler, M., Renaissance: Weltseele und Kosmos, Seele und Körper, *in*: Jüttemann, G., Sonntag, M., Wulf, Ch., Die Seele, Ihre Geschichte im Abendland, Weinheim 1991, pp. 180-197.

[326] See section 6.1.1

Further, the fact is stressed that it is in the *hand* of Pauli that the third egg—symbolically the potential 'life essence'—becomes the bipolar energy term. This means that he would have '*Hand*lungsfähigkeit,' the ability to act concerning the bipolar energy term; he would be able to observe the twin process and thus the singular quantum leap. However he does not realize this, on the one hand since he cannot accept the violation of the energy conservation law on the psychophysical level, and on the other since he knows nothing about the Eros ego.

/ / /

We can resume the essence of the two dreams as follows: The 'stable substance,' animated as well as inanimated matter, possesses a psychophysical and thus a magic matter-psyche aspect. With the help of it matter is able to change its quality in processes that follow the nexus of the singular acausal quantum leap, based on the 'subterranean connection' between the inner world and the universe ruled by the third type of law of nature. Such a transformation is however only incarnated in a positive way if there is a conscious observation of the process with the help of the Eros ego. The incarnation itself is symbolized by the sphere music of the Pythagoreans, which is an attribute of the Hermetic *coniunctio*. Actually in the practice of a healer one can empirically realize such sphere music exactly in the moment in which the patient enters the *coniunctio*. The goal of this process, of the *unio corporalis*, is then the observation of increased order of the vegetative body on the one hand and of the world soul on the other. The necessary precondition for the observation of the process, of the singular quantum leap, is the acceptance of the fourth as the *rotundum*, symbolically equivalent to the Seal of Solomon. The process and its goal are demonstrated in the Nobel laureate's visual-auditive experience of the eggs: The development into the bipolar energy term. Only this development allows for the twin process, the singular quantum leap as an incarnation act, in which the re-union of the quantitative/causal and the qualitative/acausal energy takes place.

6.16.6 The 'Chinese revolution,' the *Spiegler* (the maker of reflections) and the twin process

Twenty-six years after the invention of the neutrino/antineutrino by Pauli, at the end of 1956, a catastrophe happened the reaction of the Nobel laureate to which was 'quite a shock to myself and other physicists.'[327] Very soon physicists began to call it the 'Chinese revolution,'[328] since it were two Chinese physicists, Dr. Tsung Dao Lee, and Dr. Chen Ning Yang, who showed that in the radioactive beta decay the so-called principle of conservation of parity is violated.

On August 5, 1957, half a year after an article about the revolution, Pauli sent Jung a copy of an article[329] in the New York Times of January 16, 1957, in which a physicist shows the effects of the above discovery. How deep the shock in physical circles was shows the comment of the Nobel laureate I. I. Rabbi[330]:

> In a certain sense...a rather complete theoretical structure has been shattered at the base and we are not sure how the pieces will be put back together...It might take a long time to evolve a new concept on the basis of the recently achieved results. One scientist said that the nuclear physics, in a sense had been battering for years at a closed door only to find that it is not a door at all but a likeness of a door painted on the wall. Now science is at least in a position to hunt for the true door again, he observed.

As we will see, the image of the door and its likeness painted on the wall is very well chosen to describe the situation as well as the way out of the problem.

In the article the parity principle and its violation is delineated for a layman[331]:

> Assume that one motion picture camera is photographing a given set of actions and that another camera simultaneously is photographing the same set of actions as reflected in the mirror.

---

[327] AaA, p. 162; PJB, p. 161
[328] AaA, p. 161; PJB, p. 160
[329] Added as Appendix 10 to AaA, p. 218-220; PJB, p. 213-219
[330] AaA, p. 219; PJB, p. 214
[331] AaA, p. 218; PJB, p. 213

If the two films are later screened, a viewer would have no way, according to the principle of parity, of telling which of the two was the mirror image. The recently completed experiments indicate that there is a way of determining which of the two images is the mirror image.

In communicating with people in an intelligent civilization on another world, the Columbia Report explained, it would be impossible, with the principle of parity in effect, to tell whether or not they and we meant the same thing by right-handed and left-handed. This could be true and still the basic physical laws in both worlds would behave exactly alike. The recent experiments indicate that this is not the case for weak interactions [the radioactive decay; RFR] of sub-atomic particles.

The situation is also described as the 'handedness' of an atom or elementary particle, an attribute which is exactly characterized by Pauli's invention, the spin. Since 1925, the year of the postulation of the spin, physicists were convinced that every elementary particle can have a positive or a negative spin, i.e. be right-handed or left-handed. As the experiments of Yang and Lee showed, for the neutrino/antineutrino this is not true: The matter particle neutrino is always left-handed, the antimatter particle antineutrino always right-handed; neutrinos with a right-handed spin and antineutrinos with a left-handed spin do not exist. Thus, in contrast to most other particles nature does not mirror them.

On March 12, 1957[332], two months after the above publication of the parity's violation of the neutrino/antineutrino Pauli had the following dream[333]:

PAULI'S DREAM OF THE REFUSAL OF READING THE BOOK OF THE MAN IN FAINT LIGHT[334]:

> A youngish, dark-haired man, enveloped in faint light, hands me the manuscript of a work. I shout at him: 'How dare you presume to ask me to read it? What do you think you are doing?' I wake up feeling very upset and irritated.

The Nobel laureate comments the dream as follows:

> *Comment:* The dream...shows my conventional objections to certain ideas—and my fear of them. For only someone who is afraid can shout

---

[332] *The dating of the following two dreams is corrected according to the footnote in AaA, p. 164*

[333] *For the following see AaA, p. 164-165; PJB, p. 163-164*

[334] *My dream's title*

as loudly as I did in the dream...But with such methods as the ones used in this dream my ego is always guaranteed to lose against the unconscious. The unconscious in fact reacts immediately with the following *dream of March 15, 1957*:

THE DREAM OF THE *ANIMA MUNDI*, THE *SPIEGLER* AND THE TWIN PROCESS[335]:

I am driving along in my car...and I park it at a spot where parking seems to be permitted. There is a department store. Just as I am about to get out of the car, someone gets in on the passenger side; it is the young man who had handed me the manuscript in the dream three days earlier. He is now a policeman: 'Come with me!' he says to me brusquely; sits at the wheel, and drives off with me. (Sudden thought: the car driver Krishna.) He pulls up in front of a house, which seems to be a police station, and pushes me into the house.

'And now I suppose you'll be dragging me from one office to the next,' I say to him. 'Oh no,' he says. We come to a counter where an 'unfamiliar dark woman' sits. Turning to her, he says in the same brusque, militaristic voice as before: 'Director *Spiegler* [Director Reflector; literally: The maker of reflections; RFR], please!'

On hearing the word *'Spiegler,'* I am so taken aback that I wake up.

But I fall asleep again, and my dream continues: The situation has changed completely. Another man comes up to me; he bears a faint resemblance to C.G. Jung, and I take him to be a psychologist. At great length I explain to him the situation in physics—the one that has come about as a result of the recent experiments on the violation of the parity law—I assume that he is not familiar with the situation. His replies are rather brief, and when I wake up I cannot remember them.

Pauli then spontaneously relates the end of the dream with his and Jung's hypothesis of complementarity between physics and depth psychology. He realizes that in the dream dissociation is shown. There is a physicist who 'can master physics but is not fully aware of the archetypal background of this new situation,' and 'a psychologist who typically knows nothing about physics.' Then he adds:

---

[335] *My dream's title*

> Obviously, the *Spiegler* [the maker of reflections; RFR] is attempting to bring the two together, and in the manuscript of the young man, which I refused to read, there must have been something about that.

The reader remembers that this man was 'enveloped in a faint light.' In the esoteric tradition it is the subtle body, which is described like this. Thus we can interpret the young man as the subtle or vegetative body aspect in Pauli, which he should become conscious of. He, however, refuses to read the concerning book, i.e., is not willing to become conscious about the subtle body/world soul phenomenology in himself. As we have seen above, this inability is the result of the definition of the relationship between physics and depth psychology as being complementary, instead of developing a concept corresponding to the Taoist yin/yang bipolarity or the Hermetic spirit-psyche/matter-psyche principle with its possibility of the twin process and its result, the creation of energy/matter with altered order.

Let us return to the beginning of the dream. There the 'subtle body man' takes over. In German 'car' means 'Auto' and symbolically seen is mostly interpreted as an automatism. Thus, an automatic, spontaneous process begins. This process leads Pauli first to the 'dark woman' in whom we recognize of course the Chinese *anima mundi*, the ruler of the *unus mundus*. To her shortly after the dream Pauli associates the following[336]:

> For the instinct of the 'Dark Woman,' there seems to be no essential difference between mirror symmetries in radioactive beta decay and multiple manifestations of an archetype. For her, the latter are just 'reflections' of the 'one invisible One' or '*unus mundus*,' which is then responsible for the symmetry of these reflections. In this connection it is also important that my dream language always uses 'radioactive' as a synonym for 'numinous' or 'synchronistic.'

What does this mean exactly? With great surprise we notice that Pauli talks now of symmetry in the radioactive beta decay. Just before he had shown Jung the asymmetry of the radioactive beta decay proven by Yang and Lee. Thus, he seems to realize that the 'dark woman' compensates his conscious standpoint and to anticipate that behind the asymmetry of the beta decay there could be symmetry. According to the 'dark woman' this symmetry is equivalent to the 'multiple manifestations of an archetype.' With this term Pauli usually describes the synchronicity principle. In fact, synchronicities, multiple manifestations can empirically be observed when an archetype is constellated, and a new content of the collective unconscious would like to become conscious.

---

[336] *AaA*, p. 165; *PJB*, p. 164

As we have realized before, the physicist stresses that in his dream language the term synchronicity is always replaced by radioactivity. As synchronicity is a psychophysical term, we can assume that Pauli has a presentiment of what in a physical-symbolic language I call psychophysical radioactivity, the twin process of the *coniunctio* with its microcosm-macrocosm identity in the moment of the singular quantum leap, and its result, the physical-psychophysical *multiplicatio*[337]. However, as he writes as a comment at the beginning of the dream, he has 'conventional objections.' We see now that these conventional objections concern the 'subtle body man.' Since according to my hypothesis the creation of subtle matter/energy with altered order can only be observed when the bipolarity of the energy term is accepted, thus only when one realizes the matter-psyche aspect of energy, the objections relate to this inability of the physicist. This is exactly also the reason why he is not able to overcome the complementarity hypothesis between physics and depth psychology, and as a consequence cannot find a psychophysical theory of the events happening in as well as out of the *unus mundus*, the twin processes.

The dream tells us further that after passing by the Chinese *anima mundi*, the ruler of the psychophysical reality and of matter-psyche, he would have had the task to confront himself with the *Spiegler*, the maker of reflections or of the 'mirror images.' The *Spiegler* behind the world soul becomes like this a symbol of the twin process, in which in fact a mirroring happens: In the observation of the singular (acausal) quantum leap the unknown X is transformed into matter-psyche with potentially altered order, and the latter is mirrored back into spirit-psyche with realized altered order. In this way this the asymmetry of the parity's violation of the neutrino/antineutrino is replaced by the symmetry of the twin process. Since in this process an altered quality of energy is created, the symmetry contains also an asymmetry. As we have seen, the altered quality is the result of the *coniunctio* of the causal/masculine and the acausal/feminine principle, the collapse of the psychophysical wave function, so to speak.

We can conclude that the dream would like to call Pauli's attention to the fact that on the psychophysical level the neutrino/antineutrino hypothesis and its asymmetric spin have to be replaced by the bipolar energy term and the psychophysically nonlocal twin process. As we have realized above, using the physical-symbolic language this would mean the acceptance of the charge of the acausal condenser of matter-psyche in the *unus mundus*, which then in the process of the creation of energy/matter with altered order discharges acausally and spontaneously—for example in UFO encounter and abduction.

---

[337] Here the question arises if astrophysics does not simulate this identity with the help of the inflation hypothesis shortly after the big bang, since in it in an unimaginable small time span the 'point-universe' becomes the real, thus inflated, universe.

Though the Nobel laureate two months before the dream realized that these *Spiegler* dreams may have to do with parapsychology[338], he is not able to understand them. This is why at the end of the dream the mentioned dissociation happens; physics and depth psychology remain complementary sciences, and the space-, time- and massless psychophysical reality with its nonlocality principle cannot be explained; Pauli's 'conventional objections,' his prejudice of the unipolarity of the energy term, prevent the development of a psychophysical theory that would overcome the complementarity of physics and depth psychology on the deeper level of the psychophysical reality. The same is true for C.G. Jung, since also objective psychic energy is defined as unipolar, and not as bipolar. Only the hypothesis of the bipolar spirit-psyche/matter-psyche principle can solve the problem. Only this way science does not think anymore of the likeness of a door painted at the wall as being the door itself and 'is in a position to hunt for the true door again.' It realizes the real door to a psychophysical theory and opens it.

/ / /

A synopsis of the dream of the *Spiegler* leads to the following crucial result: On a psychophysical level the asymmetry of the neutrino/antineutrino's parity conservation violation of physics has to be replaced by the 'asymmetric mirror' of the bipolar energy term, which only allows for the twin process, in which spirit-psyche with altered order is produced. Only such a replacement leads to the creation possibility of inner spirit-psyche with increased order in the case of the realization of the meaning of a synchronicity, and to the creation possibility of outer spirit-psyche with increased order, be it as increased order of physical energy in the body in the case of SST, be it as increased order of physical energy in the universe in the case of BCI (see figure 6.33).

---

[338] *In letter [2471] of Jan 24, 1957 to Fierz, WB 4/IVA, p. 111. Pauli states that he had the dream during working on his article for the Festschrift to Niels Bohr's 70th birthday (1955). Bohr pled in favour of the violation of the energy conservation law. This dream belongs into the context of the* Spiegler *dream Pauli describes in more details in letter [76P] of Aug 5, 1957 to Jung, AaA, p. 162; PJB, p. 161; WB 4/IVA, p. 508-509*

The Two Twin Processes of the Magical World View

Body-Centered Imagination

Physical Energy (outer spirit-psyche)

Magical Energy of the Psycho-physical Level (matter-psyche)

Process:
Physical energy transforms into magic energy, and magic energy transforms back into physical energy of higher negentropy (higher order)

Synchronicity

Objective Psychic Energy (Inner spirit-psyche)

Magical Energy of the Psycho-physical Level (matter-psyche)

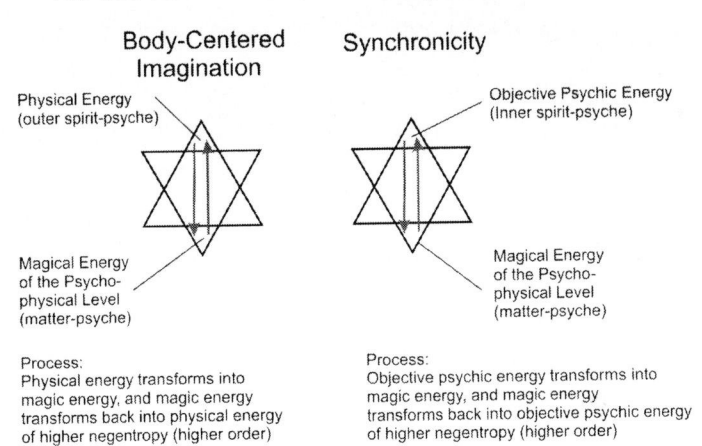

Process:
Objective psychic energy transforms into magic energy, and magic energy transforms back into objective psychic energy of higher negentropy (higher order)

Figure 6.33

The acceptance of the bipolar energy term and the possibility of the twin process have a further decisive effect: Since the background of the matter-psyche, the psychophysical reality is space-, time- and massless and matter-psyche obeys the attribute of psychophysical nonlocality, physical spacetime and mass are annulled. In a spacetime- and mass-less world neither a distinction between (masculine) force/energy on the one hand and (feminine) matter on the other exists anymore. Since it is the spin, which defines this distinction, also its definition becomes worthless.

As we realized above, it is the *unus mundus*, the psychophysical reality, the attributes of which are described by spacetimelessness and psychophysical nonlocality. The Beyond belongs also t this realm. Thus, with the help of the processes happening in SST/BCI we also approach the world of the deceased. In the next section we will realize that in the Nobel laureate's last synchronicity such a development happened concretistically, since because of his 'conventional objections' he was not able to consciously realize the above described deepest background of his dreams, visions and auditions.

6.16.7 Wolfgang Pauli's fine structure constant/death room synchronicity

Many physicists, especially Pauli, were and still are fascinated by the so-called fine structure constant. Richard Feynmann for example says[339]:

> It has been a mystery ever since it was discovered more than fifty years ago, and all good theoretical physicists put this number up on their wall and worry about it. Immediately you would like to know where this number comes from…Nobody knows. It's one of the *greatest* damn mysteries of physics: a *magic number* that comes to us with no understanding by man.

The fine structure constant is a measure for the electric charge[340]. It is a dimensionless number, more or less the inverse of 137, which means that it does not contain any of the physical base units of space, time and mass (m, s and kg). However no one knows the deeper reason why the constant has exactly this amount. If, however, it would only be a little different, the universe would have developed in a completely other manner, since it has a great influence on almost all physical phenomena.

For the epistemologist Pauli it was annoying that the fine structure constant was not at all empirically verifiable[341]. It is also a measure for the field strength in the inside of the electron. Since as any force the field strength is only defined as the force affecting a specimen and there is no smaller specimen than the electron, it is principally impossible to measure and thus to verify the electrical field strength. Thus the term electrical field strength becomes just an empty fiction without any content. Since according to Pauli in physics one should only operate with observable units, he states that 'progress in quantum field theory [is] linked to a [deeper] understanding of this number.'

Close to the end of 1958 Pauli in his office at the Physikalische Institut of the ETH at Gloriastrasse in Zurich completely out of the blue suffered a heavy pain in his upper belly. He immediately was brought to the *Rotkreuz Hospital*

---

[339] Feynman, R.P., QED—The strange theory of light and matter, *Princeton University Press* 1985, p. 129

[340] A *very good explanation of the background and mysteries of the fine structure constant see in* Miller, Arthur, I., Deciphering The Cosmic Number, The Strange Relationship of Wolfgang Pauli and C.G. Jung, W. W. Norton & Company, New York, London, 2009, p. 247-259

[341] For the following see Enz, Ch. P., Wolfgang Pauli (1900-1958): A Biographical Introduction, *in:* Pauli, W., Writings on Physics and Philosophy, *Springer, Berlin, Heidelberg, N.Y.,* 1994, p. 23

situated exactly at the other side of the street. After an emergency surgery the physicians realized that he was suffering from pancreatic cancer and that they were not able to help him anymore.

When Pauli's last assistant, Charles P. Enz on December 8 visited him in the hospital[342], he asked him alarmed: 'Did you realize the room's number?' '137!' There in the room carrying the numerical value of the 33rd prime number he died on December 15, 1958.

This synchronicity is highly meaningful. With the 33rd prime number we remember of course immediately the symbolism of 3/3, the bipolarity of the energy term on the psychophysical level of reality, and the Seal of Salomon or Star of David as the energetic background of it. Thus, there is a direct connection with the world beyond the split into a physical and a depth psychological realm shown as being complementary by the Nobel laureate of physics.

As we realized further the fine structure constant is the only physical constant without any physical base unit. It does not contain any space, any time, and any physical mass. This means that in every physical measurement system it has the same value; the fine structure constant is the constant of the constants, so to speak—eternally unchangeable.

In connection with my comments above we are reminded of the fact that also the *unus mundus*, Pauli's psychophysical reality he looked for but did not yet find, is a 'realm' without any physical base units. It is space-, time- and massless and possesses the attribute of psychophysical nonlocality. Thus, we can conclude that the 'mystical' aspect of the fine structure constant is its relation to the *unus mundus*. It is however exactly the connection of the ego with the *unus mundus*, which corresponds to the third phase of Dorneus' *opus* following the second, the *unio corporalis*. As may have become evident, in a modern terminology we describe this third phase as Body-Centered Imagination.

As Charles Enz writes further (in German)[343], the fine structure constant is connected to the Jewish Cabbalah: Written without vocals, as usual in Hebrew, 'Cabbalah' is 'HLBQ' (from right to left), where Q = 100, B = 2, L = 30 and H = 5.

---

[342] *The following according to Enz, Ch. P.,* Rationales und Irrationales im Leben Wolfgang Paulis, *in:* Atmanspacher, H., Primas, H., Wertenschlag-Birkhäuser, E. (editors), Der Pauli-Jung-Dialog und seine Bedeutung für die moderne Wissenschaft, *Springer, Berlin, Heidelberg, N.Y., 1995, p. 30. Today also published in English in Enz, Ch. P.,* On Matter and Spirit, Selected Essays, *World Scientific, 2009, p. 160*

[343] Enz, Ch. P., Rationales und Irrationales im Leben Wolfgang Paulis, *in:* Atmanspacher, H., Primas, H., Wertenschlag-Birkhäuser, E. (editors), Der Pauli-Jung-Dialog und seine Bedeutung für die moderne Wissenschaft, *Springer, Berlin, Heidelberg, N.Y., 1995, p. 30. Today also published in English in Enz, Ch. P.,* On Matter and Spirit, Selected Essays, *World Scientific, 2009, p. 160*

Thus, the sum is 137[344]. Cabbalah, the Jewish mysticism, is determined by magic procedures. On the other hand, we have realized that it is a magic procedure, which connects us with the *unus mundus*: The realization of the twin process and its singular quantum leap that is the essence of Body-Centered Imagination.

Wolfgang Pauli was intensely interested in the Cabbalah, especially in its application in East-European Jewish mysticism, in Chassidism. This shows for example the fact that he possessed the book *Der Golem* by Gustav Meyrink (1868-1932), which is still exhibited today in his personal library in the Pauli chamber in CERN in Geneva, Switzerland[345]. He even writes in a letter to Aniela Jaffé that he was always very fascinated by this book[346] describing the mentality of the Cabbalah in Chassidism. Further, Pauli was also conscious of the fact that Robert Fludd was directly influenced by the Jewish Cabbalists[347]. Thus we can imagine what deepest archetypal roots were constellated in him: The magic of the Cabbalah, which is intensely interwoven with a direct mystic relationship with God. In my terminology we could say that the constellated archetype was the mystical/magical relationship of the Eros ego with the Eros Self[348], the empirical application of which is Symptom-Symbol Transformation and Body-Centered Imagination.

In not realizing the deepest meaning of the above interpreted dreams, the Nobel laureate was not anymore able to relate to the psychophysical reality and the Beyond; his belief in the absolute truth of the energy conservation law made it impossible for him to deal with the challenge of the creation of the subtle or vegetative body and as a consequence to reach 'the other side of the street,' the realm of the matter-psyche during this life. Thus, in a concretized way he entered 'the other side of life's street,' the Beyond, without having solved his deepest life problem.

The great tragedy of the physicist's life, who was so intensely involved in C.G. Jung's depth psychology and clarified some of the latter's most important terms, lies in the circumstance that he in fact was convinced that physics should not only be combined with depth psychology and parapsychology, but also with mysticism. He did not, however, have the means to reach this state. We see this

---

[344] In a personal letter of April 8, 2008 Ch. P. Enz wrote to me that he was informed of this fact by Yuval Ne'eman, Haifa, in 1971. In WB 4/III, p. 366, the editor K. v. Meyenn notes that also Victor Weisskopf, the 5th president of CERN, was informed of the strange connection between the Cabbalah and the fine structure constant.

[345] See note 4 of the editor in WB 4/I, p. 201

[346] WB 4/I, p. 198

[347] WB 4/II, p. 291

[348] Pauli dealt intensely with the principle of Eros, especially with its role in the Renaissance. See my digital publication Wolfgang Pauli, das Prinzip des kollektiven Eros und dessen kosmogonische Bedeutung, http://www.psychovision.ch/synw/pauli_kosmogonischer_eros.htm

conviction especially in a letter to Pauli's sister, Hertha Pauli-Ashton, of 11th October, 1957. There he writes[349]:

> I do not believe in a future possibility of mysticism in its old form; I believe however that *natural science out of itself* in its representatives will produce an opposite pole, which ties in with old mystical elements. [Translation and emphasis mine]

As also the following passage in a *published* paper shows, intellectually, the Nobel price winner was prepared to accept this task of combining science with mysticism[350]:

> According to the alchemist conception, the deliverance of substance by the man who transforms it, which culminates in the production of the stone, is, in consequence of a mystic correspondence between macrocosm and microcosm, identical with the redeeming transformation (Wandlung) of the man through the *opus*, which comes about only 'Deo concedente.'

In the same paper[351] he writes that in certain periods of history it is 'the aim…to try to include science in a more comprehensive spiritualism involving mystical elements,' and continues:

> In contrast to science, the mystical attitude is not characteristic of the occident (Abendland); in spite of differences in detail it is common to occident and orient…Mysticism seeks the unity of all external things and the unity of the inner man with them; this it does by seeking to see through the multiplicity of things as illusory and unreal. Thus there comes about, stage by stage, man's unity with the Godhead—Tao in China, Samadhi in India or Nirvana in Buddhism…Thoroughgoing mysticism does not ask 'why?' It asks 'How can man escape evil, the suffering, of this terrible,

---

[349] 'Ich glaube nicht an die Zukunftsmöglichkeit der Mystik in der alten Form, [wohl] aber glaube ich, dass die Naturwissenschaften [aus] sich selbst heraus *einen Gegenpol in ihren Vertretern hervorbringen werden, der an die alten mystischen Elemente anknüpft.*' [Emphasis mine] [WB 4/IVA, letter [2707], p. 566]. Then he mentions that he had written about this problem in his Kepler essay and in his lecture 'Die Wissenschaft und das abendländische Denken' ('Science and Western Thought'). To the problem of a new union of science and mysticism see also Pauli's short correspondence of 1956 with Aldous Huxley in WB 4/III, letters [2269], [2294] and [2322]
[350] Pauli, W.: Science and Western thoughts, *in:* Writings on Physics and Philosophy, p. 145
[351] For the following see Pauli, W.: Science and Western thoughts, *in:* Writings on Physics and Philosophy, p. 139

menacing universe? How can it be recognised as appearance; how can the ultimate reality, the Brahman, the One, the Godhead (no longer personal for *Eckhard*) be seen?'...I believe that it is the destiny of the occident continually to keep bringing into connection with each other these two fundamental attitudes, on the one hand the rational-critical, which seeks to understand, and on the other the mystic-irrational, which looks for the redeeming experience of oneness. *Both* attitudes will always reside in the human soul, and each will always carry the other already within itself as the germ of its contrary. Thus there arises a sort of dialectical process, of which we do not know wither it is leading us. I believe that as occidentals (Abendländer) we have to commit ourselves to this process, and recognise the pair of opposites as complementary. We cannot and will not completely sacrifice the ego-consciousness which observes the universe, but we can also accept intellectually the experience of oneness as a kind of limiting case or idea limiting conception. While allowing the tension of opposites to remain, we must also recognise that on any path to knowledge or to salvation we are dependent on factors beyond our control, which religious language has always designated as Grace.

Theoretically, with the help of his incredibly great mind, the Nobel laureate realized the problem and its solution. Empirically, however, he was not able to enter its verification. Thus he died without having reached the real psychophysical quaternity, the Logos ego/Logos Self connection combined with the Eros ego/Eros Self unification.

6.16.8 The Nobel laureate's visual-auditive experience of the dancing Chinese woman, the Seal of Solomon, the quintessence and the square, and the World-clock vision

The interpretation of the above dreams of Wolfgang Pauli prepared us for the understanding of one of his most impressive visual-auditive experiences already presented in section 4.3.3 in Part I. When one reads the letters to Marie-Louise von Franz of Nov 6 and Nov 11, 1953, one feels that the Nobel laureate was deeply moved by this extraordinary vision. As we have seen, he first presents the change of his consciousness between the invention of the neutrino in 1930 and the early fifties, and shows it in abstract form as two successive Seals of Solomon. He is convinced that one can demonstrate the change by a transformation, a rotation of the first Seal which leads into the second. In the first the feminine triangle is pointed upwards, the masculine downwards. With the help of the transformation this situation changes into its opposite: The masculine triangle points now upwards, the feminine downwards. Since in this way the goal corresponds to Robert Fludd's Seal, the symbol of Hermetic alchemy, which Pauli published shortly before, in 1952 in the book *Naturerklärung und Psyche,* he is convinced that the two Seals correctly describe his development.

Then, however, he dreams the mentioned dream, which compensates his obviously wrong conclusion. In it he is the fourth, besides the Chinese *anima mundi* and two other men. As we realized, the fourth is nothing else than the Seal of Solomon. We can interpret this motif in the way that he 'is' the Seal, which would mean that he should become conscious of its real meaning, the bipolarity of the energy term. On the level of consciousness this means the transformation of the Logos ego into the Eros ego.

On the other hand the Chinese is the only woman besides the three men. Thus, we can also interpret her as the different fourth, the Seal, i.e., the double triadic structure of her 'realm.' In this way, also the Chinese would correspond to my solution of the enigmatic Axiom of Maria Prophetissa: the fourth corresponds to the Seal, the bipolar energy principle. As a consequence the Eros ego can meld with the Eros Self.

Pauli is forced to play chess, obviously with the Chinese. Since it is a Chinese with whom he is obliged to play the game, we have to amplify with the Chinese chess game. It is a great advantage that in *Number and Time* Marie-Louise von Franz presents this game to us[352]. It looks very different to the Western chess board (see image 6.35 below). We immediately realize that its structure is similar to the 'square' in the visual-auditive experience following the dream; both stress the middle and thus present much more what alchemy knew as the quintessence, #5 demonstrated as four points creating a square and the fifth point being the center. Thus it looks like #5 on a dice (see image 6.36 below):

---

[352] *P. 297*

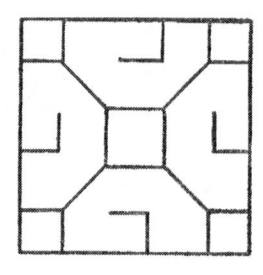

Figure 6.34:
The Chinese chess

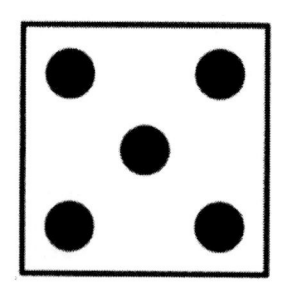

Figure 6.35:
The quintessence on a dice

In Hermetic alchemy of Gerardus Dorneus the lily plays an important role. It is insofar symbolically equivalent to the Seal as the petals are arranged in the way that three of them are below, the other three however above. In this way also the lily symbolizes the double-triadic structure. Dorneus tells us that the lily is the indispensable precondition for the creation of the quintessence[353]. Thus, he anticipates a development, which we can describe as the transformation of the Seal/lily, of the double-triadic structure, into the quintessence. We can therefore interpret the symbolic term 'playing Chinese chess' as the observation of this transformation. As we will realize, it is this development which is also presented in Pauli's visual-auditive experience.

As we have already seen[354], Dorneus' *opus* is the Hermetic continuation of the Neoplatonic *opus*. In the latter the 'spirit' is extracted from 'matter' and unified with the 'soul' in the Heavens. This first phase, in which matter or the body is deadened, is called the *unio mentalis*. The product is known as the *mens*. Hermetic alchemists, however, add a second phase, in which the *mens* has to come down from the Heavens to an intermediary realm. Simultaneously matter or the body ascend to this sphere in the middle. Here, as we realized, the *coniunctio* takes place, in which the quintessence is produced. In Dorneus' work the *coniunctio* is called the *unio corporalis*: Dead matter or the dead body are unified with the *mens*, and the result of this Holy Wedding is the red tincture or the quintessence, both symbolizing a revitalizing essence, the subtle matter.

'Playing Chinese chess,' the transformation of the Seal or of the lily into the quintessence, the subtle or vegetative substance, is therefore a process, which belongs to the Hermetic *coniunctio*, the continuation of the Neoplatonic first phase. The dream compensates thus Pauli's too Neoplatonic worldview as well as the one of science in general. As we know, in the *coniunctio* the so-called exchange of attributes takes place, which as we have seen in Pauli's dreams is also symbolized

---

[353] *CW 14, § 689*
[354] See section 6.12.3.3

by the oscillation, which should be transformed into a rotation. On the other hand, in the vision the world soul is also talking about 'rhythms and rotations.'

Thus we receive a symbolic equivalence between the terms 'playing Chinese chess' of the dream and 'rhythms and rotations' in the vision: both mean the twin process on the background of the bipolar energy term. As we know, Hermetic alchemists expressed this procedure as the extraction of the red tincture out of the *lapis* or as *the distillation of the quintessence out of the Seal of Solomon or the lily*. In an abstract language this would mean the transformation of the Seal into the quintessence—exactly the content of the visual-auditive experience. Presented is the twin process requiring the double-triadic structure, the Seal, which with the help of the product of the singular acausal quantum leap, the quintessence, leads into a new 'stable state' of the 'psychophysical radioactive core.' Later we must therefore realize what the latter could be.

With the dream of playing Chinese chess and the motif of the 'rhythms and rotations' the Chinese *anima mundi* would obviously like to correct the Nobel laureate's conclusions. He thinks that with the transformation of one Seal into the other he has fulfilled his '*opus*.' The Chinese, however, tells him that 'in your drawings one element is…transitory and false.' Obviously meant is the second Seal, which seems not yet to be the final goal. Such a transformation would lead into a new static goal—exactly the stagnation of the creative mind Pauli felt since 1951[355]. Thus, 'symmetry cannot be *statically* produced.' What is meant is a continuation of the process, the transformation of the second Seal into the quintessence, symbolically equivalent to the transformation of the oscillation into the rotation, which *dynamic* process leads to a new symmetry. As we will realize, this is the main message of the vision, and it describes Pauli's task and challenge.

Here I would like to shortly come back to the Chinese chess. As Marie-Louise von Franz tells us[356], it served the purpose of reincarnation, insofar as it was played to bring back the deceased into life. This motif reminds us of course of the one in my turtle/UFO/Anubis/Osiris BCI, in which by my long lasting observation I finally realized that the veiled figure was Anubis, who is the bringer of new life in the Beyond. As we have seen, in a modern terminology we could say that as a consequence the psychophysical reality/*unus mundus*/Beyond obtains a higher quality, which on the one hand shows that the order in it has increased, on the other that new vegetative life in the *unus mundus* as well as in our world has been created. I interpreted this phenomenon as the creation of higher quality of the world soul as well as of the vegetative or subtle body, which, because of the

---

[355] *Expressed for example in a letter to Marie-Louise von Franz from April 21st, 1951;* WB 4/I, p. 292. *On May 17th, he writes to her that the reason for the stagnation is that his Anima would like to abandon physics;* WB 4/I, p. 307. *In my opinion, addressed is the anima mundi. See also letter to Markus Fierz from Jan 19th, 1953,* WB 4/II, p. 15, *in which he describes dream motifs that deal with this subject.*

[356] Number and Time, p. 296

psychophysical nonlocality, with the help of Body-Centered Imagination leads to higher order in the physical and psychic universe, by applying Symptom-Symbol Transformation in the physical body.

The *anima mundi* continues: 'It is correct that the lines number six, but it is false to draw six points.' Thus, correct is to draw the square with the center, the quintessence with its six lines. They correspond to the six strokes of the I Ching. The I Ching is the representation of the yin/yang bipolarity—of the bipolarity of the energy term. The Chinese corrects thus the Nobel laureate's idea that the energy term is unipolar. On the contrary the bipolarity of the energy term is stressed as the background of the process, as demonstrated in the Seal of Solomon and the lily.

Surely, the reader remembers my remarks in Chapter 5[357], where I showed how Pauli reduced the dynamic bipolarity of yang and yin leading into the Tao, to the static complementarity between physics and depth psychology, and in this way *prevented the dynamic exchange of attributes*. It becomes now obvious that the world soul would like to show the Nobel laureate that this reduction had been wrong on the psychophysical level, and must be corrected.

The diagonals of the quintessence correspond to the third principle. As we know, the third principle can be translated into a modern language as being the energy term. The two thirds, the two energy terms are 'irrationally related'—the acausality of the singular quantum leap, the transmutation of the X into matter-psyche and its retransformation into spirit-psyche with altered quality happening during the twin process. As a consequence a 'dance' is created, in which in a dynamic way the places are exchanged. The latter corresponds to the exchange of attributes as a result of the *coniunctio*. Since in the transformation of the Seal into the quintessence 'the symmetry is not statically produced'—instead the symmetry is created by the spontaneous singular quantum leap—'a dance results'—the rotation as the way out of the oscillation. Therefore 'the *coniunctio* refers to the exchange of places during this dance'—the twin process.

But could the last remark about the visual-auditive experience mean that in some way C.G. Jung's formula of the four squares is perfect, since it is dynamic? Obviously it describes a repeated *dynamic* process, a replicative transformation of one quaternity into another with a new quality. A repeated process would be described, the beginning of which is the Seal of Solomon, and over an intermediary state, the quintessence, the psychophysical radioactive decay, leads into a renewed quaternity. Presented as an image the process would look like this (see figure 6.37):

---

[357] See section 5.4.8 in Part 1

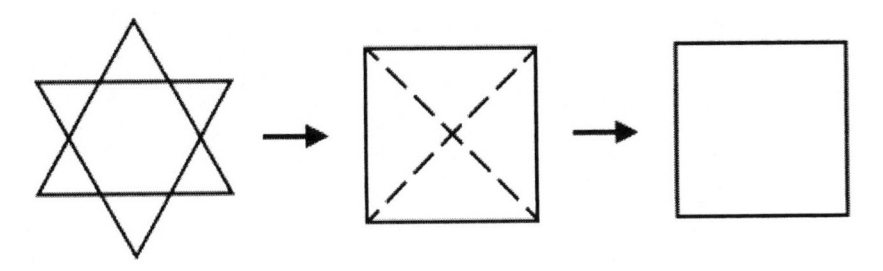

Figure 6.36:
The Seal of Solomon, the quintessence and the square

I confess to the reader that I would not have been able to interpret the end of this decisive dream of Wolfgang Pauli without the help of the preconscious knowledge of the unconscious presented in two early dreams. On February 19, 1986 I dreamed the following, completely abstract dream:

DREAM OF THE DEVELOPMENT OF THE FIRST SIX WHOLE NUMBERS:

A voice tells me: 'The real series of natural numbers is not 1, 2, 3, 4, 5, 6, but 1, 2, 3 → 6, 5, 4.'

On August 26, 1988 the above dream was followed by a second:

DREAM OF THE SOLUTION TO THE PROBLEM OF FIVE AND SIX WHICH HAS TO PRECEDE THE SOLUTION TO THE PROBLEM OF THE THIRD AND THE FOURTH:

In the dream I instinctively know the following: For the solution of the problem of the transition from the third to the fourth, the solution of the enigma of the Axiom of Maria Prophetissa, it is first necessary to solve the problem of five and six. This statement is equivalent to the following series of whole numbers: 1, 2, 3, 6, 5, 4.

These two dreams show in a nucleus the grave problem and its solution presented in my book: The third is the energy term, which however must first be extended to the six. Thus the fourth becomes two times three, the double-triadic Seal of Solomon, the bipolar energy term. Only then a development becomes possible, in which the quintessence as the fifth is reached. This development leads into the sixth, which is a renewed quaternity.

Of course, the two dreams speak of exactly the same problem and its solution, as does Pauli's visual-auditive experience. They tell us first that the energy term has to become bipolar. Only in this way can the quintessence or the red tincture be produced, which corresponds to the singular acausal quantum leap of the twin process. This acausal, 'irrational' exchange of attributes eventually leads into a new quaternity, the 'stable product' of the acausal process. Shown is nothing other than what I call the singular psychophysical radioactive decay which in a deeply introverted state the Eros ego has to observe.

In a modern language we can interpret the quaternity as Einstein's spacetime. Obviously, in singular acausal quantum leaps, represented as the quintessence in Pauli's dream, 'a new spacetime' is created, which means that the quality of spacetime is changed. Like this, Jung's formula in *Aion* becomes in fact true, with the exception that the transition from one quaternity to the other is not a causal process, as thought of by C.G. Jung, but acausal—the consciously observed singular acausal quantum leap.

This conclusion is verified by a further remark of the world soul at the end of the dream: 'The image of the World-clock in its way is right, since in it the three rhythms are contained.' We have therefore to return to this other absolutely crucial vision of the Nobel laureate of the year 1932[358], 21 years before the vision of the Chinese woman (see figure 6.4 above).

The horizontal circle with the four manikins arranged in a square symbolizes spacetime. The manikins are creative potentials[359] and connected to the rhythm's phenomenon[360], thus to oscillation as a symbol of the constellation of the singular acausal quantum leap. This is demonstrated in the World-clock vision by the fact that the manikins possess pendulums, oscillating tools. Using one of the above physical-symbolic images we could say that the four manikins with their pendulums correspond to the spacetime aspect of what I called above the charged acausal condenser, i.e. empirically observable effects. Actually, in doing BCI sometimes one can even sense such a charge as physical oscillations, which Lee Sannella describes as a standing wave in the aorta[361].

The vertical circle represents the *unus mundus*. The transition from one world to the other happens with the help of the twin process, the singular (acausal) quantum leap. This is first demonstrated by the above mentioned turning of 90

---

[358] As already mentioned in Chapter 1, Mr. U. Hoerni of the 'Erbengemeinschaft C.G. Jung' wrote to me in a private letter of July 1st, 2004: 'Die Vision der Welt uhr findet sich mit grosser Wahrscheinlichkeit in einer Traum-Aufzeichnung Paulis vom 4.11.1932.' (The World-clock vision is found with a great likelihood in Pauli's dream notes of November 4th, 1932;' Translation mine.).

[359] CW 5, § 180

[360] CW 5, § 183

[361] Sannella, Lee, Kundalini, Psychosis or Transcendence?, H.S. Dakin, San Francisco, 1981, p. 76-77

degrees, from horizontal to vertical. It is the transmutation of the X into matter-psyche, the first part of the twin process. Then the vertical circle inclines back into the horizontal position. As we know, in a physical-symbolic language this second part of the twin process corresponds to the singular quantum leap or the discharge of the acausal condenser. In this way, a new situation is reached, spacetime containing altered quality, with new laws of nature. Thus, the Nobel laureate's hypothesis already discussed in Chapter 5[362] is confirmed: *'There is room left for a new type of law of nature with life phenomena.'*

This interpretation is backed by an instinctive anticipation of the Nobel laureate. In a letter to his friend C.A. Meier of 1950[363] he realizes that the three rhythms presented in the vertical circle are discontinuously connected, which means that they symbolize acausality, while the symbolism of the four in the horizontal circle means the continuum (of Einstein's spacetime; RFR). Thus, in the World-clock vision 'the relationship between the problem of "three and four" and the problem "discontinuum/continuum"'[364] is demonstrated. This means that the Axiom of Maria Prophetissa—the transition from the third to the fourth (and not from three to four)—deals with the transition of a continuous state, static spacetime, into a discontinuous state, and back to a continuous state; demonstrated is nothing less than what I call the singular acausal quantum leap, here connected to a singular change in spacetime. As I mentioned above, it is exactly what the Nobel laureate anticipated as the 'third type of law of nature'[365] besides the causal and the statistical causal laws of physics. However, since Pauli does not accept that the fourth is the bipolarity of the energy term, he is convinced that the third is #3 and the fourth corresponds to #4.

In a note[366] Pauli even realizes that such a development must somehow have to do with the *abaissement du niveau mental*, a 'slackening of the tensity of consciousness'[367]. However, he is not able to realize that the latter is not just an unconsciousness but a consciously and empirically reachable state, the Eros ego.

I hope that the reader realizes the revolutionary implications of my last remarks: Since spacetime is the background of all physical processes as well as of human life, in the universe a change of the quality of spacetime could mean nothing less than a definite alteration of the laws of nature on the one hand and the alteration of physical/psychic constitution of humans on the other. In UFO abduction exactly this alteration constellated today is shown, however in a

---

[362] *Section 5.3.2*
[363] *WB 4/I, p. 146-147; letter to C.A. Meier of August 1st, 1950.*
[364] *'[Die] Beziehung zwischen dem Problem "der drei und der vier" und dem Problem "Diskontinuum-Kontinuum"' WB 4/I, p. 146*
[365] *WB 4/II, p. 310-311 (letter to Kröner), p.335-336 ('Die Klavierstunde' in letter to M.-L. von Franz) and p. 387-389 (letter to Heisenberg)*
[366] *WB 4/I, p. 147, note ***
[367] *CW 9/I, § 213; § 264*

non-sustainable way. In the former case for a short moment a potential change of collective spacetime is shown, in the latter of the individual. As we realized, UFO abduction means on the one hand the (potential) healing of the disease of the earth, on the other the healing of individual disease. However, a really sustainable effect is only possible in applying 'conscious UFO abduction'—Symptom-Symbol Transformation and/or Body-Centered Imagination.

CONCLUSIONS AND OUTLOOK

At least since the dream of the brass tones engraved in a metal plate of March 1948 Wolfgang Pauli seemed more and more convinced that not only living but also so-called inanimate matter possesses psyche though only in a very weak way. This conclusion, which he looked at as being 'reasonable,'[368] he adopted from the zoologist Bernhard Rensch, who argued that 'the psychic parallel components impossibly could spontaneously have bursted open in usually steady ontogenesis.'[369] Thus, Pauli argues that also 'so-called inanimate matter [must] contain "weak psychic parallel components".'[370] Further, the physicist explains that Rensch however does not give us any hint how such phenomena could express itself. Looking for a solution he continues with the conviction that such processes 'and thus life' first manifest themselves in non-reducible phenomena. The latter he equates with C.G. Jung's synchronicity principle. Then he adds that in this way he imagines the beginning of life.

As we know, synchronicity leads to an incarnation process on the level of the mind/spirit. It does not have anything to do with evolutionary life processes. However, the physicist does not know the Hermetic magic process as described in this book. Thus he tries to use the synchronicity principle for the description of evolutionary processes.

In the same letter[371] to Fierz he also sketches an idea how he imagines 'die Lebensprozesse im Grossen,' life processes on a large scale[372]:

> [Synchronicity phenomena] I always imagine as a transitory state, as temporary. Then, somewhere a causal fixation takes place anew, which

---

[368] For the following see WB 4/IVA, p. 289-291, letter [2555] of March 5th, 1957 to Markus Fierz; Pauli quotes from Rensch, B., Neuere Probleme der Abstammungslehre, 2. Aufl., 1954, p. 361 u. p. 281. See als letter [2173] to Marie-Louise von Franz, WB 4/III, p. 383

[369] 'Die psychischen Parallelkomponenten ... unmöglich in der sonst stetigen Ontogenese plötzlich aufgesprungen sein [können]'

[370] 'Sogenannte unbelebte Materie "schwache psychische Parallelkomponenten" aufweisen [müsse]'

[371] For the following see WB 4/IVA, p. 290

[372] '[Die Synchronizitäts-Phänomene] stelle ich mir ... immer nur als Durchgangsstadium vor, als temporär. Es tritt dann wieder irgendwo eine kausale Fixation ein, welche [sie] quasi überflüssig macht und den weiteren Verlauf festlegt.'

makes them more or less unnecessary and fixes the further course. [Translation mine]

Pauli anticipates that 'life processes on a large scale,' obviously the evolution of life in general, could be explained by phenomena, in which from time to time the causal flow is spontaneously, i.e., acausally interrupted and then again causally fixed. It seems that he foresees the process that I circumscribe as the acausal singular quantum leap. However, since he uses synchronicity, the principle that tries to explain meaning, i.e. spirit-psyche with increased order on the spirit/mind level, for the explanation of negentropic life processes, he cannot succeed.

Further, Pauli includes the following distinctive restriction[373]:

> I imagine this fixation as follows: Seen from the standpoint of the ordinary physical/chemical laws it must always be 'possible,' would however according to these laws be more or less unlikely. [Translation mine]

With this restriction the Nobel laureate remains in the frame of the quantum physical hypothesis. He assumes that in synchronistic processes very unlikely events happen, which one, however, still can explain with this theory. Since he cannot accept the idea of the bipolar energy term and the possibility of the creation of matter-psyche with potentially increased order, he cannot escape the quantum physical limitation. He cannot advance to a psychophysical theory, in which with the help of the twin process outer spirit-psyche, physical energy with increased order is created. Thus, on the one hand Pauli accuses Einstein[374] of 'regarding as an imperfection of quantum physics within physics what in fact was an imperfection of physics within life,' but cannot open to a real life science that includes paranormal phenomena; an 'extended physics' he himself asked for.

To recap: Without the knowledge of the bipolarity of the energy term, the twin process and the singular acausal quantum leap connected to it, neither a deeper understanding of synchronicity nor of its complementary process, the magic singular quantum leap influencing the psychophysical reality as well as matter is possible. Thus, a further differentiation is necessary, which I tried to develop in the course of the book: The inclusion of the creation of increased order on the spirit/mind level with its background, the interpreted synchronicity, *and* a complementary evolution process on the material level, caused by singular magic quantum leaps. Since only the Eros ego is able to observe such singular quantum leaps, Pauli and Jung do not know however this complementary consciousness to the Logos ego, they remain in the world of the Logos and thus on the level of

---

[373] 'Diese Fixation stelle ich mir so vor, dass sie vom Standpunkt der gewöhnlichen physikalisch-chemischen Gesetze aus zwar stets "möglich" sein muss, dass sie gemäss diesen Gesetzen jedoch mehr oder weniger unwahrscheinlich wäre.'
[374] For the following see AaA, p. 121-122; PJB, p. 121; WB 4/II, p. 164

complementarity of physics and Jung's depth psychology. Because of this, neither are able to advance to a psychophysical theory.

Further, C.G. Jung produces a conflict of two mutually exclusive theories, causal complex and archetype theory and acausal synchronicity. We have seen that Pauli's visual-auditive experience of the dancing Chinese woman, the Seal of Solomon, the quintessence and the square contains the solution to Jung's problem. It consists in the fact that in BCI the causal flow is interrupted by the acausal singular quantum leap that leads to a new causal flow of unpredictable extent. Since one enters the Eros ego consciously, incarnation in the new world is constructive.

In physics Pauli's adherence to the Logos principle has the consequences that he cannot accept the violation of the energy conservation law by the twin process with its production of energy with altered quality. Instead of the postulation of the matter-psyche aspect of the energy term (equivalent to negative energy), he postulates the antineutrino, which—corresponding to Paul Dirac's transformation of negative energy into antimatter—in fact consists of antimatter, but contains conventional energy, what I call the (outer) spirit-psyche without increased order. Further, with the help of the spin Pauli divides the physical world into 'masculine,' space-less energy and 'feminine' matter, which according to Descartes is only *res extensa*, and does not contain a specific energetic principle on its own. By this decisive reduction implicitly the matter-psyche, actually the archetypal 'female' space energy and its magic effects, is excluded[375]. In this way modern physics became able to define the so-called standard model. Since it is a materialistic theory, consequently it does not contain any form of a 'psychic parallel component of matter' proposed by the Nobel laureate.

However, if the hypothesis of the antineutrino as not just consisting of antimatter, but as being the matter-psyche aspect of energy on the deeper layer of the psychophysical reality or *unus mundus* is correct, it is to be expected that its artificial production as an effect of fission in the bomb and in nuclear power plants will lead to non-planned and unanticipated incarnation phenomena. Since according to my further hypothesis matter-psyche is space-, time- and mass-less

---

[375] *As we have seen, this other aspect of the bipolar energy term Hermetic alchemy of the Renaissance called the Pneuma or the Logos spermatikos. It is a form of energy that is not lead by the first cause, by God, but is the autochthonous energy form of the feminine principle. See Stadler, M., Renaissance: Weltseele und Kosmos, Seele und Körper, in: Jüttemann, G., Sonntag, M., Wulf, Ch., Die Seele, Ihre Geschichte im Abendland, Weinheim 1991, pp. 180-197.*

It seems that this space aspect of the energy term comes now unconsciously back in Einstein's cosmological constant or in its modern form, the quintessence (!) postulated by Lawrence M. Krauss and others. Further, according to Yakov B. Zeldovich this macrophysical energy acts precisely like the energy associated with virtual particles of the microphysical vacuum. [See Lawrence M. Krauss, Cosmological Antigravity, Scientific American, January 1999, p. 53-59.] Therefore, physics unconsciously comes back to the statement of 'smaller than small yet greater than great,' an attribute of god (or of the goddess, the world soul).

and obeys psychophysical nonlocality, it is very likely that fission will lead to parallel events which make a mockery of physical laws. Since such incarnation phenomena happen out of the psychophysical reality beyond the split into the outer, physical and the inner, psychic world, phenomena on the psychic level are also to be expected, which neither materialistic brain research nor modern psychology can explain. Since all these phenomena happen unconsciously, it is very likely that they lead to catastrophic and very destructive effects.

As the reader may have realized in the course of reading my book, besides the Pauli effect I also add UFO encounter and abduction to these effects, which, as we know, can have a destructive impact on the psychic as well as on the physical level. According to my theory, during the experience of these encounters and abductions the consciousness is forced into the Eros ego, which only is able to observe these phenomena on the level of the Eros Self, of the psychophysical reality or *unus mundus*. It thus seems that behind this rape there is an 'intention' of the world soul, since only the observation of a human can incarnate the potential phenomena. Since such an observation happens however unconsciously, the incarnation is non-sustainable and leads to destructive phenomena. As we know, for example from the observations of John E. Mack[376] and his collaborators, especially in the case of UFO abduction the effects are absolutely traumatizing.

Ultimately Wolfgang Pauli's invention of the spin and the exclusion principle and of the antineutrino prevents him from empirically penetrating into the world of the psychophysical reality which he theoretically anticipated. Since dreams compensate the conscious prejudice, the dream of the objectification of rotation would have shown him the decisive possibility of the overcoming of the physical/reductive worldview: The Taoist exercise of the (reversed) circulation of light, which he mentions in connection with the above dream as well as with the dream of the Chinese woman contracting space and finally letting it rotate[377]. In contrast to C.G. Jung and the Nobel laureate I regard the circulation of light not only as a mandala, a static symbol of the goal of a merely spiritual individuation process, but on the basis of Taoist philosophy use it as a meditative exercise. Since our effort consists in the transformation of the Logos ego into the Eros ego, which only is able to observe the singular inner quantum leaps, I turn the circulation around and reverse it: Beginning at the head the 'light', the inner energy is lead down into the belly and turned at the level of the coccyx. Since this motion can be imagined as number 6, I call it the exercise of number 6. With its help the vegetative nervous system in the region of the belly is activated, which leads to a sudden 'shift' of the Logos ego in the head into the Eros ego in the belly. The latter is able to observe acausal impulses out of the *unus mundus*, spontaneous images and

---

[376] Mack, J.E., Passports to the Cosmos, Human Transformation and Alien Encounters, Crown Publishers, N.Y., 1999, p. 207-219

[377] Pauli also mentions the circulation of light in his Kepler/Fludd essay in Naturerklärung und Psyche, p. 132 (English in Writings on Physics and Philosophy, p. 234, note 16).

vegetative sensations out of the belly, the products of the twin processes and their singular inner quantum leaps. As I explained above, these results correspond to the final goal of the Hermetic alchemical *opus*, to the creation of the red tincture or the quintessence. The result of such a procedure is outer spirit-psyche, physical energy with increased order or higher quality, which leads to the recovery and cure of individual as well as of collective disease.

To be able to describe this result in the terminology of quantum physics, we have first to go back to a decisive theorem of the mathematician Emmy Noether (1882-1935). In 1918 she had proven[378] that the energy conservation law is equivalent to the physical statement that the flow of time is homogenous. Likewise she showed that the conservation law of momentum corresponds to the idea of the homogeneity of space. This means that the two conservation laws disarray space and time of any quality. In this way they prevent qualitative transformation, in the world of physics as well as in the psychophysical reality.

We can now understand even better that with the postulation of the neutrino/antineutrino for the defense of the energy conservation law Wolfgang Pauli had excluded this qualitative transformation. The denial of energy's bipolarity and thus of matter-psyche, the energy of the *unus mundus*, to salvage the conservation law of energy prevented him from further penetrating empirically into the world of psychophysical reality.

Thus, he was also unable to experience the phenomena of Body-Centered Imagination and Symptom-Symbol-Transformation that had empirically proven the theoretical postulation of this world proposed and looked for by him together with C.G. Jung.

Before we can continue, we have to clarify the physical term 'momentum.' In German, the usual term for the physical momentum is 'Impuls' (impulse).

In colloquial language this term means something other than 'momentum.' It describes a *spontaneously* occurring motion or emotion. Thus, it has much more to do with the singular acausal quantum leap than with the conception behind the physical momentum. In the following I will use the term 'impulse' in this way.

We have seen that the idea of the energy conservation law is equivalent to the conception of the homogeneity of time. The consideration of the *kairos*, the spontaneous (i.e., acausal) moment of time during the twin process, in which meaningful events would like to happen, brings back quality to time. Since the spontaneous process violates the energy conservation law, energy of higher order or increased negentropy is created and incarnation in the meaning of *creatio continua* has happened[379].

---

[378] Noether, E., Invariante Variationsprobleme. *Nachrichten der Akademie der Wissenschaften, Göttingen, Mathematisch Physikalische Klasse*, 1918, p. 235-257
[379] *This result also shows the incredibly deep but unconscious conflict in Wolfgang Pauli: on the one hand he created the neutrino/antineutrino for the rescue of the energy conservation*

In such specific moments of the *kairos* during the consciously observed *coniunctio,* the twin process, acausal impulses out of the *unus mundus* are observable which, because of their spontaneity (acausality) violate the conservation law of the momentum (of the 'Impuls' in German). Thus, they also bring back quality to the impulse, and the idea of the homogeneity of space is broken through.

Since the physical impulse (the momentum) is defined as the product of mass and velocity, one can on the one hand imagine that the quality of mass is changed; the idea of the creation of the subtle body, the astral body of Paracelsus comes back into our considerations. Matter of the living body as well as so-called inanimated matter of the universe receives the quality of the subtle body/world soul, especially their quality of psychophysical nonlocality.

In this way Rensch's and Pauli's conjecture could become true that living as well as so-called inanimate matter could possess psyche; in my terminology matter-psyche. Further BCI/SST could be the empirical way of increasing this qualitative aspect of matter and in this way become an Alexipharmakum, a 'counter-poison' to the black mass of producing artificial radioactivity in the bomb and in nuclear power plants.

On the other hand, also the term 'velocity' receives qualitative meaning. Velocity is always connected to motion. In German the term 'motion' means on the one hand physical motion, 'Bewegung,' on the other 'Bewegtheit.' psychical motion, emotionality. In this way the qualitative aspect of motion, the ability of letting onself psychically move, comes back.

The above acausal impulses are empirically observable as singular inner (acausal) quantum leaps during BCI or SST, as spontaneous observation of inner images and vegetative bodily sensations. Since the term 'image' is always defined on the background of space, also the latter receives the qualitative aspect.

With the help of the restitution of qualitative space, time, mass and motion in the state of the Eros ego the physical/materialistic energy conservation law as well as the conservation law of momentum (impulse) are transcended, and a constructive incarnation on a qualitatively higher level or with increased negentropy has happened.

It is my deepest hope that there are some individuals in our space- and time-bound world that begin this constructive process of the relationship with the psychophysical reality or *unus mundus,* and in this way compensate the destructive effects of artificial fission in the physical as well as in the psychical world. In fact, they will be the modern Knights of the Holy Grail who can redeem the Grail king suffering from his severe wound in his hip.

In his letter 'To be or not to be' to the depth psychologist Pauli compares complementarity of physics with the Hermetic alchemical *coniunctio*. There he calls the complementarity between particle and wave of the Copenhagen

---

law, on the other he was fascinated of the kairos, *the qualitative moment in time, in which incarnation (creatio continua) would like to happen.*

interpretation of quantum physics 'die kleinere *coniunctio*,' the smaller *coniunctio*, which we surely also can equate with the complementarity between physics and Jung's depth psychology proposed by the Nobel laureate and the depth psychologist. Then, however, he continues that it is only 'a model or example of that other, more comprehensive *coniunctio*'[380], which in my opinion should overcome and replace the small one. In the course of my book I tried to present to the reader the theory as well as some empirical results, especially the twin process, that address the problem of how to realize the more comprehensive *coniunctio*.

---

[380] '*Eine Art Modell oder Vorbild für jene andere, umfassendere* coniunctio;' WB 4/II, p. 52; PJB, p. 92-93, AaA, p. 91; Translation adopted of Charles P. Enz, No Time to be Brief, A Scientific Biography of Wolfgang Pauli, Oxford University Press, Oxford, 2002 p. 463.

BIBLIOGRAPHY

Anonymous, *Rosarium philosophorum*, Frankfurt, 1550
Atmanspacher, et al., *Der Pauli-Jung-Dialog*, Springer, 1995
Avalon, Arthur (Sir John Woodroffe): *Die Schlangenkraft. Die Entfaltung schöpferischer Kräfte im Menschen*, Barth, Weilheim; O.W. Barth bei Scherz, München, 2nd ed., 1975; English original: *The Serpent Power*
Bair, Deirdre, *Jung: A Biography*, Little Brown, New York, 2004
Bender, H., *Unser sechster Sinn, Hellsehen, Telepathie, Spuk*, Rowohlt, Reinbeck b. Hamburg, 1972
Dossey, Larry, Space, Time and Medicine, Shambala, Boulder, Colorado, USA, 1982
Enz, Charles, P., *No Time to be Brief, A scientific biography of Wolfgang Pauli*, Oxford University Press, Oxford, 2002
Enz, Charles, P., *Rationales und Irrationales im Leben Wolfgang Paulis*, in *Der Pauli-Jung-Dialog und seine Bedeutung für die moderne Wissenschaft*, ed. Atmanspacher, H., et al., Springer, Berlin, 1995
Enz, Ch. P., *Wolfgang Pauli (1900-1958): A Biographical Introduction*, in: Pauli, W., *Writings on Physics and Philosophy*, Springer, Berlin, Heidelberg, N.Y., 1994
Enz, Ch. P., *On Matter and Spirit, Selected Essays*, World Scientific, Singapore, 2009
Erkelens, Herbert van, *Wolfgang Pauli und der Geist der Materie*, Königshausen & Neumann, Würzburg, 2002
Feynman, R.P., *QED, The strange theory of light and matter*, Princeton University Press, 1985
Fischer, E. P., *An den Grenzen des Denkens, Wolfgang Pauli, Ein Nobelpreisträger über die Nachtseiten der Wissenschaft*, Herder, Freiburg, Basel, Wien, 2000
Fludd, Robert, *Utriusque Cosmi Maioris scilicet et Minoris, Metaphysica, Physica atque technica Historices Mundi* [1621]
Franz, Marie-Louise von, *Zahl und Zeit, Psychologische Überlegungen zur einer Annäherung von Tiefenpsychologie und Physik*, Stuttgart, 1970;
Franz, Marie-Louise von, *Number and Time, Reflections Leading toward A Unification of Depth Psychology and Physics*, Northwestern University Press, Evanston, 1974
Franz, Marie-Louise von, *Spiegelungen der Seele, Projektion und innere Sammlung*, Stuttgart, Berlin, 1978
Franz, Marie-Louise von, *Creation Myths*, Spring Publications, University of Dallas, Irving, Texas, US, 3rd ed., 1978

Franz, Marie-Louise von, Hillmann, James, *Lectures on Jung's Typology, Part I: The Inferior Function,*, Spring Publications, N.Y., 1971

Franz, Marie-Louise von, *The Golden Ass of Apuleius: The Liberation of the Feminine in Man,* 1980

Gershon, Michael, D., *The Second Brain,* New York, 1998

Goodchild, V., Eros and Chaos, The Sacred Mysteries and Dark Shadows of Love, 2006

Granet, Marcel, *Das chinesische Denken,* Piper, München, 2nd ed., 1971

Gieser, Suzanne, *The Innermost Kernel, Depth Psychology and Quantum Physics. Wolfgang Pauli's Dialogue With C.G. Jung,* Springer, Berlin, 2005

Gribbin, John, *In Search of Schrödinger's Cat. Quantum Physics and Reality,* Wildwood House, London, 1984

Heisenberg, W., Die Kopenhagener Deutung der Quantentheorie, In: *Über den anschaulichen Inhalt der quantentheoretischen Kinematik und Mechanik,* Armin Hermann, ed., *Dokumente der Naturwissenschaft, Abteilung Physik.* Vol. 4, Ernst Battenberg

Holton, G., et al., *How a Scientific Discovery is Made: A Case History,* American Scientist, Volume 84, July-August, 1996

Jung, C.G., *Wandlungen und Symbole der Libido, Beiträge zur Entwicklungsgeschichte des Denkens,* 1911/12

Jung, C.G., *Psychology of the Unconscious. A Study of the Transformations and Symbolisms of the Libido. A Contribution of the History of the Evolution of Thought,* New York, 1916

Jung, C.G., *Collected Works,* volumes 1 to 18, especially:

Jung, C.G., *Collected Works,* vol. 8, Princeton University Press, 1969

Jung, C.G., *Collected Works,* vol. 5, Routledge & Kegan Paul, London, 1956

Jung, C.G., Pauli, W., *The Interpretation of Nature and Psyche,* Bollingen Series LI, Pantheon Books, N.Y., 1955

Jung, C.G., *Memories, Dreams, Reflections,* ed. A. Jaffé, Fontana Press, London, 9th edition, 1995; abbreviated as MDR

Jung, C.G., *Letters,* Princeton University Press, Princeton, New Jersey, 1973, two volumes

Jung, C.G. et al., *Der Mensch und seine Symbole [Man and his Symbols],* Walter Verlag, Olten, 1968, p. 78

Jung, C.G., Pauli, W., *Naturerklärung und Psyche,* Rascher Verlag, Zürich, 1952

Jung, C.G., Wilhelm, R., *Das Geheimnis der Goldenen Blüte, Ein chinesisches Lebensbuch,* Dornverlag, München, (1929), 10th edition, 1973

Kaku M., *Hyperspace, A Scientific Odyssey Through Parallel Universes, Time Warps, and the 10th Dimension,* New York, Anchor Books, Doubleday, 1995

Kennedy-Xypolitas, Emmanuel, ed., *The Fountain of The Love of Wisdom, An Hommage to Marie-Louise von Franz,* Chiron, Wilmette, Illinois, 2006

Lindorff, David, *Pauli and Jung, The Meeting of Two Great Minds,* Quest Books, Wheaton, Illinois, 2004

Mack, J.E., *Passports to the Cosmos, Human Transformation and Alien Encounters,* Crown Publishers, N.Y., 1999

Meier, C.A., (ed.), *Wolfgang Pauli und C.G. Jung, Ein Briefwechsel 1932-1958,* Springer, Berlin, 1992; abbreviated as PJB

Meier, C.A., (ed.), *Atom and Archetype, The Pauli/Jung Letters 1932-1958,* Princeton University Press, New Jersey, 2001; abbreviated as AaA

Meyrink, Gustav, *Der Golem,* Kurt Wolff, Leipzig, 1916

Miller, Arthur, I., *Deciphering the Cosmic Number, The Strange Relationship of Wolfgang Pauli and C.G. Jung,* W.W. Norton & Company, New York, London, 2009

Noether, E., *Invariante Variationsprobleme.* Nachrichten der Akademie der Wissenschaften, Göttingen, Mathematisch Physikalische Klasse, 1918, p. 235-257

Pauli, Wolfgang, *Wissenschaftlicher Briefwechsel mit Bohr, Einstein, Heisenberg, u.a, Band 2: 1930-1939,* ed. Karl v. Meyenn, Springer, Berlin, 1985; abbreviated as WB 2

Pauli, Wolfgang, *Wissenschaftlicher Briefwechsel mit Bohr, Einstein, Heisenberg, u.a, Band 3: 1940-1949,* ed. Karl v. Meyenn, Springer, Berlin, 1993; abbreviated as WB 3

Pauli, Wolfgang, *Wissenschaftlicher Briefwechsel mit Bohr, Einstein, Heisenberg, u.a, Band 4/I: 1950-1952,* ed. Karl v. Meyenn, Springer, Berlin, 1996; abbreviated as WB 4/I

Pauli, Wolfgang, *Wissenschaftlicher Briefwechsel mit Bohr, Einstein, Heisenberg, u.a, Band 4/II: 1953-1954,* ed. Karl v. Meyenn, Springer, Berlin, 1999; abbreviated as WB 4/II

Pauli, Wolfgang, *Wissenschaftlicher Briefwechsel mit Bohr, Einstein, Heisenberg, u.a, Band 4/III:1955-1956,* ed. Karl v. Meyenn, Springer, Berlin, 2001; abbreviated as WB 4/III

Pauli, Wolfgang, *Wissenschaftlicher Briefwechsel mit Bohr, Einstein, Heisenberg, u.a, Band 4/IV:1957-1958,* ed. Karl v. Meyenn, Springer, Berlin, 2001; abbreviated as WB 4/IV

Pauli, Wolfgang, *Physik und Erkenntnistheorie,* Braunschweig/Wiesbaden, 1984

Pauli, Wolfgang, *Writings on Physics and Philosophy,* ed. Charles P. Enz and Karl von Meyenn, Springer, Berlin, 1994

Peuckert, W.-E., *Paracelsus Werke,* Schwabe, Basel, Stuttgart, 1968

Roth, Remo F.: *I Cercatori di Dio, Una riunificatione della mistica cristiana e della fisica dei quanti nella sincronicità die C.G. Jung,* Di Renzo, Roma, 1994. Revised Italian translation of *Die Gottsucher,* Frankfurt, 1992

Roth, Remo, F., *Holy Wedding, C.G. Jung's and Wolfgang Pauli's Inner Development and the Creation of a New Hermetic science,* digital publication, http://www.psychovision.ch/hknw/holy_wedding_alchemy_modern_man_contents.htm

Roth, Remo, F., *Return of the World Soul, Wolfgang Pauli, C.G. Jung and the Challenge of Psychophysical Reality, Part I: The Battle of the Giants*, Pari Publishing, Pari, Italy, 2011

Sannella, Lee, *Kundalini, Psychosis or Transcendence?*, H.S. Dakin, San Francisco, 1981

Scholem, Gershom: *Kabbalah*, Keter Publishing House, Jerusalem, 1994

Schrödinger, E.: *What is life, The Physical Aspect of the Living Cell*, Cambridge University Press, 5th ed., 1955

Selleri, Franco, *Die Debatte um die Quantentheorie*, Braunschweig/Wiesbaden, 1983

Spaemann, R., Löw, R., *Die Frage Wozu?, Geschichte und Wiederentdeckung des teleologischen Denkens*, Piper, München, 1981

Stadler, M., *Renaissance: Weltseele und Kosmos, Seele und Körper*, in: Jüttemann, G., Sonntag, M., Wulf, Ch., *Die Seele, Ihre Geschichte im Abendland*, Weinheim 1991, pp. 180-197

Stöckler, M.: *Philosophische Probleme der relativistischen Quantenmechanik*, Berlin, 1984

Wei Po-Yang, *An ancient Chinese treatise on alchemy entitled Ts'an T'ung Ch'i*, transl. by Lu-Ch'iang Wu, ISIS, International Review devoted to the History of Science and Civilization, Volume XVIII, 1932

Wilhelm, R., Jung, C.G., *The Secret of the Golden Flower, A Chinese Book of Life*, Routledge & Kegan Paul Ltd., London, 8th ed., 1950

Zabriskie, B., *Jung and Pauli, A Meeting of Rare Minds*, in: *Atom and Archetype, The Pauli/Jung Letters, 1932 – 1958*, ed. Meier, C.A., Princeton University Press, Princeton, New Jersey, 2001, p. xxvii-l

Zukav, Gary, *The Dancing Wu Li Masters, An Overview of the New Physics*, 1979

Zumstein-Preiswerk, Stefanie: *C.G. Jungs Medium, Die Geschichte der Helly Preiswerk*, Kindler, München, 1975

Finito di stampare nel mese di maggio 2012
presso Universal Books Srl, Rende (CS)
per conto di Pari Publishing Sas di Eleanor F. Peat & C.

Pari Publishing is an independent publishing company, based in a medieval Italian village. Our books appeal to a broad readership and focus on innovative ideas and approaches from new and established authors who are experts in their fields. We publish books in the areas of science, society, psychology, and the arts.

Our books are available at all good bookstores or online at
www.paripublishing.com

If you would like to add your name to our email list to receive information about our forthcoming titles and our online newsletter please contact us at newsletter@paripublishing.com

Visit us at www.paripublishing.com

Pari Publishing Sas
Via Tozzi, 7
58045 Pari (GR)
Italy

Email: info@paripublishing.com